Cookin' with Queen Ida

REVISED 2ND EDITION

Queen Ida Guillory
with **Naomi Wise**

*Interviews by Michael Goodwin
and Irene Namkung*

Prima Publishing

PRIMA PUBLISHING and colophon are trademarks of Prima Communications, Inc.

Concept and Producer: John Ullman
Cover photo: Irene Young

Library of Congress Cataloging-in-Publication Data
Ida, Queen
    Cookin' with Queen Ida: "bon temps" Creole recipes (and stories)
    from the queen of zydeco music/Queen Ida Guillory, with
    Naomi Wise.—2nd ed.
       p.   cm.
    Includes index.
    ISBN 0-7615-0006-5
    1. Cookery, American—Louisiana style.   2. Cookery, Creole.
    3. Ida, Queen.   I. Wise, Naomi.   II. Title.
TX715.2.L68I33 1995
641.59763—dc20   95-1517
                                                CIP

96 97 98 99 00 AA 10 9 8 7 6 5 4 3 2 1

Printed in the United States of America

How to Order:

Single copies may be ordered from Prima Publishing, P.O. Box 1260BK, Rocklin, CA 95677; telephone (916) 632-4400. Quantity discounts are also available. On your letterhead, include information concerning the intended use of the books and the number of books you wish to purchase.

*I dedicate this book
to my mother, Elvina Lewis,
who was a great
inspiration
throughout my life.*

"While filming Queen Ida, the opportunity to sample her great cooking was a major fringe benefit. Ida cooks food like she plays music—with a straightforward, good-hearted approach that wins over anyone who is lucky enough to get a little taste. *Cookin' with Queen Ida* gives the reader some real insight into how food and music combine to infuse Louisiana life with joy."

Les Blank

Filmmaker and creator of the "food/music" genre. His latest work is *Yum, Yum, Yum,* the definitive Cajun food film.

ACKNOWLEDGMENTS

This book was made possible by the efforts of many people.

The memoirs arose from interviews carried out by Michael Goodwin, Irene Namkung, John Ullman, and Naomi Wise. Michael Goodwin also provided superlative assistance as a valiant computer-wrestler, patient roux-stirrer, and acute food critic. Most of all, his skillful editing suggestions were invaluable in helping to condense the largeness of a life into the compactness of a memoir. We are also indebted to Sara Akemi Ullman for transcribing and proofreading.

Queen Ida's family and friends generously contributed their most precious recipes: special thanks to Hazel Bellow, Ledra Guillory, Mabel Joan Guillory, Ray Guillory, Thelma Lewis, Vera Lewis, Willie Lewis, Pam Guillory, Marc Savoy, Rena Scott, and Yvette Sims. And, of course, this book might have been possible but it would have been unlikely without those who contributed to Ida's musical career: Gary Cristal, Garrison Keillor, Gene and Neil Norman, Margaret Moos Pick, and all the musicians.

Naomi Wise would like to extend special thanks to Madame Dorothée Brodin, an inspired and inspiring teacher whose lessons were finally put to use here.

We also especially thank the following for their encouragement and moral support: Dewey Balfa, Les Blank, Karen Brooks, Meryl Korn, Kathy Millard, Poki Namkung-Stewart and George Stewart, Ann Allen Savoy, Marc Savoy, Chris Simon, Chris Strachwitz, and Vivian Williams.

Thanks are also due to the folks of the Portland Party Crew, who, during the early stages of this book's history, tried out many of the recipes and brought them to a party for Ida to taste and evaluate. It was a great party, and it gave us a real sense that the recipes worked: Gwendolyn Blake, Les Blank, Karen Brooks, Barbara Dvorak, Bill Foster, Carol Foster, Marcella Gauther, Virginia Hand, Doug Henry, Jeannie Henry, Millie Howe, Carol Ivy, Eric Johnson, Kumi Kilburn, Lee Kilburn, Meryl Korn, Charles Laird, Tobie Liss, Lilly Meiners,

Grace Merchant, Alan Meyers, Kathy Millard, Kevin Mooney, Peggy Nauman, Poki Namkung-Stewart, Michael O'Rourke, Mary Orr, Billy Oskay, Georgia Peterson, Robyn Pokorny, Phyllis Reynolds, Michael Rose, Sura Rubenstein, Julia Sakahara, Patricia Salsich, Judy Shepherd, Tim Sills, Chris Simon, Nancy Skakel, George Stewart, Chris Strachwitz, Emlin Thomas, Charlotte Uris, Joe Uris, Joe Vinikow, Barbara Weissman, Eric Weissman, Leon Williams, Don Wright, Wanda Wright, and Cathy Wygant.

Last but not least, we'd like to thank Jennifer Basye for her persistence—without her, the book would still be sitting in the word processor; Ben Dominitz and Laura Glassover for their encouragement, help, and patience; and Carol Dondrea and Robin Lockwood of Bookman Productions for helping us through the editorial process.

CONTENTS

INTRODUCTION

Early on, we realized the wisdom of skipping lunch when we had a business meeting at Queen Ida's. After several hours of discussing tour logistics and promotional materials, Ida would step over to the stove, lift the lid off a large pot, and say "John and Irene, sit down and try just a little of this!" "A little of this" usually turned out to be boudin, neck bone stew, okra and tomatoes, gumbo, catfish courtbouillon, hog's head cheese, or another of the marvelous recipes contained in the following pages. This food had the same strength, subtlety, and ebullience as Ida's zydeco music (see About Zydeco at the back of the book). It was everyday cooking for Ida, but it was a whole new culinary world for us.

Ida's career took off in the mid-1970s at the same time that the strong interest in indigenous American cooking emerged. Since food and music are inexorably linked in Louisiana, it didn't take concert promoters long to turn Queen Ida concerts into dinner dance events. Offering Cajun/Creole food at Ida's performances became so popular that we began sending out recipes with the promotional materials, and the idea for this book was born. (There was one unmitigated disaster, however, perpetrated by a rather "new age" promoter. He took it upon himself to alter Ida's jambalaya recipe by using brown rice, eliminating the salt and cayenne and substituting tofu for the smoked sausage. The result was decidedly un-Creole!)

During our business discussions and impromptu feasts, we heard Ida's stories about her childhood in the rural, French-speaking communities of Louisiana and Texas, and her family's joining the Creole emigration to postwar urban California. These stories sounded very much like the experiences of our own ancestors when they emigrated from Europe or Asia, except that it all happened within the United States! Ida's personal story, making a mid-life career change from a school bus-driving mother to a Grammy Award winning leader of a hot band, seemed plenty interesting too. We saw that this book could be more than a compilation of tasty, somewhat exotic recipes, so we began the hours of interviews that were fascinating for us and hopefully not too tedious for Ida.

As this project continued, we became increasingly impressed with how Ida's family in particular and the Creole community in general maintained their traditional values of family, community support, and celebration. The unwavering adherence to these values is the implicit gift that Ida transmits in both her concert performances and her cooking.

A large part of Queen Ida's success as a performing artist has come in the fine arts field. Ida often appears on the same series as symphony orchestras, dance companies, and theatrical attractions. Fifteen years ago it was almost unheard of to have a folk arts group on these series. By pioneering in this area (with much-appreciated initial help from the National Endowment for the Arts), Ida has helped numerous other folk artists find a place in the mainstream fine arts market.

By adamantly keeping many traditional zydeco and Cajun elements in her music, singing roughly half her lyrics in the original French and keeping her many delightful innovations within the context of her musical heritage, Ida has managed the very rare feat of increasing her popularity with Louisiana people at the same time she has been winning over the general public. This was exemplified a few years ago when Ida played two Los Angeles engagements back to back. One was at Verbum Dei, a Catholic parochial school serving the Creole community, and the other was at UCLA's Royce Hall, one of the most prestigious venues on the West Coast. Both shows were sold out and neither audience was really aware that the other show existed.

Queen Ida's career has taken her from Lake Charles and All Hallows Church Hall to Lake Wobegone and Carnegie Hall. She has brought zydeco music to Europe, Africa, and Asia as well as across the United States and Canada. An Australian tour has just been confirmed for March 1991. Many major radio and television shows over the years have sought out Ida's zydeco music, including "Saturday Night Live," "Austin City Limits," "A Prairie Home Companion," "Mr. Rogers' Neighborhood" and "Entertainment Tonight." Now that word is getting out about her skills in the kitchen, she is being asked to be a guest chef on shows such as the ABC "Home" show and the Lifetime channel's "Attitudes."

Queen Ida's philosophy can be captured in a phrase: "Va pour ça!"—"Go for it!" In the dozen years we have been privileged to provide Ida with agency and management services, we have been continually impressed with her ability to make decisions quickly and intelligently and then pursue her projects with the same unwavering commitment and immense energy she puts out on stage.

Ida has a full touring schedule mapped out for the next season, and now her spare time is starting to fill up with book signings and cooking shows. With her son, "Freeze" Guillory, already launching his own zydeco career, and one or two grandchildren beginning to show signs of having Ida's talent, we soon may see a three-generation zydeco dynasty on stage! There has also been talk about a Queen Ida Cafe in San Francisco. Right now, Ida and her career are in high gear, and whatever the future may hold, one thing is certain: Ida will definitely va pour ça!

John Ullman and Irene Namkung,
Traditional Arts Services,
Berkeley, California, 1990

1

Louisiana Baby

L ife in Louisiana is like life in another country. The culture is different. The music is different. People there cook differently from people in any other state. Even the language is different. We speak what we call "Cajun patois," which is a form of French, and the Creole, which is almost the same. Even English is spoken so differently—we seem to forget to use all the letters in a given word. The celebrations, the festivals, are unique. Mardi Gras is one of the biggest festivals in America and was found only in Louisiana for many, many years—right up until the '50s. I don't know why we were so isolated. Louisiana is such a melting pot, like New York or San Francisco, but somehow, it's different.

My earliest memory of Louisiana, and of being alive, is of the big yard on my family's farm. There was all this open land, and you felt free. Whenever you got out from under your mom's apron strings, you felt free to do things on your own.

I was born on January 15, 1929. My father was Ben Lewis. He came from Mallett, Louisiana, in the Cajun country northwest of New Orleans. My mama's maiden name was Elvina Broussard, and she came from Eunice, Louisiana, about 50 miles away from Mallet. After they got married, they moved to Lake Charles, Louisiana, to raise their family. All seven of us children were born there. I have three sisters and three brothers, and I'm number four.

All of us children were born two to three years apart. The oldest was Agnes, who got married very young and lived in Lake Charles all her life. Next is Hazel, who lives in Clear Lake, California. Willie (real name: Wilbert) lives in San Francisco. I live in Daly City, just south of San Francisco. Mabel Joan lives in Concord, California, a suburb across the San Francisco Bay. Paul lived nearby in Daly City until his death. Al lives in San Francisco and works as a musician under the name of Al Rapone. He reminds me a lot of my oldest sister.

My mom was taller than me, about five feet four. She was a pretty big woman; her normal weight was about 145, and after Willie was born her weight went up to about 170 for a while. She had a tiny little chin like I have, and tiny lips. She hardly ever wore lipstick because she said, "Who's going to see my lips?" She had a dark olive complexion, long, wavy hair, and greenish hazel eyes. My dad's eyes were hazel also, and he was fair-skinned. He was not a tall man, five-nine probably, and not large of build.

My parents were not musicians, although my dad played Cajun waltzes and two-steps on the harmonica for himself and for the family. My uncles Marius and Louis Broussard played accordion, and another uncle, "Chub" Thibodeaux, played violin. Most of the time they would visit during the warm part of the year, so they'd go out on the porch or by the barn or someplace where it was cool and play Cajun music. There was a nice ring about it because it was outdoors. Of course, they played inside the house during Christmas. I can't say I loved the music at that time. It was just there, part of life, c'est la vie. It never occurred to me that I might actually play music myself until I found myself doing it.

The city of Lake Charles was named after the big lake that's right next to it. It's a seaport area right off the Gulf, so there's a lot of moisture in the air. Moss would hang from the trees, and the limbs would get so heavy the branches dipped almost to the ground. It was really pretty. People used to pick the moss and dry it and make moss mattresses. The moss came in very handy.

Our farm was approximately ten miles outside of the city of Lake Charles, by gravel roads. We had a big, old-time ranch house, a barn, a chicken yard, chicken houses, pigpens, and pasture for the cattle. My dad was sharecropping: he was a rice cropper and also grew a little cotton. The land he sharecropped wasn't on the farm we rented, but farther inland, farther away from the city. He also had his own little truck patches and grew corn, potatoes, and sweet potatoes to sell, and that was another part of the family's income. On Saturdays, he and the other farmers would go through the neighborhoods where there were no farms nearby. People expected to see him on weekends; all he had to do was drive through the streets slowly and beep the horn of his pickup truck. He was gone all day Saturday, or until he got rid of what he had. Sometimes my older brother Willie went with him.

My mother had a truck garden, too—a big one. In fact, we thought it was *too* big, because we had to help tend it. My mother grew turnips, cabbage, mustard greens, tomatoes, peas, string beans, lima beans, okra, butter lettuce, watermelon, cantaloupes, banana squash and scallop squash, cayenne peppers, cucumbers, onions, garlic, green onions, and beets. Maybe that's why we were so healthy. All we ever got were just the normal childhood diseases, although whooping cough was very prevalent in our area.

We weren't well off but we were comfortable. At the time the Depression started, I was less than a year old, so I really don't remember it, but later my parents told me about that Depression. It wasn't easy for them; it wasn't easy for anyone. They did say, "Well, thank God we managed to live through it."

My earliest memories are of playing with the animals, the chickens and pigs and a few cattle. We'd go out and play with them like pets. We had to feed the chickens. Actually, we overfed them. Just like people, there are certain times of day when chickens should have their meals, in the morning and afternoon, but we would feed them all day long, whenever we wanted to. We were fortunate that we didn't have to pay a big price for chicken feed. We went to the other rice growers after they harvested their rice, and they let us have the rice that they couldn't sell, the rice left in the combines and on the ground, and we'd use it for feed.

And the pigs—each time you'd go out there, the pigs would come over to you because they thought you were going to feed them. It didn't matter what time of day it was, unless it was a very hot day and they were bathing in the mud. They didn't want to be bothered. That was strange for a youngster. When we saw them wallowing, we'd go, "Ooh, that pig's all dirty!" and we'd tell our mom that they were out lying down in the mud. Once I asked her, "They're so dirty; should we wash them?" And she said, "No, no. That's the way they keep cool. They'll clean themselves up later."

We didn't have horses, but we had mules to bring in the hay. Once, when I was 10 or 11, we really got in trouble with my father one time when we played with one of the farm mules. One mule, named Judy, was so tame and gentle my dad would ride her to the fields and ride her back. One day, we heard our dad tell our mom that somehow he'd fallen off that mule, and Judy just stopped and looked at him and didn't move until he got back on. "That's a smart mule," he said. Well, I can't remember which of us got the idea, but we decided we wanted to try this out. Three of us went out and put the bridle on her and got on her, and we were falling on the ground, on purpose. And we'd grab her tail and let her pull us. It was really dangerous—how did we know that she wouldn't step on us or kick us, and we'd be crippled for life or even killed? When Dad got that report, he made sure we wouldn't try such a stunt again.

Because we grew most of our own food, all we had to buy from the store were baking powder, spices, black pepper, salt, and coffee. We also bought sugar, flour, and cornmeal in bulk. Sometimes my parents would make their own cornmeal, but it was too coarse because they didn't have the machinery to grind it. We bought syrup from a small company of sugarcane growers; they made their syrup thicker than others in the area, so my dad would always buy from them. They had a big wooden table where the syrup ran out, called a trough. They'd press the sugarcane, cook it, and skim off all the foam. It was so pure, it was like water from a cistern. It was so sweet and pure that before the beginning of the next season there were crystals at the bottom of the cans—rock candy!

We never bought cottage cheese; my mother would make it by putting a ball of curds inside a bag made of cheesecloth and hanging it in a tree to cure. It tasted a little stronger than today's cottage cheese, drier and less creamy, like feta—but it wasn't salty. We ate it plain or mixed with milk and cereal, or we ate it with sweet French bread.

My mom used to make candies, too, for the weekends when people would visit: pecan praline or peanut praline, or peanuts with caramel syrup. And we'd make caramel taffy. We'd pull and pull and pull, and as we pulled, it turned a beautiful amber color. We'd make popcorn, too, and during the winter we'd make caramel popcorn balls with syrup while sitting by the stove. They were great, tasty. And I remember Mom used to make what we called "café au lait," although it had no coffee in it. It was our version of chocolate milk, made with caramel. She would heat sugar until it browned and then add the milk to it. The adults' version of café au lait was just hot milk in their coffee.

We'd have soda pop only when our parents did their shopping, about once a week. If you wanted anything cold, it was iced tea with lemon, or lemonade, or milk. If you were lucky you had lemon trees; or you'd get lemons from a neighbor who did. Aside from lemons, we never had many fruit trees. A plum tree here and there, a peach tree here and there, and a few canning pears, which were very grainy, not smooth like the eating pears. We didn't like to eat the canning pears, so my mom would preserve them and then we'd eat them as dessert.

Everything was made at home: anything that you could raise, you could can, or preserve. My mom had pressure cookers for canning. She and her generation knew just how long to cook their string beans or green peas, and what the temperature should be for each. They seldom lost a jar, but whatever didn't get sealed properly was fed to the hogs. My mom had a whole room just off the kitchen filled with shelves of canned fruits, vegetables, meats, and jams and jellies, and you always knew exactly where you could find whatever you needed. Later, when we moved to Texas, my dad built her a similar pantry there.

They had large kitchens in those days, nothing like today, with all our cabinets, appliances, and sinks. We had none of those; we had to wash dishes in one dishpan and rinse them in another dishpan, and drain them on the cupboard on top of towels. If we didn't have time to drain, one would wash the dishes and another would put them in the rinse water, then dry each dish and put it away.

We had our own chickens and ducks, so we always had enough eggs for the family, farm-fresh eggs. My mom used the duck eggs as well as chicken eggs, but we didn't like them. She sold eggs at some of the local stores, and customers would come by the farm to buy them, too. We had a few geese, and occasionally a few turkeys (although usually we'd buy our holiday turkeys "on foot" from a turkey farm). Mom would use the wings of the ducks and geese: She'd cut off the first joint of the wing and dry it in the sun to cure it. This left a hard stick covered with feathers, which she used for dusting—but if you were naughty, she used it to dust your pants as well.

There was no electricity where we lived, so there was no refrigeration, no radio, no electric lights. My mother did all the cooking on a wood-burning stove. My dad chopped the wood and put it into cords, although sometimes my sister Hazel helped. My mother wouldn't allow us little ones to play with an axe, but we were responsible for bringing in kindling as soon as we could carry it. We always had to make sure there was enough wood and kindling in the woodbox. If there wasn't enough, the one that was responsible would be awakened early in the morning when Mom got up to make breakfast and you'd have to go out and get it. You wouldn't forget twice: Even during the summer you hated to be awakened early, and on winter mornings, it was too cold to go out there!

It gets very cold in Louisiana in winter. There's rarely any snow, but there's ice on the ground, and icicles on the houses, and the ground is too hard to grow anything. We had one big wood-burning heater. The whole house was on one level, with no upstairs or basement, and all the doors inside the house were left open so the heat would go from one room to the other. The fire was kept going all night. My dad would get up in the middle of the night and add more wood to the stove. He wouldn't use kerosene heaters because they're dirty and dangerous. If you run out of oil, they emit a lot of soot, and they can set a place on fire.

There may have been battery-operated flashlights by then, but we used lanterns that burned kerosene or coal oil. In the house, we had kerosene lamps, and we had lanterns hanging on the porch like porch lights at night. I know there are a lot of people today who live in the mountains, still don't have electricity, and I think back and say, "Wow! Still?"

We had to get our water from a well about 50 yards from the house and bring it home in a big bucket. Each of us had to start bringing the water as soon as we could walk and carry a bucket at the same time. To carry water while you walk, you have to learn to balance. We kids did not come by that skill naturally.

Mom would say, "Put just a little water in this bucket, because you can't carry it full."

We'd say, "Yeah, sure I can. I'm big. I can carry it full." By the time you got home to Mom you had a quarter of a bucket of water. You'd bump it on your leg because it was heavy, and the water would go zoop, shamp, zoop, and your leg would get wet. In the winter, only the bigger kids would go out for water. My sister would bring two buckets—*two at a time*. I thought that was great!

As soon as you were old enough to handle the bucket and pump, you had to draw your own water for your bath. Some people used to laugh and say, "Oh yeah, the weekly bath," but even during the winter my mother made us take baths at least twice a week—complete baths. (On days we couldn't have a full bath, we'd take sponge baths.) Mom would have to heat the water. There was a certain bucket they called the "little foot tub," and one of our parents would bring it in and put it on the stove to heat. We used to paddle around and play in the water; it just felt good to be in that tub. You had to wait in line to take your bath—today, if you only have two bathrooms, and you have a family of five, it's the same: you still have to wait in line for your shower.

Summer months, you'd want to take a bath not just every day, but all day. Every few hours we'd draw water and splash it on ourselves, cold, just getting the dust off.

The toilet was outdoors, too. It was quite a ways from the house because it had to be far away from the well. If the well was on the west, this would be on the east. They had it all figured out. It was near the barn and it was always kept neat and clean with lime, and whitewashed so that it looked freshly painted. During the winter nights, we used the *pot de chambre,* a covered chamber pot, but in summer we had to use the outdoor toilet, and I was always afraid to go out there by myself, in that absolute darkness of a moonless country night.

What was I afraid of? There were no wolves or other bad animals there—or if there were, we never knew about it. There were no water moccasins or rattlers, just king snakes, garter snakes and little lizards. I wasn't afraid of the lizards, but I *was* afraid of the snakes. Those snakes were not poisonous, but I didn't trust any—and I still don't.

I was more afraid of ghosts—and of men. I was afraid a strange man would suddenly come grab me and take me away. Mom had always told us, "You don't take anything from strangers, people you do not know, and you don't ask anything from strangers, because someone can take you away and never bring you back. We will never see you again and you will never see us again."

My mother told us scary stories to make that point. She told us not to go into any empty houses or barns, and she told us the story of "Monsieur Barbe-Bleue," Bluebeard. It was my favorite story when I was a child:

In a certain small town, women would disappear and nobody knew where they had gone. Monsieur Barbe-Bleue lived in that town. He was a bad man. He lived in a big house with many, many rooms. All the young girls were forbidden by their parents to go near his house. However, a young lady went to his house one day despite the warnings, taking her little dog Annette to keep her company. She was curious, and decided she was going to go and peek through the window to see what was inside. She peeked through the first window and she saw a woman hanging by her neck. She moved on to the window of another room and there was another woman hanging by her neck. Every window she looked in, she saw the same thing. While she was going from one room to the other, old Bluebeard came out from behind her and seized her, shouting, "Ahh!" The girl's little dog started crying and jumping up and down.

Monsieur Barbe-Bleue took the girl and asked, "What do you want?" The girl answered that she just wanted to see what was in his house, and he said, "Well, now you're mine. I'm going to keep you." And he told her to go to the powder room. He told her, "Go comb your hair, Madame" (he called her Madame; he was polite), "make up your face, and when I'm ready, I'll come and get you." So after seeing what she'd seen—the women hanging by their necks—she told her little dog, *"Annette, va chercher mes parents,* go get my parents!" So Annette took off and barked and barked and barked—you know how dogs try to get your attention if something has happened.

Meanwhile, every now and then the old guy would come and say, "Aren't you ready yet?" And the young lady would answer, "No. No. A few more minutes. A few more minutes." And Barbe-Bleue said, "Okay," and would go away again—he was very patient. And the little dog ran back to the young lady. *"Annette, où est mes parents?"* she asked the dog again. The little dog would run to the door and look, but when she didn't see anything, she'd come back and bark at the girl, and sit by her like she was guarding her.

Again Monsieur Barbe-Bleue came back to ask, *"Tu es prête?* Aren't you ready yet?"

"No. A few more minutes, a few more minutes," said the girl. And singing, so that Barbe-Bleue would think she was just singing a song and not talking to her dog, she asked Annette again, *"Annette, où est mes parents?"* All of a sudden, looking out through the window, she saw a trail of dust and knew that someone was approaching and hoped it was her parents. Then Annette came running to her, barking and barking, and she sang to the dog, *"Je vois 'tite poussière là-bas, là-bas, là-bas* (I see a little stream of dust way, way far away). *Annette, où est mes parents?"* And then Barbe-Bleue looked out the window, and he said to her, *"Madame, les parents est à la porte* (your parents are at the door)." So she was saved, and they seized Monsieur Barbe-Bleue because they saw the other women that he had killed.

So that's the story of Barbe-Bleue, and that was to tell us, "Don't go into those empty houses or barns that you see over there or into strange men's homes."

Another of my mom's favorites was a very old story from France called "Rosa Majeur." It was about a young lady who wanted to go out to a Saturday night street dance that was being held on a bridge called Pont du Nord. Her parents didn't want her to go, and warned her that she might fall off the bridge, but they couldn't stop her because she was legally of age—that's why they called her Rosa Majeur, Rose of legal age. So she went to the dance despite her parents' warning, and the bridge collapsed and Rosa drowned. The story ends, "So see what happens to children who don't mind their parents." That was a little story to make us obedient. My brother Al eventually turned the story into a song, and I liked it so much, it's the first song on our first album. Recently I met two professors from France who had come to Quebec and to Louisiana to research the way the French language is spoken in those two areas. They had the album with "Rosa Majeur" on it, when they visited me here in California. One of them told me, "That's a story my parents used to tell us when we were youngsters. The generation today probably doesn't know anything about it, but it's a very old story." (They also said that some of the French that we speak is like the older French. I thought, "That's great coming from two professors in Paris.") We had a great time; we ended up dancing.

Our part of Louisiana was very rural, so we had to do things on our own. We'd make our own toys, and I think it was more fun than kids have today with all their store-bought toys. The boys would get one of the old brooms and ask my dad to saw off part of the handle, and they'd put a string through it and pretend it was a horse. The straw was the head, and we'd tie ribbons on it to dress up the horse. The boys would often want to play with the girls. We'd play with our dolls, playing "mother" and "sister." And we used to make our own stilts. My dad made great stilts, but sometimes when they broke we couldn't wait for him to replace them, so we'd make our own. It was very dangerous because we didn't make them as well as he did. My sister Hazel cut her leg very badly when her foot slipped off the footrest and was cut by a nail that was sticking out.

We had a lot of old spare tires—big and small—and they made great toys! You'd curl up inside of one and hold onto the groove, and somebody would roll you—and you'd go lumpety-lumpety across the yard or down the driveway. Once you'd get one push, the momentum would keep you going. Another thing you could do with an old tire was hang it in a tree with a rope, attaching it to one of the bigger limbs, and use it for a swing.

Or you could just climb the tree. There weren't that many trees, but whatever we had, we'd climb. The aim was to get higher in the tree than the other guy. Both the girls and guys would climb. The girls always wore dresses and skirts, so if we were going to go climb a tree, we had to borrow pants from the brother whose pants fit the best. The legs were always too long for me, and sometimes the waist was too big so I'd have to use a piece of rope as a belt.

We used to play some of the same song-games that kids sing today, like "Ring Around the Rosies." And we'd play a finger game where we'd put our fingers in, one on top of the other, while we sang a nonsense rhyme that went *"Pain 'ti peau l'eau rond la 'ti' fait atten' l'eau RA!"* With that last word, the person whose finger was on the bottom was out of the game. It would go round and round and round until the last person left was the winner.

Often we had water fights. We would get water all over the porch and make a muddy mess. My mom would get mad at us for using up all the water and getting the porch all wet.

We usually got our spankings with Dad's belt. My mom was a very, very gentle person, and while she'd give us a slap if we were doing something really outrageous, she would hardly ever use that belt. There was a special place Dad would hang it where we'd see it—to remind us to be good. When one of us was bad, Mom always reported to Dad: "This kid was naughty." Sometimes we'd eavesdrop, and we'd hear him answer, "Why do you wait to tell me when I come home? I have to come back from the fields and correct these kids, and I'm not angry with them. Why didn't you just give them a spanking when they were naughty?"

Dad was a serious person. He'd tell us what to do, and ask how our day was, but it wasn't the "big smile" situation. He was very jovial with adults, though. On summer Sundays, when all the men were together, sitting under a tree and talking, you'd hear him joking and laughing out loud. The women would sit and talk, doing their sewing and quilting, and the men would go off under a tree and talk and smoke and have their beer or wine.

Everybody in that area made their own beer and wine. It wasn't considered a big deal. The wine was usually made from blackberries because they were plentiful; you could go out along the sides of the roads, and in the fields, and pick as many as you wanted. Sometimes the blackberries were mixed with peaches or strawberries. A few people made wine out of grapes, or made peach brandy. I don't recall the taste because I wasn't old enough to taste any of it.

I realize now that some people also made moonshine, the homemade corn whiskey they called "mash"—but as kids we didn't know that. They never made whiskey anywhere near the house. It was always way out in the country, far from the eyes of the law. My father didn't like it. In fact, my father didn't drink for many, many years, even after we came to California. Maybe to toast the New Year he'd have his little drink, but he and my mom would never drink alone. I found out later, when I was in my teens, that he had friends who drank too much, and he didn't like it because he said their conversations were repetitious and not worthy of anything.

During planting and harvest, farm families had only one day off each week: Sunday. Saturday nights the grownups might get together for a party or a "fais-dodo" (a dance). Sundays, after church, folks would visit and talk together for a few hours. They would get out the wine when company came, and we always had cookies and cakes in the house for the weekend. In those days chocolate was not that easy to come by, so my mama mostly made yellow or white cakes. I couldn't wait for her to start baking so I could lick the bowl.

Sometimes we'd make hand-cranked ice cream. We didn't have a refrigerator or freezer (in fact, I don't think refrigerators really existed at that time), so we made only as much as we were going to eat immediately.

On our birthdays we always had birthday cake and lemonade and ice cream, and if we wanted to we could invite the neighbors to come over and enjoy it with us. There were seven of us children, so Mom had seven birthdays to think about. That's a lot of baking, but when it was your birthday Mom would specify, "This is particularly done for you. It's not just dessert. It's not because I felt like making a cake." So it made you feel real great. The thought behind it was, it's for you. And of course you'd always get a little gift.

The best gift I ever received was at Christmas. Christmas was the time of year when the things you wanted, and hadn't gotten, finally came in abundance. Most of the time they'd give you clothes (just like we do with our kids); they'd give you dolls, socks, underclothes, or a real nice "Sunday dress." One year, when I was only about five years old, I told Mom and Dad I wanted one of those spinning tops—the big round ones that whistle. They didn't say anything—they just listened.

The night before Christmas, we hung up our stockings, and I wanted so many things I took my dress and tied the bottom of it so Santa could just fill my dress with gifts. (Afterwards, my dad told me, "From now on, use a stocking. Not a dress. No more dresses.")

The next morning we got up and went running to the Christmas tree, and there was that top! I was so happy, so excited, I'll never forget it. I didn't think I was going to get the top! Of course we were always pleased with the gifts we received, no matter how big or how small, because we were taught to accept whatever was given: "Whether you like it or not, you should appreciate it because that person is thinking of you." But when I got that top, that was the most joyful moment that I can remember as a child.

Our holidays would start with close friends and relatives gathering on Christmas Eve; everyone would come by for a bowl of gumbo and a glass of eggnog, or a little wine or corn whiskey. Gumbo and eggnog were always served on Christmas Eve. That's a tradition I've kept every year (except once, when I was touring).

My mom and dad both came from large families, so we'd see relatives who lived in the area, and others who might have come a distance of 40 or 50 miles to spend Christmas with us. They were all farmers and they came in their pickup trucks. I don't remember, because I was too young, but I know they used to travel by buggy or wagon until they were able to get a car or truck. (We always had two vehicles, a truck for the farm and a car for taking the family out. Of course, we had to take turns. Nine of us couldn't fit in one car.)

I was happy to see them all, but especially those who lived the farthest from us—my aunt and cousins from Beaumont, Texas. They didn't come that often. It couldn't have been more than 65 miles, and they had good cars, but in those days that was still a long way. They'd write and say they were coming and we'd wait for them, just standing in the yard asking, "When are they going to get here?" They would only spend a day with us. They rarely spent the night.

Christmas Day, sometimes there'd be a turkey, or big roast hens. Or maybe we'd have a pork leg, pork roast, or roast beef, and the dressing and the sweet potato pies. As an hors d'oeuvre to serve to company who dropped in, we always had boudin—a delicious fresh (unsmoked) sausage made with pork and rice. (If you travel in southwestern Louisiana, you'll still find every little grocery offering homemade boudin, and no two versions of it will be identical.)

Christmas was a very religious holiday for us. You weren't supposed to miss midnight Mass. New Year's Eve, though, was celebrated the way it is in the rest of America, with partying and drinking. Since it wasn't a religious holiday, you didn't have to go to Mass that night, just the next day. On New Year's Day it was the custom to visit, to have some sweet wine and to try out each other's cakes. My parents served hog's head cheese (page 113) and boudin (page 124) as hors d'oeuvres, and coffee or wine with cake, cookies, and sweet potato pawn (a baked pudding made from grated sweet potatoes, also called "pone"; see page 37).

It was quite rare for women to sing—except sometimes in church. They hummed instead. Occasionally, during the Christmas season, my mom would sing Christmas carols. I think they were mainly translations of some of the hymns sung in church. Church was open to anybody, and they didn't care if you communicated with each other in French—but most of the songs in church were in English. The priest sang in Latin, and we'd answer him in English. The songs the choir sang were in English, too. They didn't want you to speak French— anywhere! When I started school, I found out more about that.

A CREOLE CHRISTMAS

About Roux (Required Reading)

Roux is the vital thickener of most Creole cooking; it's used in gumbos, stews, and étouffée (smothered) dishes, and gives their flavor some of its smokiness. Roux need not be reserved for Louisiana cooking; it can be used anytime a fat-and-flour thickener is called for in a recipe. The darker the roux, the less it will thicken a liquid, but the stronger a taste it contributes. The roux that follows is typical of western Louisiana: Unlike the fairly light "peanut butter roux" that's usual in New Orleans cooking, this "red roux" will be nearly as dark as bittersweet chocolate by the time it has cooled. (A peanut butter roux can be used in gumbo, however.)

Cajuns and Creoles usually make their roux in advance in large quantities, to have on hand as needed. Roux will keep, refrigerated, for many months. It gets very hard when chilled; store it in a plastic or metal container, not glass, so that the container won't shatter when you're digging out a few spoonfuls.

Roux should always be at room temperature when it's introduced into dishes. If the roux is chilled, let it soften a few hours. If the roux is freshly made, let it cool about a half hour before using it.

To add roux to liquid, bring the liquid to a boil. Remove the pot from the heat, and start stirring in the roux by large spoonfuls. (A wooden cooking spoon is the best implement for this.) Return the pot to the heat. (On an electric stove, you may have to move it to a different burner, not the hot one you've been using.) Adjust the heat between medium and low, so that the liquid bubbles slightly but never returns to a full boil; stirring constantly, add additional roux by large spoonfuls, until each addition of the roux is completely blended. (Be sure to stir from the bottom of the pot, where roux may settle and burn if it's not absorbed.) Continue stirring in roux and letting the liquid absorb it until the mixture is as thick as you desire. This process will take about 10 minutes.

Once roux has been added, never cover the pot during the remainder of the cooking time, or the steam will thin out the roux. Nor should you allow the liquid to reach a full boil again after adding roux, as this, too, will break up the roux and thin the liquid. Liquids containing roux should be kept at a simmer until cooking is complete.

〰〰〰〰〰〰〰〰〰〰

ROUX

Note: If you expect to do a lot of Creole cooking, you can double or triple the recipe; it will take longer to cook, of course. Once roux has started to color, never leave the stove: ignore telephones, doorbells, children, and pets, and keep stirring. If a roux burns (it will develop a burned smell and blackened patches), throw it out and start over. Roux can't be rushed: it's a gradual process, and needs patience. When cooked too rapidly, roux may brown but it won't develop its characteristic flavor. When roux is done, it will smell like well-cooked flour; it may taste and smell slightly bitter when sampled "as is," but this does not mean it is burned.

1½ cups oil   **2 cups flour**

Mix oil and flour in a heavy iron skillet (or as heavy a skillet as you have). Do not use a Teflon-lined pan. If the mixture is not as soft as pancake batter, add more oil. Cook over low to medium heat, stirring gently but constantly with a wooden spoon so that the mixture won't burn, making sure to lift roux from the bottom and sides of the skillet. If any lumps develop, whisk with a wire whisk until they break up. Cook until the color is nearly the red-brown of mahogany or chili powder. This will take anywhere from 30 to 60 minutes (depending on the material of your pot and the heat of your stove). Be patient.

After the roux is done, set it off the heat to cool, but keep on stirring constantly for the first few minutes. Then stir frequently about 10 more minutes, since roux will continue to cook from its own heat for a few minutes. As the roux cools, some of the oil will float to the top; spoon it off. (There will still be some oil in the mixture, but when you cook with the roux you can skim off excess oil before serving.) Turn roux into a plastic or metal container and store in the refrigerator. Before using, skim any additional oil that has separated from the roux, and let roux return to room temperature.

VERA'S CANE RIVER MEAT PIES

My sister-in-law Vera Lewis comes from Cane River, which is near Shreveport, Louisiana, in the north of the state. I remember Vera's aunt making these meat pies every New Year's and Christmas. We looked forward to her making those meat pies. She was so good at it— she never used a recipe, and it was always the same, and always good.

This dish is only made for holidays, and for special occasions like weddings—not for the wedding reception itself, but for when family members drop in before or after the wedding. The pies can be made smaller and used for hors d'oeuvres, but we prefer to make them as large hors d'oeuvres. They can also be made larger yet, so that each one makes a meal-size portion.

One reason these savory pies are mainly eaten during the winter holidays is that the rich dough (which becomes ethereally light and flaky when deep-fried) is liable to fall apart in hot weather. Inexpert dough-rollers may find it easiest to chill the dough briefly (about 20 minutes) and then roll out the pastries (a few at a time, leaving the major portion of the dough in the refrigerator) between 2 sheets of well-floured waxed paper, changing the paper whenever it gets wrinkled. Even so, novices may not get as many pies from the dough as experts like Vera. Although leftover filling is delicious in other dishes (such as shepherd's pie), you may want to make only half the filling the first time you try the dish.

Makes about 40 hors d'oeuvres

FILLING:
1½ **pounds ground beef**
1½ **pounds ground pork**
1   **cup chopped green onions**
1   **cup chopped yellow or white onion**
1   **heaping teaspoon salt (or to taste)**
1   **teaspoon coarse-ground black pepper (or to taste)**
1   **teaspoon coarse-ground white pepper**
1   **teaspoon cayenne or dried crushed red pepper (or to taste)**
⅓   **cup all-purpose flour**

PIE SHELLS:
2   **cups self-rising flour (unsifted)**
     Generous ½ cup shortening, at room temperature
1   **egg, beaten**
¾   **cup milk**
     About 3 cups oil for deep-frying

To make filling: In a large skillet, brown the meat, stirring constantly, then add both types of onions and the seasonings. Continue cooking until onions are very soft. Taste and correct seasonings. Sift the flour over the mixture and stir until well combined. Remove from heat, place mixture in a colander to drain off excess grease and juice, and cool to room temperature.

To make pie shells: Combine flour, shortening, egg, and milk. Stir until dough forms a ball. (This can be done in a food processor, or in a large bowl using a wooden spoon.) Turn dough onto a well-floured board. Flour your hands thoroughly and knead dough until it becomes smooth and elastic. (If desired, chill dough 20 minutes after kneading.) Pinch off a small handful of dough, about the size of a medium egg, and roll it lightly in extra flour. On a well-floured surface (or between 2 floured sheets of waxed paper), using light strokes in all directions, roll it out very thin (thinner than piecrust, but not so thin it will break when filled) to the size of a 5½-inch circular saucer. (You can use a saucer to mark the circle and cut it out with a knife.)

Place a heaping tablespoon of the filling inside the pastry circle, dampen the edges, fold over and press the edges with a fork or fingers to seal. With the tines of a fork, poke a few holes in the pastry. Repeat until all the filling or all the dough is used up. Keep pastries cool until ready to fry. (They may be refrigerated a few hours, if desired.)

Heat the oil in a deep skillet to 350 degrees. Fry meat pies (1 or 2 at a time) until golden brown on all sides. If desired, meat pies can be frozen, uncooked. Cook frozen; do not thaw first. If preferred, pies may be baked in a 350-degree oven about 15 minutes, or until pastry is golden brown. (Note: Baking is less fattening, but less tasty, too.)

wwwwwwwwww

PIG'S FEET

These make a nice snack on New Year's Day or any other social occasion.

Serves 4–6 as hors d'oeuvres

4	pig's feet	2-3	cloves garlic
1½	teaspoons salt		Vinegar

Have the butcher split the pig's feet lengthwise and then cut them into 3-inch pieces. Wash the pieces well and scrape with a knife to clean thoroughly. Cover with water, bring to a boil, and add salt and garlic. Simmer covered until meat is tender but not falling off the bone (prick with a fork to test). Drain, sprinkle pieces lightly with vinegar, and serve as an hors d'oeuvre.

About Gumbo

Gumbo is a hearty soup that's served over white rice, usually as a main dish. Gumbo should be about the consistency of a beefy vegetable soup or a thin cream soup—not quite as thick as pea soup. There are several types of gumbo, based on the ingredient that thickens the broth. Some gumbo is thickened with roux only. Okra also thickens gumbo, so when using it, use less roux.

Filé gumbo (a spice consisting of ground sassafras, often with a little powdered thyme) is another thickener for gumbo, but it's never added to the pot. Filé is quite strong as both a flavor and a thickener, and when heated it develops an unpleasant musky flavor and turns the gumbo dark and stringy. Instead of adding it to the pot, put a little filé (¼ teaspoon or less) on each plate and stir it into the portion of gumbo.

For chicken gumbo, buy a whole chicken (what we call a "chicken poulet for four"), because you'll need the neck and back to make a rich broth. You can use as much or as little of the rest of the chicken as you wish, according to taste and how many people you're serving. Smoked sausages add the smoked flavor typical of our Cajun-Creole gumbo. You want that smoked flavor to become part of your broth. (Do not add liquid smoke to your gumbo! Some people do that and then say that it wasn't very good. You need to add sausages to get the flavor.) No matter what you find in canned "gumbo," we don't use tomatoes in this gumbo. The tomatoes take the taste of the roux away. One taste sort of contradicts the other.

CHICKEN AND SAUSAGE GUMBO
(Gumbo Filé)

The amount of roux needed to thicken this gumbo will vary with the type of chicken used, since some of the liquid will evaporate during the long cooking needed with a stewing hen or a large roaster. If using small fryer pieces that cook quickly, use 1¼ cups of roux; if using a larger or tougher chicken, use just 1 cup. For the richest flavor, start the stock cooking first, and let it simmer while you measure and cut up the other ingredients.

Serves 5–6

1-1¼	cups roux (see above), at room temperature	1	tablespoon cayenne (or to taste)	
6	cups (48 ounces) chicken broth, homemade or canned	1½	teaspoons black pepper	
*6½	cups water	1½	pounds smoked sausages (page 122 or store-bought) or smoked links (spicy or mild), cut into ½-inch slices	
3½	pounds chicken, cut into serving pieces, with neck and upper back separated	1	cup chopped parsley leaves	
	Stalks of 1 bunch parsley, chopped	¾	cup chopped green onions	
¼	of a medium-size yellow onion	½	cup chopped celery	
1	tablespoon salt (or to taste)		About 1½ teaspoons filé powder (optional)	
			Cooked rice (about 8 cups)	

*Note: If there is no time to simmer the neck and back, replace water with a light (uncondensed) chicken broth.

Let roux come to room temperature. In a large stockpot, bring chicken broth and the water to a boil. Add the neck and back (and wingtips, heart, gizzard, and feet, if desired), the parsley stalks, and the yellow onion. Return to a boil; skim, reduce heat, and simmer while preparing other ingredients.

Mix the salt, cayenne, and black pepper, and season the remaining chicken pieces on both sides with the mixture (reserving any extra seasoning). Film a large skillet with oil and, over high heat, lightly sauté the chicken pieces on both sides just until they begin to color. Or you can broil chicken briefly (about 5 minutes per side), turning once. Do not totally brown the chicken; cook it only long enough to tighten the meat and seal in the juices. Reserve chicken pieces. Add any juice from the bottom of the broiling pan to the stock.

Return the stock to a boil, remove from heat, and stirring strongly, blend in a large spoonful of the room-temperature roux. Return pot to low heat so that the liquid bubbles gently but does not boil, and gradually stir in the remaining roux, a little at a time, until the liquid thickens slightly. This process will take 5–10 minutes.

Add sausages and parsley to the stock and simmer uncovered 20–30 minutes. Drop the chicken pieces carefully into the stock, add any reserved seasonings, and simmer uncovered, stirring occasionally, 20–30 minutes. Adjust heat to maintain a steady simmer; do not boil. Add green onions and celery, and continue to simmer until chicken is cooked through but not yet falling off the bone (about 15 minutes longer for a fryer, 1 hour longer if using a tough stewing hen). As chicken simmers, tilt the pot and with a large metal spoon skim excess fat from the surface of the broth. Taste carefully and correct seasonings if needed, and remove any chicken parts you don't want to serve (such as feet, neck, upper back). If liquid has gotten too thick (it should not be as thick as a stew), stir in a little more broth or water and simmer briefly to blend flavors. Serve gumbo hot over a mound of rice.

To make this a "gumbo filé," sprinkle a little filé powder (about ¼ teaspoon) into each person's empty gumbo bowl, then spoon in the gumbo and rice and stir together.

Chicken Okra Gumbo: Wash 1 pound okra, trim off the heads and tough tails, and cut it into slices about ¼ inch thick. Make gumbo as above, but decrease roux to ⅔ cup. Once the roux has been stirred into the liquid, add all the okra at once. (Gumbo liquid will suddenly become much thicker.) Proceed as above, cooking the gumbo at least 45 minutes after adding the okra, or until okra is very tender. Although gumbos combining both okra and filé powder are rare, filé powder may be sprinkled into the gumbo bowls if desired.

〰〰〰〰〰〰〰〰

SEAFOOD GUMBO

In seafood gumbo, pieces of crab are cooked in their shells so that none of the meat will get lost. (The shells give flavor to the broth, too.)

Serves 5-6

1 cup roux
6 cups water
4 cups chicken broth
½ pound dried shrimp
¾ cup parsley, divided
2 tablespoons coarsely chopped yellow onion
½ cup chopped green onions
½ cup chopped celery
2 Dungeness or Alaska crabs, cracked (or 6 blue crabs, or 5 pounds King crab legs)
   About 12 clams (optional)

2 pounds prawns or shrimp, peeled, deveined, and rinsed
1 pint jar shucked oysters (optional)
2 teaspoons salt (or to taste)
2-3 teaspoons cayenne (or to taste)
1 teaspoon black pepper (or to taste)
   Cooked rice (about 8 cups)

Let roux come to room temperature. Meanwhile, bring the water and chicken broth to a boil. Add the dried shrimp with 2 tablespoons of the parsley and the yellow onion. Simmer 20 minutes. Return the broth to a boil, remove from heat, and stirring strongly, blend in a large spoonful of the room-temperature roux. Return pot to low heat and stir in remaining roux, a large spoonful at a time. When all the roux has been absorbed and the liquid is lightly thickened, add the green onions, celery, and the remainder of the parsley and continue to simmer uncovered.

Clean and scrape the legs, claws, and bodies of the crabs and add crab legs and claws to the gumbo (reserving the bodies), along with clams if you are using them. Simmer uncovered about 20 minutes. As the gumbo cooks, skim any excess fat from the surface of the liquid with a large metal spoon. When gumbo is almost done, about 10 minutes before you're ready to serve it, season it carefully to taste with salt, cayenne, and black pepper. Add the prawns and the bodies (center part) of the crab, broken into 4 pieces each if large. (These are added later than the legs because they take less time to cook.) If using oysters, drop them into the broth just before serving the gumbo; the heat in the pot will be enough to cook them. Serve over rice.

VERA LEWIS'S OKRA GUMBO WITH CHICKEN, SAUSAGE, AND SEAFOOD

Every Creole and Cajun has her or his own version of gumbo. My sister-in-law makes a gumbo thickened only with okra. Her gumbo does include tomatoes, since there is no roux.

Serves 8–10

CHICKEN MIXTURE:

6-pound roasting chicken, cut into serving pieces
1½ teaspoons salt
1½ teaspoons cayenne
1½ teaspoons black pepper
1½ teaspoons paprika
1 teaspoon garlic powder

1 teaspoon onion powder
½ cup oil
2 large cloves garlic, finely chopped
1 medium onion, finely chopped
⅔ cup chopped bell pepper
12 cups water

OKRA MIXTURE:

2 packages frozen chopped (or sliced) okra, 20 ounces each, thawed
½ cup oil
2 teaspoons salt
½ teaspoon cayenne
½ teaspoon black pepper
1 medium onion, finely chopped
⅔ cup chopped bell pepper
2 large cloves garlic, finely chopped
1 tablespoon flour

14½-ounce can stewed tomatoes
1 cup water
½ pound Polish sausage (or other smoked sausage)
1 pound snow crab legs or 1 cracked Dungeness crab
1 pound medium-size shrimp, peeled, deveined, and rinsed
1 bay leaf
Cooked rice (about 12 cups)

To make chicken mixture: Season chicken pieces with the salt, cayenne, pepper, paprika, garlic powder, and onion powder. In a large stockpot, heat the oil and fry chicken over high heat until lightly browned. Add garlic, onion, and bell pepper. Continue to fry, stirring occasionally, until vegetables are soft. Add 12 cups water. Cover, bring to a boil, and reduce heat. Simmer over low heat while preparing okra mixture.

To make okra mixture: Place okra in a large heavy skillet with the oil. Add salt, cayenne, and pepper. Sauté over medium heat, stirring frequently and scraping the bottom of the skillet to incorporate the browned bits, until okra is lightly browned and okra seeds turn light pink. Add onion, bell pepper, and garlic and continue sautéing until vegetables are soft and okra has stopped stringing. Stir in flour and cook a few seconds. Stir in tomatoes and 1 cup water. Cook over medium heat 2 minutes. Pour okra mixture into the chicken mixture. Add sausage, crab, shrimp, and bay leaf. Simmer uncovered over medium heat 30 minutes, stirring occasionally. Serve in a soup bowl over rice.

About Rice

Many Creole rice dishes, including Dirty Rice (page 214) and Jambalaya (page 149) call for plain rice, cooked in advance and cooled. (This keeps it from becoming mushy when it's stirred into a liquid.) In addition, rice is served as an accompaniment to almost all Creole and Cajun dishes.

I always use the pearl rice. It's easier for a beginner, and it's what my family always used. Cook pearl rice cup per cup with water. If you're cooking long-grain rice, use 2 cups of water for every cup of rice, or a little less liquid if the rice is going to be used in Jambalaya. I use an electric rice cooker, but you can cook rice on a stove almost as easily.

It's better to cook rice in fairly large quantities (at least 2 cups raw rice). If you cook just a little rice you risk burning the bottom layer. (If the leftover rice isn't going to be used for Jambalaya or Dirty Rice, it can be buttered and gently reheated, covered, in a moderate oven.) If using an electric range, be aware that electric burners maintain their heat well after their settings have been lowered. After the rice has come to a boil, move it to another burner set to "warm" (if "low" is too high), or insert a flame-tamer pad between the burner and the pot.

PLAIN RICE

Serves 3–4

2 cups short-grain pearl rice (such as Blue Rose or Calrose)

2 cups water
Salt to taste
1 pat butter (optional)

Rinse rice in a strainer under cold running water until water runs clear. Place rice in a heavy saucepan with a tight-fitting lid. Add an equal amount of water (plus an extra 2 tablespoons if halving the recipe), a little salt, and a pat of butter if desired. (Butter will help prevent burning.) Bring to a full boil, stir well a few seconds, and cover immediately. Reduce heat to a simmer and cook rice very gently 15 minutes. This will make 4 cups of rice.

Long-Grain Rice: To make rice as a side dish, use a ratio of 1 cup long-grain rice to 2 cups water (for example, 1½ cups rice and 3 cups water to make 4½ cups cooked rice). To make the drier rice needed for Jambalaya or Dirty Rice, use just 1¾ cups liquid to each cup of long-grain rice. Proceed as for pearl rice but increase simmering time to 20 minutes.

BAKED TURKEY

Corn Bread Dressing (following), Dirty Rice (page 214), or Chaudin (page 125) can be served as a dressing with an unstuffed turkey. If desired, the turkey can be stuffed with a dressing of choice and cooked about 20 minutes longer.

Serves 10–12

	10-pound turkey
2	**teaspoons salt**
1¼	**teaspoons paprika**
1	**teaspoon cayenne**
½	**teaspoon white pepper**
4	**large cloves garlic, minced**
2	**tablespoons butter**
¼	**cup water**

STOCK/GRAVY:

Neck and giblets (and wingtips, if desired) of turkey

3	**cups water**
3	**sprigs parsley**
½	**rib celery**
2	**tablespoons chopped onion**
3	**tablespoons flour dissolved in ⅓ cup cold water**

Preheat oven to 325 degrees. Start cooking the turkey stock (below). In a small bowl, mix salt, paprika, cayenne, and white pepper. With a small, sharp knife, cut small pockets under each side of the turkey breast and between each thigh and the body. In each pocket, insert some of the seasoning mixture and a quarter of the garlic. Rub turkey all over, inside and out, with remaining seasoning mixture. Place turkey in a roasting pan with a cover (if you don't have one, see Cookware in the Appendix). Melt butter and brush turkey with it, and pour ¼ cup water into the roasting pan. Bake turkey uncovered 30 minutes. Cover and bake an additional 2–2½ hours, basting occasionally, until turkey is cooked. (Leg will move freely; when thigh is pierced with a knife tip, juice will be golden or clear, not pink.) Remove from oven and let stand about 15 minutes before carving.

Stock/Gravy: Combine turkey neck, giblets, and wingtips in a saucepan with 3 cups water. Bring to a boil, reduce heat to moderate, and skim foam and particles for about 10 minutes or until no more foam appears. Add parsley, celery, and onion. Simmer partly covered (but never completely covered) until liquid tastes like a rich broth (about 1 hour). Strain the stock and return to the saucepan. Baste turkey lightly with small amounts of the stock. When turkey is done, pour the pan drippings into the stock. Skim fat from the surface. Bring liquid to a boil. Remove from heat. Gradually stir in the flour paste, a little at a time, until gravy has reached the desired thickness, returning the pan to medium-low heat after the first spoonful. Simmer a few minutes to cook the flour, then serve hot.

~~~~~~~~~~~~~~~~

PAM'S CORN BREAD DRESSING

"A moist and spicy holiday dressing" is how my daughter, Ledra, describes this piquant dish as prepared by my daughter-in-law. The dressing is fully cooked, and needs only a few minutes in the oven or microwave to reheat. Despite the modern shortcut (a muffin mix), it takes a little time to prepare, but the giblets and broth can be cooked a day early, cooled, and refrigerated until the next morning. Ingredients may be halved to serve 6 as a dressing to accompany roast chicken or duck.

Serves 10–12

1 **pound chicken or turkey giblets**
5 **cups water**
1 **rib celery, halved**
1 **medium carrot, halved**
1 **small onion, quartered**
½ **teaspoon salt**
2 **boxes corn muffin mix, 1 pound each**
1 **cup minced fresh parsley**
¾ **cup finely chopped green onions**
¾ **cup finely chopped celery**
½ **cup finely chopped green bell pepper**
1 **teaspoon minced fresh garlic (or ½ teaspoon garlic powder)**

¾ **teaspoon black pepper**
¾ **teaspoon cayenne**
½ **teaspoon poultry seasoning**
1 **pound uncased sausage mixture (page 122) or seasoned breakfast sausage (preferably spicy)**
½ **cup butter**
2 **cups reserved giblet broth (fat skimmed from top)**
As needed: about 1¾ cups uncondensed chicken broth (or a 14½-ounce can)

Place giblets, the water, celery halves, carrot, quartered onion, and salt in a large, deep saucepan. Bring just to a boil, skim until foam (if any) subsides, reduce heat, and boil slowly until giblets are tender (about 1 hour). Drain, reserving solids and liquids separately. Chop giblets or pulse in a food processor.

While broth cooks (if you are making the dressing all in one day), prepare corn muffin mix according to package directions and bake in a cake pan until golden brown. Let cool; crumble into small pieces.

Meanwhile, chop the vegetables and mix the garlic and seasonings; reserve.

In a large skillet or Dutch oven, brown the sausage. Drain off the fat and add the butter, vegetables, and seasonings. Cook, stirring occasionally, over medium-high heat, until vegetables wilt. Add reserved giblet broth and giblets and bring to a simmer. Simmer about 20 minutes. Stir in crumbled corn bread. Stir in additional chicken broth a small amount at a time, folding together well, until mixture is moist but not soggy. Taste carefully and correct seasonings. Dressing should be spicy to your palate. Pack mixture into an ovenproof or microwaveable pan, and reserve while preparing the remainder of the meal. Reheat shortly before serving.

~~~~~~~~~~~~~~~~~~

DAY-AFTER TURKEY NOODLE SOUP

Serves 8–12

	Turkey bones and scraps	1¾	cups strong chicken broth (or a 14½-ounce can broth)
7	cups water		
1	large onion, quartered	2	cups dry medium-size noodles
2	ribs celery		
3	sprigs parsley	1	cup chopped carrots
3	cloves garlic	3	cups cooked turkey meat cut into small pieces
1½	teaspoons salt		
¼	teaspoon cayenne	1	cup peas
¼	teaspoon black pepper		

In a 4-quart soup pot, combine turkey bones and scraps with the water, onion, celery, parsley, garlic, salt, cayenne, and pepper. Bring to a boil, reduce heat, and simmer 1½ hours, partly covered. Let cool a little, then strain the stock and return it to the pot. Add chicken broth and bring mixture to a boil again. Add noodles and carrots. Boil 10 minutes, or until noodles are tender. Reduce heat, add turkey meat and peas, and simmer until peas are tender and turkey is heated through (about 5 minutes).

∿∿∿∿∿∿∿∿∿∿∿

RÔTI DE BOEUF
(Baked Beef)

Roasting over liquid in a covered pan produces moist, tender meat, even from the tougher roasting cuts. In this recipe, the beef comes out well-done but juicy; cut the cooking time if you prefer a rare roast. (If you don't have a covered roasting pan, see Cookware in the Appendix for how to improvise one.)

Serves 4–6

3-4	pounds boneless beef roast from the round or chuck (such as cross-rib roast, top round, rump roast)	1	teaspoon black pepper
		1	teaspoon cayenne
		1	teaspoon garlic powder
		½	cup minced bell pepper
1	teaspoon salt	3-4	cloves garlic, minced

Preheat oven to 350 degrees. If meat is thickly covered with fat, trim off all but a thin layer. In a small bowl, mix salt, pepper, cayenne, and garlic powder. Separately, mix bell pepper and minced garlic. Make several small slits in the meat and fill them with the bell pepper mixture, and with a total of 1 teaspoon of the seasoning mixture. Rub the remaining seasoning mixture over the outside of the roast. If possible, let meat stand about 1 hour to absorb seasonings.

Place on a rack in a covered roasting pan and pour ½ cup water under the rack. Add leftover bell pepper mixture to the water. Cover and roast 1 hour, basting every 15–20 minutes with pan juices. (For rarer meat, cut covered cooking time to 30–45 minutes, depending on the size of the roast.) If water evaporates, add more. Uncover and brown 30 minutes longer, basting again halfway through. Let stand a few minutes before carving, and serve with the pan juices.

~~~~~~~~~~~~~~~~~~~

BLACK-EYED PEAS

In the Southern tradition, eating black-eyed peas on New Year's Day is supposed to bring good luck for the rest of the year. And what harm could it do?

Serves 6–8

1 pound dried black-eyed peas	1 cup chopped onion
6 thick slices bacon	¼ cup chopped bell pepper
3 cloves garlic, chopped	1 tablespoon oil
2 medium jalapeño peppers, trimmed, seeded, and chopped	1½ teaspoons salt, or to taste
	¼ teaspoon black pepper
	8 cups water

Combine all ingredients in a 4-quart Dutch oven or heavy saucepan. Bring to a boil, cover, reduce heat, and simmer until peas are tender (about 1 hour). Check liquid from time to time, adding more water if liquid is evaporating too quickly. When peas are done, check liquid again. If it is too thin, increase heat to moderate, uncover pan, and cook until liquid thickens.

CANDIED CARROTS

We often serve candied carrots with fowl—chicken and turkey—and with pork, but not so much with beef. The sweet flavor goes real well with those kinds of meat, much the way the Chinese use a sweet-and-sour sauce with chicken or pork.

Serves 3–4

5–6 **carrots, pared**	4 **tablespoons (½ stick)**
½ **cup water**	**butter**
¼ **cup sugar**	

Slice carrots into pieces about 3 inches long and place them in a 2-quart saucepan. (It's best to crowd them close together.) Add the water, sugar, and butter. Bring to a boil, cover the pan, and reduce heat to maintain a light boil, slightly stronger than a simmer. A light syrup will form; stir occasionally to coat each carrot. Cook until tender (15–25 minutes, depending on the thickness of the carrots).

THELMA LEWIS'S
SWEET POTATO PAWN

This dessert comes from my sister-in-law Thelma (Willie's wife). Leftover pawn, reheated, makes a delicious breakfast.

Serves 10–12

About 1¾ pounds (4 medium) raw sweet potatoes or yams, pared (to make 4 cups, grated)	4 eggs, well beaten
	½ cup all-purpose flour
	2 teaspoons cinnamon
	1 teaspoon nutmeg
1½ cups sugar	¼ teaspoon salt
½ cup (1 stick) butter, at room temperature	¼–⅓ cup milk, if necessary Sour cream or whipped cream

Preheat oven to 350 degrees. Thoroughly grease an ovenproof rectangular pan, about 12″ × 8″ × 2″. Grate the sweet potatoes on the coarse holes of a hand grater, or in a food processor (use the shredding disk, then briefly pulse with the steel knife to cut the shreds short), until you have 4 cups. (Discard any extra, or save for another use.)

In a large bowl, using a wooden spoon (or in a food processor), cream the sugar with the softened butter. Thoroughly blend in eggs, flour, cinnamon, nutmeg, and salt. Stir in sweet potatoes and mix well. If mixture is too dry, add milk. Turn mixture into the greased pan and bake until golden brown (about 1 hour). Serve hot or at room temperature with sour cream or whipped cream.

ALMENA'S THREE-LAYER CAKE

This exceptional cake is moist, fine-grained, and light. Begin by letting about 2¼ sticks of butter come to room temperature, and the rest will be surprisingly easy. Prepare the filling as soon as the cake goes into the oven, and make the icing while the filled cake sets.

Makes a 3-layer cake

¾ cup (1½ sticks) butter at room temperature
¼ cup shortening, at room temperature
1½ cups sugar
4 eggs, separated
1½ cups milk
1½ teaspoons vanilla
3 cups cake flour, sifted before measuring

2 teaspoons baking powder
*Lemon Pudding Filling (below) or other filling
White Butter Icing (below) or a favorite chocolate icing
About ½ cup shredded sweetened coconut (optional)

*Note: If desired, a simpler, old-fashioned cake filling can be made by turning the contents of a 14-ounce jar of raspberry (or other flavor) jelly into a saucepan and gently heating it until it melts.

Preheat oven to 350 degrees. Grease three 8- or 9-inch cake pans with a little shortening. Cream together butter, shortening, and sugar until fluffy. Stir in milk and vanilla. Stir in flour and baking powder until well mixed; do not overbeat (or cake will be heavy).

Beat egg whites until stiff peaks form and gently fold into the batter. Pour batter equally into the greased pans. Bake until a toothpick inserted in the middle of each layer comes out clean (about 25 minutes). Remove cakes from oven and let cool. Turn out of the pans.

Turn out bottom layer of the cake upside down and spread with Lemon Pudding or other filling. Place the second layer on top of the first and spread filling on it. Place the third layer on top, and let cake stand 1 hour to set. Then frost the top layer and the sides of the cake with White Butter Icing or a favorite chocolate icing. If desired, scatter coconut lightly over the icing.

LEMON PUDDING FILLING

2   egg yolks (white spot removed)
⅓   cup plus 2 tablespoons sugar
1   cup milk (or water)
2   teaspoons butter (preferably unsalted)
1   tablespoon cornstarch dissolved in 2 tablespoons water

1   teaspoon vanilla
½   cup shredded sweetened coconut
About 4 tablespoons fresh lemon juice (from 2 or more large, ripe lemons; see Appendix)

In a very heavy saucepan, combine egg yolks, sugar, milk, and butter. Stir constantly over low heat until butter melts. Stir in cornstarch paste and vanilla. Continue simmering, stirring almost constantly, until mixture is thick and creamy. Stir in coconut and remove from heat. Stir in 2 tablespoons of the lemon juice, taste, and continue stirring in lemon juice until tartness and flavor are as desired. (Bear in mind that the icing is very sweet, so filling can be quite tart.) Let cool before spreading on cake.

~~~~~~~~~~~~~~~~~~~

WHITE BUTTER ICING

⅓   cup butter (preferably unsalted), at room temperature

¼   cup whole milk
2½   cups powdered sugar
½   teaspoon vanilla

In a bowl (or food processor) beat butter, milk, and half the powdered sugar together until smooth. Stir in remaining sugar and the vanilla and beat until creamy (about 3 minutes with a spoon or hand-held electric beater or about 30 seconds in a food processor). If too stiff, add a few additional drops of milk.

OLD-FASHIONED CARAMEL POPCORN BALLS

Don't hang these Christmas treats on the tree—they're too tasty to waste as decorations.

Makes 10 baseball-size popcorn balls

⅓ **cup raw popcorn**   1 **cup pure cane syrup**
⅛ **teaspoon salt**   1 **tablespoon butter**

Pop the popcorn according to package directions, salt it lightly if desired, and set aside in a large bowl or pan. Pour syrup into a saucepan; bring to a boil. Reduce heat. Cook slowly until syrup makes a fine string when poured from a spoon. (That is, the string will form almost at the last drop pouring from the spoon.) Add the butter and continue cooking until melted. Pour syrup mixture over the popcorn and stir well to mix. Wet your hands in cold water and form popcorn into baseball-size globes, rolling the mixture between your palms until it clings firmly together.

QUICK PECAN PRALINES

These tender, fudgy candies take just a few minutes once you've assembled the ingredients and tools—but make them when you're sure there'll be no interruptions.

Makes 12 large or 18 medium pralines

1   **cup packed brown sugar**   3   **tablespoons butter**
1   **cup white sugar**   ½   **teaspoon vanilla**
⅔   **cup evaporated milk**   1½ **cups pecan pieces**

Grease a sheet of waxed paper or a cookie sheet with a little butter and set in a convenient place. Have on hand a candy thermometer, or place a small bowl filled with ice water near the stove. In a saucepan, mix brown and white sugars with evaporated milk. Bring to a boil, stirring constantly. Reduce heat to medium and boil lightly, stirring constantly, until mixture reaches 238 degrees on a candy thermometer (about 7 minutes). (Lacking the thermometer, test by dropping a few drops of the mixture into ice water; it should form a soft ball.) Remove from heat and let cool until temperature drops to 200 degrees or less (5–10 minutes). With a wooden spoon or a wire whisk, beat in butter and vanilla. Beat until mixture thickens and becomes creamy, but not until it loses its gloss. Stir in the pecans and drop mixture by spoonfuls onto the waxed paper or cookie sheet. Let stand a few hours before serving or storing.

wwwwwwwww

ELVINA GUILLORY'S
OLD-TIME EGGNOG

This eggnog can be served hot on a cold winter's night, or it can be chilled.

Serves 8

4	eggs, separated	1	cup rum or Jack Daniel's
⅓	cup sugar		(optional)
1	quart half-and-half		Pinch of salt
1	quart whole milk	4	teaspoons nutmeg, or
			to taste

Remove the little white spot from each of the egg yolks. In a 3-quart saucepan, cream the egg yolks and sugar. Add half-and-half and heat very hot, but do not boil. Slowly add milk. Remove from heat. Add the spirit you choose. Beat 2 of the egg whites very stiff with a pinch of salt, and fold gradually into the mixture. (The leftover whites can be refrigerated overnight and used for scrambled eggs, or frozen for later use; see Appendix.) Gradually stir in nutmeg to taste (or if serving immediately, sprinkle some nutmeg over each portion, or over the serving bowl).

GIN FIZZ

I serve this cocktail at my New Year's Day parties, but it's just as delicious at a summer brunch. The egg yolks make it very foamy, but those who don't like them (or who want to use up some leftover egg whites from the Eggnog) can substitute whites only. In either case, since the eggs aren't cooked, make this drink only if you are confident of the eggs in your area.

Makes 2 tall glasses

2 whole eggs, or 3 egg whites	1½–2 ounces gin (or to taste)
4 heaping teaspoons sugar	1½ teaspoons fresh lemon juice
4 ounces orange juice	1½ teaspoons fresh lime juice
3 ounces club soda	1½ cups ice cubes
3 ounces half-and-half (or light cream)	

Pour all ingredients into a blender and blend at the highest speed until slushy (20–30 seconds). If using a food processor, first crush the ice separately by whatever means available and then add to the other ingredients.

2

Ici On Parle Français

As any Cajun or Creole can tell you, when you start school, you're in for a shock. The teacher will tolerate you speaking French for only the first few days before she tells you, "I'm sorry. You'll have to speak English here."

At home we spoke French, our Creole patois. My oldest sister knew some English, but she didn't bother with it among the family. The rest of us could understand it a little, but we didn't have a radio and television didn't exist yet, so we weren't exposed to English very much.

It was only when we started going to school, where we spoke French but many of the other kids spoke English, that I learned we were Creole. We went home and told our parents about it, and started asking questions about it. "Well, what are we?" we asked.

They told us that we were Creole. People often ask me what is the difference between Cajuns and Creoles. Cajuns are the

Acadian people, originally from France, who migrated to Louisiana from Nova Scotia (formerly called Acadia), in Canada. Creoles were originally French and Spanish, migrating directly from Europe (not from Canada) about 300 years ago. Then, of course, the Creole group was broadened by mixing with all the other Louisiana nationalities: Native American (my own lineage is part Cherokee), West Indian, African, German, etc., no one is sure what the mixture is. But the mixture that I am is always referred to as Creole, not Cajun. When my mother described her cooking, it was always "Creole cooking"—never Cajun—although there's really very little difference between the cooking styles.

I can remember starting school feeling very excited—"I'm big enough to go to school!" The letdown came when I discovered that it was very difficult to communicate with the teacher: she's telling me something in English and I'm telling her something in French, and we're not understanding each other at all. I kept trying to tell her, in French, "I don't speak English." Some of the older children translated, and told me that she said I had to speak English in school. I told them to tell her I would, as soon as I could learn the language.

I went through that for a couple of weeks, and suddenly the English just came. You keep hearing the same things over and over, and somehow it all gets locked in. Suddenly you're saying, "I'm going," "I went," "I will go." It's the way a baby learns to speak. The teacher didn't want us to revert to French. In fact, we got spanked if she caught us; she actually slapped our hands. She felt that we *could* speak English, and so we should.

At home, I would practice English with my sisters. When I didn't know a word, I'd ask my big sister. And then I'd teach my little sister, which gave me an incentive to try and learn quicker. It made me feel important: "Oh, I'm teaching someone else, I'm helping someone." That has always been a part of me, knowing that I'm helping. But you know, even now I still sometimes find myself thinking in French.

That little white and green schoolhouse probably held no more than 100 students. It was a community school for Creoles and blacks, and it went up to the 12th grade. A farmer donated the building and the land, because the nearest school was so far away that some of the kids couldn't have gotten any education. There were no school buses, some of the kids had to walk three and four miles a day since the parents couldn't drive them to school because they had to work on the farms. Luckily, we lived just one mile from school. One mile isn't really that bad—except when it's rainy or cold.

We were taught all in the same room. All the youngsters sat in the front, while the higher grades sat in the back. The teacher would teach the lesson on the blackboard and then she'd recess the younger kids while she'd take care of another grade. She'd give us an assignment that kept us busy while she worked with another group. And she was a good teacher. I tell you, we learned.

There were no hot school lunches; we had to bring our own: milk, fruit, sausage sandwiches (with Mom's homemade smoked sausages), or leftover fried chicken. Often we had butter and jelly, because Mom made her own butter and jelly. Then, when we came back from school, Mom always had something for us. She had cookies and gingerbread, or freshly baked sweet bread, or little cakes and muffins, or tea cakes (which are little cookies that aren't as sweet as a cake). We could smell them in the air as we walked home. As they do in England, we had teatime before we started our chores and homework.

Having to dress for school, I became more conscious of being the middle child of seven. I thought about it many times:

"I'm the fourth one, and my sister is passing on her clothing to me. Why couldn't I be before her?" But the clothes were just too good to throw away. I had my own new clothes, too, just not as many as I wanted—or as I could have had, had I not been the middle child. I thought my sister's hand-me-downs were too big for me, but they really fit well enough. I had to use them. Actually, they were nice dresses; they might have been a little faded, but they were all starched and ironed and clean. (We never wore pants. Never *ever* wore pants to school!)

At major holidays like Christmas, we'd go into town to try on dresses and buy shoes, but most of our dresses were handmade. We wore little muumuu dresses, and faille dresses, which would take more time to make, with the little gathers at the bottom, and ruffled jumpers and pinafore aprons over the dresses.

Even our undergarments were handmade. At home, and working in the fields, and playing in the yard, we wore homemade underpants. For school we wore store-bought undergarments. The homemade panties were beautiful, with ruffles around the legs, but we felt we wanted some from the department store, too. That was a treat for us.

Our shoes were store-bought, but my grandfather had a shoe repair shop, so he would repair them as they wore down— and our everyday shoes were passed from one sister to another. For our dress-up shoes, we had the little black patent leather shoes like youngsters have today; they were made from really good patent leather, not that imitation patent leather they have today. And how we used to polish and keep those shoes nice! We'd use lamb oil—we put it on the patent leather like saddle soap. We had little purses to match our shoes. Sometimes my mom would make us little cloth purses to put our nickels and dimes in, and she made our hankies too. Each girl always had a little handkerchief—no Kleenex. My mom would embroider one corner of it with a little flower or some other design, and sometimes she crocheted all around it to make it very dressy.

We didn't like to wear shoes in the summer months to go out to play. But going barefoot was dangerous, especially if we played where we shouldn't have (like around the barns), because there were always nails and things we could step on— and we did.

My father sang a Cajun dance tune called *"Papier dans mes souliers,"* which means "paper in my shoes." When we asked him what it meant, he told us that times were hard for lots of people, and when the soles of their shoes wore through they couldn't afford to fix them. Once, when he was young, he wore the soles of his own shoes until they had little holes in them, but he didn't notice until he went outside and felt the dampness. They were his best shoes. So he took paper bags or pieces of cardboard and put them inside his shoes. He thought it was terrible, having to go see his girl friend with paper in his shoes, but he had to do it until his dad repaired them.

My mom used to make little beads for dress-up, but we wouldn't wear our beads to school unless it was a special day. Mom pierced our ears, too, and we wore earrings. She used a cork underneath the lobe and a hot needle, the tiniest sewing needle she could find. She burned the cork first and nothing touched it thereafter until she brought it to the ear. She cleaned the ear, then she took the cork and rubbed it over and under the lobe. She threaded the needle with silk thread, and after rolling the earlobe to push the blood away, she put the cork under the earlobe and push the needle through with a little lamb tallow— a solid block of lamb fat, which was used as a salve like we use Vaseline today. We kept the silk thread in our ears for about two weeks, or until the ears were healed. Afterwards, our parents would buy us gold earrings, which were expensive for them, two or three bucks, and that was our second Christmas present. If we had to go to the fields, we took the earrings off and used tiny pieces of broom straw oiled with tallow to keep the holes open.

We dressed up to go to school plays and pageants. It was at one of those plays that I first saw Santa Claus, live. And I was terrified. I was sitting next to my sister and my mom at the school Christmas play, and when Santa Claus appeared, I was so afraid, I got under the chair. It was just the mask, the beard, the way he was dressed. I couldn't see anything of the man beneath. I was afraid of Santa Claus for a long time. It's funny, but a lot of children are. I see little kids today in the department stores, their parents put them in Santa's lap and they slide off and start screaming.

Despite having to learn English all at once, I liked school— maybe because I was running away from all the chores at home. Everybody had chores. The oldest girl helped Mom in the kitchen. Back then I was never one for the kitchen (but look at me now!). I was always out in the yard or helping my dad in the field.

Everyone said that I was my dad's favorite, and I think it was true, because I liked the outdoors a lot better than I liked the indoors, so I'd follow him around. I was a tomboy. Having to help Mom in the house, in the kitchen, washing, mopping, sweeping, making beds, carrying water and emptying the garbage . . . well, instead, I used to go out in the field on Saturdays, when there was no school, and help my dad.

As for my sisters, when the time came when my dad needed all our hands, they were somewhat reluctant. They'd say, "Do I have to? I gotta help Mom." When he wasn't listening, they'd say, "I don't want to go out in that sun." They wanted to stay where it was cool, and I can't blame them. I don't know why I was so apt to run out in that hot sun—and it was *hot*.

I'll never forget my dad saying, "You are such a big help, I'm gonna buy you a brand-new dress. All the others are too lazy to come out and help me with this work." This was just after he'd harvested the corn. They used to rake all the dried stalks together and burn them, but there were always a few stalks that would not cooperate. My dad had to pick all those stalks by hand so he could clean the field, preparing it for the next crop, and that's what I was helping him do. It was nothing heavy, pulling these old cornstalks, bringing them to the fire and burning them.

So when he said he was going to get me a dress, I said, "Oh great! Oh wow! What else you want me to do?" And that Saturday, he did bring back a dress for me. My sisters said, "How come *she* gets a new dress?" and he answered, "Well, you remember she came and helped me in the field and I didn't get any help from the rest of you." What he meant was, "Here's what happens to girls who help."

For working in the field, we always had straw hats. People knew that the more sun you got the drier your skin would get, but they didn't worry about that, they worried about sunstroke. Sometimes, playing in the sun, we did get sunburnt to where it made little water blisters. We really got punished for that, because we stayed in the sun too long.

Women used to make sunbonnets to keep the sun from really beaming on their heads. The bonnets were made out of cloth, starched so stiff they would stand out from your forehead at least four or five inches, and they were decorated very beautifully. It was a style, a dress-up kind of a thing. They always wore long sleeves to protect themselves from the sun. As kids, we would wear long sleeves, but we rolled them up because we were too hot.

We did have some extra help in the fields. Sometimes we had four or five hired hands to help with the sowing and the harvest, but usually it was more like exchanging help. Another farmer would exchange with you: "I'll help you this week. Next week you bring your group over." It was family and friends, but they'd get paid for it. There was always so much work to do, our dad was happy to have our help.

There were a few cattle, which we used for milk and beef, and I'll never forget the time I decided I wanted to try and milk a cow. I'd seen my dad and my oldest brother Willie do it, and it seemed so easy. Of course, we didn't have a milker; you had to use your hands. The thumb was the "kingpin"—that's what you press and then squeeze. And I tried it. Milk was going all over me, all over my face—but I kept trying! When my mom saw me she said, "No, you can't do it anymore. The cow will get upset." Somehow cows are able to withhold their milk if they want to, and we needed the milk. I never did learn to milk a cow.

The chore I hated most was when my mother made cotton mattresses. She used to tell my father she needed him to grow cotton. He didn't want to grow cotton—it takes more manpower than rice, and it's hard work. He said, "What for?" She said, "So I can have cotton to make my mattresses." She didn't want to have to buy the cotton, and he could sell whatever was left over.

The cotton would come in from the fields, and we had to take it out of the bolls. To prepare the cotton, my mom would get some tough little green branches from a peach tree. There were always little buds on the limbs, and they would help break up the cotton until it was very fine and silky. The neighbors and relatives would help each other beat the cotton until it was as light as cotton candy. We had to help beat it. Mom would put the cotton on a board, and we had to beat it and beat it. I hated it with a passion. Usually we did this just after the cotton harvest, when it was very hot, and I felt like I was going to smother in that barn with all the dust. So I'd go out and take little breaks, and sometimes I'd get in trouble for taking a longer break than I was supposed to.

We stuffed the mattresses with the cotton, and Mom would sew the mattresses around. And then every year, probably twice a year, she would take the cotton out and wash it—and we had to beat the cotton all over again so it would be nice and soft again and not lumpy.

Everybody made their own quilts, too. I can remember we had to help Mom hold the quilt out—extend it and put it on a big quilting frame hanging from the ceiling of the barn. Mom stuffed her quilts with our cotton, too, and made a patchwork cover out of material from old dresses, blouses, and shirts cut up in pieces and laid out in strips running in different directions. Other women would come over to quilt together, and they filled the different areas and added smaller pieces so that it would all be nice and smooth. Then they put the top cover down, and roll it up, and start sewing it together, unrolling it as they went. They tacked it first and then they sewed. You'd be surprised at how warm those quilts were.

Years later, in Texas, my father decided that growing cotton wasn't worth the trouble, but my mom would still buy cotton in bulk, and we still had to beat it for mattresses! She kept saying, "Why should I buy them when I can make them, and make them better and tighter than they do?" Well, that was her idea. She was a very busy woman. She worked very hard and she never complained.

And though my brothers and sisters and I worked hard, too, we also played with other children, of course. During the week it was too far to walk to the neighbors' after school, but on weekends other kids would come over.

We'd visit as a family to a family. Once we were old enough to take care of ourselves, we were dropped off to visit, or an older sister or brother would take us. We would usually visit a family that had kids the same ages we were, and we'd stay for two or three hours. We played on swings, and played baseball and hop and skip [hopscotch].

On occasion, we'd go to carnivals, or our parents would take us to baseball games. There were movie theaters downtown, but they were too far away, maybe ten miles. During the week, the older guys could use the car once a week and let their hair down, but I never saw a movie until I was 10 or 11.

We loved to go out and catch crawfish for fun. This was something we started doing around age four or five, and kept doing until we were big kids, and then we outgrew it and never did it again.

The crawfish season ran from early March until early June. In the heat of summer they go down in the holes to spawn in the bottom of the mud. You could still catch some, but the most plentiful time was spring.

So we'd go out and catch a big bunch of crawfish in the canals that irrigated the rice fields. We'd take a little string, tie it onto a branch, and tie a piece of meat—fat pork or salt pork—on the end. In season, we'd get six, seven, or eight crawfish grasping at it, and we'd lift them out and drop them into a bucket. Off-season, it was different: You could see the crawfish and put the meat right next to them, and they'd come to it, bite at it or grab it—but for some reason, when you got them just about to the top of the water where they could see daylight, they opened their claws and dropped down again. In season, though, you could lift them right out of the water, and we stayed out until we had enough for a meal.

We'd bring them home and wash them off really well, and sometimes we'd cook them ourselves. "Outdoors!" my mother would shout. "Not inside with the crawfish. Make your mess out there." And we'd play house, and pretend, "Okay, you're coming for dinner and I'm cooking a meal for you." Other times, Mom would drop the crawfish into her pot of gumbo. There's not really enough meat on crawfish to make a meal, unless you've got a whole bucketful *and* time to peel the tails.

Our parents wouldn't let us go out on the bayous, the waterways linked to the Gulf. They were very deep, and dangerous—probably alligators, definitely snakes, and very swampy. They wouldn't let us go near them, no way! Canals were dangerous enough.

Fishing was great when they closed the irrigation gates to the canals; then the fish couldn't go anyplace. They were trapped, and we were ready for them. I didn't like fishing—I never caught anything—but Dad was good at it. Sometimes he'd catch fish with a pole, but other times a group of men would go "sanding for fish." It was like trolling, but they didn't have a boat—they just had a net. One guy would get on one side of the canal, another guy would go into the water, and the two of them would drag the net along. When they had gone a certain distance, they would lift the net to look and see if they'd gotten anything. Often they had a full net, sometimes nothing. The net was so wide it took two, three people to lift it, especially when it was full of fish. Sanding was illegal, I think, but everybody did it.

At night, my dad used to go frog hunting in the bayous. Hunting in the bayous was serious business; he wouldn't even take my older brother but once or twice. You had to have knowledge of the danger; this was a man's job. The frogs he caught weren't the everyday frogs that go leaping across your yard—those are not edible. The ones he caught were big bullfrogs. He used a device made of sacks and sand, or a net with heavy metal parts around the bottom, which he'd throw over the frogs. In the middle of the night he'd bring back a sackful. I don't know how he killed or cleaned the frogs; he never did it when we were watching. Next day, Mom deep fried the legs. At that time, I wouldn't eat them, but since then I've eaten fried frog legs many times. They're a delicacy.

My dad was very good at hunting game birds, too. Every time he went out he'd tell my mom, "Get the hot water on; keep it hot. I'm coming home with my limit." A group of men would go out together. Sometimes they had to go a long ways. My dad would bring home ducks, quail, geese from the fields. Then he plucked them, and poured hot water over them to get off the rest of the feathers, and my mom would take the small feathers and dry them to make pillows. They used to wait for hunting season to make different-tasting gumbo, because it does taste different with wild fowl.

Occasionally my dad would hunt possum, but you really had to have a dog to go possum hunting. We had dogs, but they were never the best hunting dogs because our dad wasn't a hunter per se. It was mainly a sport for him. He wasn't out to hunt alligators either.

Aside from hunting for fun, people would party Saturday night and Sundays, but late Sunday afternoon they would go home to get to bed early—because they knew the hard days ahead of them.

Some Sundays, the adults would go to local horse races held amongst the farmers. A few of the bigger ranchers had horses that were trained, but they were in the minority. Most often people just raced the fastest farm horses. Our parents would take us as far as the farmhouse, and we occupied ourselves playing in the yard, but we could not go to the races because they were gambling.

Another thing the adults did for their entertainment (and of course we were not involved) was playing poker. Sometimes they played cards all night. They played in the kitchen during the winter, and in summer they played in the barn. It was so far out in the country they weren't afraid of the law.

As Catholics, we had religious holidays that other people regard as just entertainment. All Saints' Day *(La Touts Saints)*, the day after Halloween, was our Memorial Day. And people looked at Halloween night as the night that the devil and the ghosts were out—bad things, bad spirits—so everyone stayed inside. There was no dressing up, no trick or treat. And the next day, *La Touts Saints*, the day the souls rested, you'd go to church to pray for those who had died. (For that matter, our funerals were also simple and sober, a church service followed by a quiet get-together, nothing like the New Orleans jazz funerals.)

Mardi Gras was a big day because there was always a giant party the Saturday before, and another one Mardi Gras evening. But no costumes. Mardi Gras means "Fat Tuesday," because the next day is Ash Wednesday. From that day forward, you didn't eat meat on Wednesdays or Fridays until Easter. And for adults it was the last chance to have big fun for seven weeks.

Our Mardi Gras was nothing like it is in New Orleans. Starting around noon on Mardi Gras day, a group of masked horsemen would ride from house to house gathering food for the party. Every year a different man played the *Capitaine de Mardi Gras*, the Mardi Gras Captain, and he gathered a group of men to go along with him. The guys would dress like Zorro, with capes and big hats and homemade masks made of cloth. Some wore hoods covering the whole face. They went galloping down the road with their capes flying out behind them, and rode into your yard on big horses.

They sang a song that went, *"Mardi Gras, Mardi Gras, vient une fois par an,"* meaning, Mardi Gras comes only once a year, and that's why I'm asking you to give something for charity.

"Yes, Capitaine!" people would say when they rode in.

"What do you have to give today for the little get-together tonight?" the Capitaine would ask.

One person would say, "I'll give chicken," another would say, "I'll give you a sack of rice," and the men went on and on until they had gathered enough food to make gumbo for the evening.

You couldn't tell who they were under their masks, and they disguised their voices as well. They didn't want anybody to recognize them. The idea was to fool the parents, not the kids— it wasn't kid's play. Often my dad would try to guess who it was. He'd say, "Yeah, I know who *you* are, and you, too." It was a lot of fun for the adults as well as the children. We watched and thought it was the funniest thing, but we were afraid, too.

They had sacks slung across the back of their horses, and whatever they could carry with them, they took. When they couldn't carry any more, they took the food to the house where the party was going to be. The Capitaine would present the food to the women who were there to cook, and then leave again and gather more. Then they rode home and changed into clean clothing for the party. They never wore their costumes to the dance.

And on that day, the children were not allowed out of the house. With their masks on, the men couldn't see very well, they were blind at the sides, and they were on horses. So it was dangerous, very dangerous for children, because those guys might run over us and never see us. Adults could get out of the way because they knew about the danger, but kids would just run around all happy about seeing the men in their capes. So we were not allowed to go near them. When we heard the horses galloping, it was back to the house and get inside! And if we were on the road, we were to stay inside the fence. I could never forget the Capitaine and his horsemen, because we were afraid of them. Those guys were rough! They never threatened anyone, but they rode fast. And those men were hitting their bottles. Our parents didn't tell us that, but we knew, because we saw them sip from their little flasks.

That night, the family would go to the party together, as one big family with kids, teenagers, parents. I remember the gumbo, because it was what I liked best.

The next day was Ash Wednesday. On Ash Wednesday no one was supposed to eat or drink until noon. The children could eat at ten o'clock. But the adults—not until noon. They had to fast all morning.

There was no dancing for seven weeks, until Easter. It was like a penance. You are supposed to cleanse your soul during that period. No dances or parties for us, the Catholic people. We could go to movies, and play the radio, and play our music, but there was no dancing, no participating in really big fun, until after 12 midnight the day before Easter Sunday.

On the afternoon of *Jour de Pâques,* Easter Day, there was always a celebration, and it took the form of an egg fight. Everyone, young and old, received an Easter basket containing several hard-boiled eggs, and would play "the clash of the hard-boiled eggs." Two people would smack the tops of their eggs together, and the winner (the one with the uncracked egg) would collect the loser's broken egg and add it to his basket. The winner of the game was the person who gathered the most eggs. When the game ended, all the eggs were used to make potato salad and stuffed eggs.

Easter dinner consisted of boudin, gumbo or roast chicken, vegetables, and dessert. There was beer and wine for the adults, and everybody was delighted to see the end of those seven long weeks of Lent.

FROM MARDI GRAS
THROUGH JOUR DE PÂQUES

STUFFED CRAB

This is a favorite Louisiana first course.

Serves 4–6

1   pound fresh white crabmeat, crumbled
5   tablespoons plus 5 teaspoons butter
⅔   cup finely chopped bell pepper
⅔   cup finely chopped onion
½   cup finely chopped celery
1   clove garlic, minced

¼   teaspoon cayenne (or to taste)
¼   teaspoon black pepper
1   cup Italian-style dry bread crumbs, divided
2   tablespoons minced fresh parsley
    Paprika

Preheat oven to 425 degrees. Rinse and thoroughly drain crabmeat to remove excess salt. Melt 5 tablespoons butter in a heavy skillet over low heat. Add bell pepper, onion, celery, and garlic. Sauté, stirring frequently, until tender. Stir in crabmeat, cayenne, and pepper. Stir in ⅔ cup of the bread crumbs. Blend well and correct seasonings. Grease scallop-shaped baking shells or an 8″ × 8″ Pyrex baking dish with ample butter. Add crab mixture. Mix remaining ⅓ cup bread crumbs with the parsley. Sprinkle crumb mixture over the crab, sprinkle with paprika, and dot with 5 teaspoons butter, cut into small pieces. Bake 20 minutes and serve hot.

CREOLE STUFFED EGGS

These are as welcome at a summer picnic as they are at Easter.

Makes 12 hors d'oeuvres

12	eggs	¼	teaspoon salt
½	cup mayonnaise	¼	teaspoon black pepper
¼	cup pickle relish		Paprika
½-1	teaspoon cayenne		Minced fresh parsley

Place eggs in cold water to cover, bring to a rolling boil, cover the pot, and turn off the heat. Let stand 17 minutes, then drain. Peel eggs immediately under cold running water, or refrigerate overnight and then peel them. Halve eggs lengthwise, remove yolks, and place yolks in a bowl, reserving the whites. Mash yolks with a fork. Stir in mayonnaise, relish, cayenne, salt, and pepper. Spoon the mixture into the whites of the eggs. Sprinkle with paprika and parsley. Serve chilled or at room temperature.

FISH SOUP PIQUANT

Serve this thick, hearty soup with French bread and butter on the side. If you have fewer than 8 people to serve, you can halve the recipe, but you can also freeze any leftover soup and reheat it at a later date.

Makes 1 gallon, to serve 8

1 cup roux (page 20)		6-ounce can tomato paste
3 pounds whole catfish (or halibut or rock cod)	1	cup chopped celery
	1	cup chopped yellow or white onions
4 quarts water		
28-ounce can whole tomatoes, chopped	⅔	cup chopped bell pepper
	½	cup chopped green onions

½ cup chopped parsley
2 teaspoons chopped garlic
2 teaspoons salt (or to taste)
1 teaspoon ground or crushed dried red pepper

1 teaspoon black pepper
½ teaspoon white pepper
½ teaspoon powdered dried thyme
2 cups diced potato
2 bay leaves

Let roux come to room temperature. Meanwhile, cut off and discard the head of the fish, clean the stomach cavity, and rinse. Place in large stockpot or Dutch oven with the water. Bring to a boil, reduce heat to medium, and boil gently 20 minutes. Lift out the fish, reserving the cooking liquid. Let cool briefly. Bone the fish well by flaking the meat off the bones; set meat aside.

While fish is cooling, bring the fish broth to a simmer and stir in roux a large spoonful at a time until it is absorbed. Add all remaining ingredients except the reserved fish, the potato, and the bay leaves. Return to a simmer, stirring well to blend, and cook over low heat 30 minutes. Taste and correct seasonings. Add potato, bay leaves, and reserved fish and simmer 20 minutes longer. Correct seasonings again (potatoes will have neutralized some of the salt and the hot pepper) and simmer briefly to blend. Remove bay leaves before serving.

CRAWFISH ÉTOUFFÉE

This dish is very similar to the better-known Shrimp Creole, except that crawfish need different preparation. We use only the tails of crawfish, as there is not enough meat in the claws. (The claws can be used for flavoring a broth, though, and they are edible. Some people crack the larger claws with their teeth and suck out the meat, but it slows you down.) In some areas of the country, fish markets carry frozen peeled crawfish tails. They are worth the extra cost if you want to make this dish. Crawfish Étouffée is usually served over rice. We always have French bread, butter, and salad with it, but instead of the salad you could serve string beans, or peas and carrots.

(Serves 4)

14 pounds fresh live crawfish or cooked whole crawfish (or 2 pounds peeled crawfish tails)	8-ounce can tomato sauce
¼ cup oil	1 cup water
¼ cup chopped onion	4 teaspoons flour dissolved in about ⅓ cup cold water
¼ cup chopped bell pepper	1 teaspoon salt
¼ cup chopped celery	1 teaspoon cayenne (or to taste)
¼ cup minced fresh parsley	¼ teaspoon black pepper (or to taste)
¼ cup chopped green onions	3 bay leaves Cooked rice
3 cloves garlic, minced	
3-4 medium tomatoes, peeled (see Appendix) and coarsely chopped (fresh tomatoes preferred)	

Wash live crawfish well and cover them with ice-cold water to stun them. Soak them about 5 minutes. Drain them and drop into boiling water a few at a time. Boil gently about 8 minutes. Drain under cold running water. (If you've gotten already-peeled crawfish or cooked crawfish, skip these steps.)

As soon as crawfish are cool enough to handle but not yet cold, pull off and discard the heads, then peel and devein the tails and reserve them. Heat the oil in a large skillet. Add onion, bell pepper, celery, parsley, green onions, and garlic. Sauté over medium-high heat 10 minutes, stirring frequently. Add the tomatoes, tomato sauce, 1 cup water, the flour paste, and seasonings. Bring the mixture to a boil, stirring constantly to dissolve flour thoroughly. Reduce heat and simmer uncovered until the vegetables are cooked through but not mushy (about 20 minutes), stirring occasionally. Taste carefully and correct seasonings; sauce should be quite spicy. Add the crawfish tails and simmer just until they're heated through. Remove bay leaves and serve immediately over rice.

Shrimp Creole: Substitute 2 pounds shrimp for the crawfish. Peel and devein them, wash them in cold water, drain, and set aside. Proceed as above, simmering the shrimps just until opaque all the way through (5–7 minutes).

~~~~~~~~~~~~~~~~~~~

DEEP-FRIED FISH

My favorite fish to cook this way is catfish, but you can cook any kind of fish you like—lingcod, trout, bass, red snapper, flounder. Perch is my second-favorite, and you don't even have to cut perch or flounder if they're small. Serve this fish with tartar sauce and lemon wedges, french fries or Hush Puppies (page 71), and salad. When the fish is done, cook the hush puppies or french fries in the same oil. Some of the cornmeal that flakes off the fish will cling to them, making them extra-tasty.

Serves 4–6

About 3 cups oil for deep-frying
2 pounds fish fillets
2 teaspoons garlic salt or garlic powder
1½ teaspoons salt
1 teaspoon black pepper
1 teaspoon cayenne
1 cup cornmeal
Tartar sauce
Lemon wedges

Preheat oil in large, deep skillet to 400 degrees. Cut fish fillets into slices about ½ inch thick, or in cross sections. Season the pieces with the garlic salt or garlic powder, salt, pepper, and cayenne, then roll them in the cornmeal. Fry them in hot oil, a few at a time without crowding, a total of 5 minutes, turning them after 2½ minutes. (Cook longer if the slices are more than ½ inch thick.) Maintain oil at 400 degrees. Drain cooked fish on paper towels and tent with foil to keep warm until all the fish is fried and the hush puppies or french fries are done. (If desired, fish may be reheated briefly in a low oven.)

Pan-Fried Fish: Proceed as above, but use only ½ cup oil, and fry fish 5–7 minutes a side (for fillets ½ inch thick), or until opaque all the way through.

~~~~~~~~~~~~~~~~~~

FRIED FROG LEGS

French people have always eaten frog legs. They're usually served as an appetizer, but you can use them as a main dish with french fries or hush puppies and a vegetable.

Serves 4–5 as main dish, 8 as appetizer

2   pounds frog legs
1   teaspoon salt
½   teaspoon white pepper
4   large cloves garlic put
      through a garlic press
      (to make about 2
      teaspoons pressed)

About 3 cups oil for deep-
      frying
⅓   cup cornmeal
Tartar sauce
Lemon wedges

Wash the frog legs, pat dry, and season with salt, pepper, and garlic. Let stand a while (preferably an hour or two) to absorb the seasonings and to approach room temperature.

In a deep, heavy pot, heat the oil to 400 degrees. Roll frog legs in cornmeal and drop them, about 6 at a time, into the oil. Fry, turning occasionally, until meat is golden brown (about 7 minutes). Cook them carefully, not too hot and not too fast, maintaining the oil at 400 degrees. You don't want them to absorb too much oil. Drain on paper towels and keep warm until ready to serve. Continue frying in small batches until all the frog legs are cooked. Serve with tartar sauce and lemon wedges.

SMOTHERED CHICKEN BREASTS
OR WILD DUCKS

When I was a child, we had domestic ducks and my parents would make stuffed roast ducks, stuffed with dressing and baked in a casserole like a turkey. With wild ducks, most of the time they made gumbo, just substituting duck for chicken in the chicken gumbo. They never used filé with the wild duck gumbo because the duck already has its foreign taste, a little gamy and with a heavier-tasting grease than chicken. You didn't ever bake or roast wild ducks, but my mother used to braise or smother them, so they were tender and had a little gravy with them.

This recipe produces moist, flavorful chicken breasts—or equally tender wild ducks. Unlike domestic ducks, wild ducks have almost no fat. When roasted, they often come out dry and tough, but when braised they're succulent and tender. I recommend serving the smothered poultry (of either type) over rice, accompanied by Steamed Carrots with Parsley (page 72).

Serves 4

4 chicken breasts	2 tablespoons chopped celery
1¼ teaspoons salt	¾ cup water
1 teaspoon garlic powder	2 tablespoons chopped parsley
¾ teaspoon cayenne	Cooked rice
¼ teaspoon black pepper	
2 tablespoons oil	
2 tablespoons chopped onion	

Season chicken breasts with salt, garlic powder, cayenne, and pepper. Heat the oil in a large skillet and brown chicken on both sides. Add onion and celery and sauté until wilted. Add the water and, over high heat, bring to a boil. Reduce heat and simmer covered 15 minutes. Sprinkle the parsley over the chicken and simmer 5 minutes longer. Tilt the pan and with a large metal spoon skim fat from the surface of the cooking liquid. Serve hot, with rice.

Wild Duck Étouffée: Replace chicken with cleaned, dressed wild ducks, using 2 or 3 small ducks (such as teal) or 1 larger one (such as mallard) for 3–4 pounds dressed weight. Cut duck into serving pieces; place pieces in water to cover, add 1 tablespoon vinegar, and soak 1–2 hours. (This will combat any gamy, fishy smells.) Pat dry with paper towels and proceed as for Smothered Chicken Breasts, but include 1 tablespoon minced fresh garlic when sautéing the onion and celery. Season generously with cayenne, until very spicy to your palate. Simmer until duck meat is cooked through and tender when pricked with a fork (20–45 minutes, depending on the size, age, and type of duck). Serve with plain rice or Dirty Rice (page 214).

〰〰〰〰〰〰〰

RABBIT ÉTOUFFÉE

You can use a domestic frying rabbit for this, or if you are a hunter, you can use a wild rabbit if you cook it a lot longer. This dish goes well over rice, of course, with any vegetable you like.

Rabbit has no fat marbling the meat, so in many preparations it is liable to dry out while it's cooking. Poaching it very gently in liquid keeps it tender. This is especially important with domestic frying rabbits, which can't take the lengthy cooking time of many traditional recipes designed for wild hares.

Serves 4

1 domestic frying rabbit, about 2½ pounds
2 quarts water
1 tablespoon vinegar
*2 large cloves garlic, minced

*About 2 small fresh hot peppers (such as fresh cayenne or serrano), seeded, minced (about 1 tablespoon), or 1 teaspoon powdered cayenne

*Note: Instead of mincing these ingredients, you can use a blender, an electric spice mill, a clean coffee grinder, or a mortar and pestle to make a paste of them.

Salt

Cayenne

Black or white pepper

¼ cup oil

½ cup chopped yellow or white onion

1 tablespoon flour

1½ cups water

2 large green onions, sliced, whites and greens included

2 generous tablespoons chopped parsley

Clean the rabbit, removing and discarding all the internal organs and all the fat (from the stomach cavity and around the joints). Disjoint the rabbit, separating front legs and hind legs from the torso. (If convenient, divide hind legs into thigh and shin pieces.) After using both hands to snap the backbone at the desired intervals, cut the back of the rabbit crosswise into pieces about 1 inch wide. (If you find all the rib bones too annoying to eat, you can snap them off the backbone and use a boning knife or poultry shears to finish separating them from the spine.) Mix 2 quarts water and the vinegar in a large bowl, and soak the rabbit pieces about 5 minutes in the liquid. Drain and pat rabbit dry.

Cut small slits in the thick part of the meat of as many rabbit pieces as possible. Mix garlic and peppers with 1 teaspoon salt and ½ teaspoon black pepper. Using the tip of a knife, stuff about ¼ teaspoon of the garlic mixture into each of the slits in the rabbit meat. Then season the outsides of the pieces with additional salt and generous sprinklings of powdered cayenne and black or white pepper.

Pour the oil into a Dutch oven or a skillet with a lid, and over low heat allow it to get warm but not hot. Add rabbit pieces and very gently turn them in the oil over low heat until they lose their raw look. Add the onion and sprinkle with flour. Cook, stirring, until onion starts to soften and flour loses its raw smell (about 3 minutes). Pour in 1½ cups water, increase heat, and bring to a light boil. Immediately reduce heat, cover, and simmer slowly until rabbit is cooked through and tender (about 20 minutes). Make sure there is always enough water in the pan.

With a slotted spoon, remove rabbit pieces and reserve. Turn heat to high and boil away any excess liquid, stirring occasionally, until broth reduces to the consistency of a thin sauce. Return rabbit to the pan, add green onions and parsley, and simmer about 5 more minutes to reheat.

Wild Rabbit Étouffée: If using a wild rabbit or a mature domestic roasting rabbit (about 5 pounds), double all other ingredients, and poach about 1½ hours, until rabbit is tender.

〰〰〰〰〰〰〰〰〰

CASSEROLE-ROASTED LEG OF LAMB

This is a lamb roast for people who think they don't like lamb. The cooking method produces a beautifully seasoned, moist, and tender well-done roast. (Cook a little less if you prefer rare lamb.) If you do not have a covered roasting pan, see Cookware in the Appendix for an improvised version.

Serves 6–8

1	leg of lamb, about 3¼ pounds	1	tablespoon minced fresh onion
1½	teaspoons salt	1	teaspoon paprika
½	teaspoon cayenne	1-2	cups water
½	teaspoon black pepper	½	cup white or red wine
1	tablespoon minced fresh garlic	1	teaspoon Worcestershire sauce

If possible, start to prepare lamb 1–2 hours before roasting it. Trim off excess fat from the exterior, leaving just a thin layer (about ⅛ inch). (If you prefer, you can trim off all the fat, and after seasoning the lamb as directed below, rub a little olive or vegetable oil all over it.)

In a small bowl, mix together salt, cayenne, and pepper. With a small, sharp knife, cut several small pockets in the meat. Using a small measuring spoon, spoon some of the spice mixture, the garlic, and the onion into each pocket. Mix leftover spice mixture with paprika and rub it over the entire leg. Let lamb rest 1–2 hours to reach room temperature and absorb the seasonings.

Preheat oven to 400 degrees . Place lamb on a rack in a roasting pan with a cover and add 1 cup water to the pan. Roast uncovered 20 minutes. If all the water has evaporated, pour another cup of water into the pan. Reduce heat to 350 degrees, cover the pan, and continue roasting. Cooking time for well-done lamb is a total of 30 minutes per pound, including the browning time (for a 3¼ pound leg, roast for an additional 1 hour and 20 minutes), or 20–25 minutes per pound for medium-rare.

A half hour before lamb is done, combine wine and Worcestershire sauce and pour mixture over the lamb. Every 10 minutes, baste lamb with liquid from the bottom of the pan. When lamb is done, remove it to a cutting board and let it stand about 10 minutes before carving it. Arrange the sliced lamb on a platter, pour the pan juices over it, and serve.

VEGETABLE STEW

On meatless days during Lent, my mother made a stew from root vegetables. When the stew was almost done, she would boil eggs for about 5 minutes, take the shells off, and then drop them into the stew. You had no meat at all, but you had protein and vegetables. It was very good. I serve it whenever I have vegetarian guests for dinner. My mother also put boiled eggs in the seafood gumbo, especially the okra gumbo. She took the shells off and dropped them into the gumbo after it was turned off. It was delicious.

Serves 4

6 cups water
2 cups beef or chicken broth
   (or a 14½-ounce can)
¾ cup roux (page 20), at
   room temperature
4 medium carrots, pared
   and diced (in about ¾-
   inch cubes)
4 medium potatoes, peeled
   and diced
3 medium turnips, pared
   and diced

1½ cups peeled pearl onions
    (see Appendix) or
    shallots
½   cup chopped yellow or
    white onion
½   cup chopped parsley
1   teaspoon salt
1   teaspoon cayenne
1   teaspoon minced garlic
¼   teaspoon black pepper
4   eggs (optional)

Combine the water and broth in a large saucepan (3 quarts or larger). Heat over moderate heat, and when broth is warm stir in room-temperature roux a large spoonful at a time until well mixed. Add all remaining ingredients except the eggs. Bring just to a boil and immediately reduce heat to a simmer. Continue simmering uncovered until all the vegetables are tender (about 30 minutes). Taste and correct seasonings. If the stew appears too thick, add a small amount of water; if too thin, cook over moderate heat (so that the liquid bubbles lightly) until the liquid is as thick as desired. During the last few minutes the stew is cooking, drop eggs carefully into a separate pan of boiling water, boil 5 minutes (until they just cohere, without being hard-cooked), drain, and remove shells. Add eggs to the stew just before serving.

Vegetable Stock: If a purely vegetarian stew is desired, substitute a strong, flavorful vegetable stock for both the water and the beef or chicken broth. Coarsely chop 3–5 pounds of vegetables. Include onions, carrots, outer ribs and tops of celery, a handful of parsley stems, 2 bay leaves, 4 garlic cloves, and fresh herbs or pinches of dried herbs (tarragon, marjoram, basil, borage) as desired. Add any or all of the following: leeks or leek trimmings, mushroom stems, asparagus trimmings, squash, green beans or trimmings, greens (lettuce, spinach, chard), parsnip and/or potato parings. In a large pot, melt 2 tablespoons butter or oil, add vegetables, and sauté slowly, stirring, until vegetables soften. Cover with water, bring to a boil, reduce heat, and simmer about 1 hour. Strain. If stock tastes too mild, return it to the pot, bring to a boil, and boil gently until reduced and flavorful.

〰〰〰〰〰〰〰〰

HUSH PUPPIES

Hush puppies are light, fritterlike puffs of batter. (Legend tells that they got their name from being invented to placate the hungry dogs running around at an outdoor fish fry.) The buttermilk in this recipe makes them light. They can be eaten as hors d'oeuvres, or they can be served instead of bread, with fried fish or fried chicken. They're always highly seasoned—hot! When they're freshly made they don't need butter, but if you are reheating them, serve them with butter to give them a fresh taste.

Makes about 20 hush puppies

1   cup white cornmeal
½   cup flour
1   teaspoon baking powder
1   teaspoon salt
¼   teaspoon black pepper
½   cup chopped green onions

1   medium jalapeño pepper (fresh or canned), trimmed, seeded, and finely chopped
1   egg, lightly beaten
¾   cup buttermilk
    About 2 cups oil for deep-frying

In a large bowl, mix cornmeal, flour, baking powder, salt, and black pepper. Stir in green onions and jalapeño, then egg and buttermilk. Let sit 10 minutes, or until batter becomes light and slightly foamy-looking.

Turn oven on to the lowest setting. While batter sits, pour at least 2 inches of oil into a deep, heavy saucepan and heat it to 350 degrees, until fragrant but not smoking. (If you don't have a frying thermometer, test by dropping a cube of bread into the oil. It should fry crisp in exactly 1 minute.) Drop batter by teaspoonfuls into the hot oil, a few spoonfuls at a time. Fry about 2 minutes, turning after 1 minute, until hush puppies are golden brown all over. Regulate the heat so that the hush puppies neither brown too quickly nor drop to the bottom of the pan. With a slotted spoon, remove hush puppies as they are done, drain them on paper towels, and keep warm in the oven. Repeat until all the batter has been used. If possible, serve hush puppies while still warm. (They may also be reheated in a moderate oven, if necessary, and served with butter.)

STEAMED CARROTS WITH PARSLEY

The young carrots of spring are so sweet, they need very little seasoning.

Serves 3–4

1½ cups water
5 medium carrots, sliced diagonally (about 2 cups)
2 tablespoons butter

2 tablespoons finely chopped parsley
1 teaspoon sugar (optional)
Pinch of salt

Bring all ingredients to a boil over medium-high heat. Reduce heat to low and simmer 15 minutes, or until carrots are tender when pricked with a fork. Drain and serve.

MRS. LEWIS'S LEEKS

This very simple, tasty recipe comes from my mother. Leeks go very well with lamb or roast fowl.

Serves 4

2 bunches leeks
4 tablespoons (½ stick)
   butter
   Salt and black pepper to
   taste

Bottled or homemade pickled
   hot peppers (page 223) as
   table condiment (optional)

Trim the root end from the leeks, along with the flabby upper portion of the greens. Wash the leeks well, ridding them of as much sand as possible. Slice the leeks crosswise into pieces 1-1½ inches long, and rinse again thoroughly. Pat dry with a paper towel, or allow to air-dry in a colander about 20 minutes. Melt butter in a skillet over medium-low heat, add leeks, reduce heat, and sauté them until tender (about 20 minutes), stirring often to prevent burning. Season to taste with salt and pepper. Some people enjoy these leeks sprinkled with the vinegar from pickled hot peppers.

POTATO SALAD

Mashing the egg yolks with mayonnaise makes the dressing rich and creamy.

Serves 6–8

10 medium boiling potatoes (about 4 pounds)	1 teaspoon salt
5 eggs	1 teaspoon prepared mustard
1½ cups mayonnaise	½ teaspoon black pepper
1 cup chopped celery	1 teaspoon minced fresh onion (optional)
½ cup pickle relish	
¼ cup oil	

Peel potatoes, dropping them as they are peeled into a large stockpot or Dutch oven with enough lightly salted water to cover them. Bring to a boil and maintain heat so that liquid boils gently. Boil potatoes until tender when touched with a fork (30–40 minutes). Drain and let cool.

Meanwhile, place eggs in a saucepan with cold water to cover, bring to a rolling boil, cover, and turn off the heat. Let stand 17 minutes. Drain and peel under cold running water.

Chop potatoes into cubes and place them in a large bowl. Halve the eggs and remove and reserve the yolks. Chop the egg whites and add them to the potatoes. With a fork, mash the egg yolks and blend with remaining ingredients in a small bowl to form a sauce. Fold the sauce into the potatoes, and chill.

EMMA KYLE'S OLD-FASHIONED TEA CAKES

The recipe for these old-time tea cakes comes from my husband Raymond's niece. They're called tea cakes, but they're really like cookies or shortbread. You can use cookie cutters, but my mom would just cut them with a knife into squares or diamonds.

Makes 3 dozen

2 eggs	½ cup white sugar
¾ cup (1½ sticks) butter, at room temperature	½ cup brown sugar
	½ teaspoon baking soda
2¼ cups all-purpose flour (unsifted)	½ teaspoon nutmeg
	Dash of salt

Preheat oven to 350 degrees. Beat eggs and butter together. Add remaining ingredients and mix well. Roll the dough on a large floured surface to ½ inch thick. Cut with your favorite cookie cutter, or use a knife to cut into squares about 3″ × 3″. Place them on a cookie sheet 2 inches apart. Bake until brown (10–12 minutes).

~~~~~~~~~~~~~~~~~~~~

GINGERBREAD

Gingerbread is a lovely teatime snack or a tasty breakfast bread. This version is subtly seasoned.

Makes 1 loaf

2 eggs	2 teaspoons baking soda
1 cup brown sugar	2 teaspoons ground ginger
¾ cup shortening	1½ teaspoons cinnamon
⅔ cup molasses	½ teaspoon baking powder
1 cup boiling water	½ teaspoon ground nutmeg
2½ cups all-purpose flour (unsifted)	¼ teaspoon ground cloves
	Pinch of salt

Preheat oven to 350 degrees. Blend eggs and brown sugar well. Add shortening and molasses and stir until creamy. Stir in the boiling water until well blended. Separately, mix remaining ingredients together. Add to sugar mixture, blending well. Pour batter into a well-greased 9″ × 5½″ × 4″ loaf pan and bake until a knife inserted in the center comes out clean (about 1 hour).

3

Texas Tornado

When I was about nine years old, in the second grade, we
moved from Louisiana to Beaumont, Texas. It was only
65 miles west of Lake Charles, just over the state line, so
everything was almost the same—the cooking, the garden, the
flat terrain. The main difference was that Louisiana was more
humid, because there was a lot more water surrounding us,
more little lakes and rivers, and the Gulf. In Texas we were
further inland.

My uncle Louis, who was my father's brother, was married
to my mother's sister Dora (two brothers had married two
sisters), and they were living in Texas. Uncle Louis was
wealthy, and when he came visiting he would tell my dad,
"Look, you're just scratching the surface here. Move on
westward, move on. You could do much better in Texas. I'm
doing very well up there. I've leased a lot of land to farm and I
have more than I can handle, so why don't you come and
join me?"

My father went and looked at the land. "I'll go for it," he said. "I'll try." My father realized he could farm more land there, and grow more rice, on top of which (for some reason) Texas rice sold at a higher price. So we moved to Beaumont, and my father went in with his brother.

Even as a child, I could see that my uncle and aunt in Beaumont were doing very well. I used to admire the way my aunt dressed when she visited us. She dressed modishly, because she didn't have to make her dresses but could afford to buy them. She had long hair, which she wore up in a chignon as she got older, and she always wore a hat—that was really the upper class! And she wore gloves with her dress clothes. I remember feeling, "Oh, one day when my dad has a larger farm, and we're making more money, we'll be able to afford some of those nice things."

I had mixed feelings, then, about moving to Beaumont. When you're a youngster making a move, it's always difficult at first. We hated to leave our friends, but we were happy to be moving on. We told them, "Oh, we're moving to Texas, but we'll come back and see you, or you come and visit us." Of course, immediately after we got settled in Texas we met the neighbors, made friends in school. Kids make friends easily.

Our farmhouse in Beaumont was larger and more modern than our house in Louisiana. It had the same sort of layout that we had in Louisiana, with barns and chicken coops; we also had the same food: chickens, pigs, beef—and another big truck garden to help tend.

We had cistern water, but our well had hard water. You could boil it to use for cooking and drinking, but it was no good for washing—for some reason, you couldn't rinse the soap out. We got our washing water from the running water in the irrigation canals, which consisted of captured rainwater. They had gates on the canals, and when the water was running low my mother wouldn't use it, because it was too still.

Eventually my dad put in electricity, but for a long time we had to use kerosene lamps. Then we got kerosene lamps with a different type of burner, called (I think) Aladdin lamps, and they gave a bright, white light like electricity, not the red flame-colored lantern light. We used them until we were able to get the electricity put in. They made it easier to study. Abe Lincoln used candlelight to study by, so we were blessed because we at least had more light than a candle.

One day my dad came home from town with a radio. It was what we called a crystal radio, which didn't need electricity, and he brought it home and laid it on the living room shelf. Most of the time we all gathered in the kitchen; we very rarely gathered in the living room. I don't remember much about that radio except that we finally had one—maybe because you had to listen to a crystal radio through earphones, one person at a time, we kids couldn't get to use it very often. Later, when we had electricity, we had a regular radio in the kitchen.

Going to a new school was our biggest worry: What's it going to be like; what are the teachers going to be like? By then I was able to speak English, I could communicate quite well, so that wasn't a big problem. But you get used to the teacher, and you have to learn what any teacher is all about: Is she going to be mean? Is she going to be nice?

Beaumont was a larger community, and not only was the school larger, but now we had school buses to pick us up and take us to and from school. There were a lot more kids in school, and a lot more activities. I actually enjoyed the change.

Our parents cared a lot about our grades. That had to do with the fact that they were both illiterate. They had gone to night school for a while and learned their numbers, learned the alphabet, how to add, how to write their names and recognize their names when they saw them written—but not reading and writing. (When we moved to Texas, I was surprised to find that other people there weren't able to read and write either.) But my parents cared more about our grades than the parents who could read and write. I found this out by talking to other kids. I would ask, "Do you get in trouble when you get a bad mark?"

"Yeah, sort of, they do this and that."

"Well, we get punished. We can't go to the movies, we can't go to the game. We have to stay home and study until we get our grades up."

Far worse than being punished for a bad grade was the punishment the weather sometimes doled out to us all. We'd had bad storms in Louisiana, and I was always afraid of thunder and lightning. I remember when there was a lot of lightning and thunder my mom would cover the mirrors, because people believed that a mirror was like a lightning rod, that lightning would strike at its reflection. And we were supposed to stay away from windows. We had to go into the center of the room, because every room had a window that was covered with shades.

I recall one storm was so bad, it probably was a tornado, although we didn't know it. Our house in Beaumont was just one level, like our house in Louisiana; there was no place to hide. (A lot of people in the area had what they call a "storm shelter" under their houses, and my dad was thinking of building one, but he hadn't done it yet so all we had were shutters.) When a storm was coming my parents would always go out and close the shutters, but that time the storm was so bad the doors and some of the windows popped open, and outside you could see things turning, lifting up and turning! Everything shook so badly, it was like an earthquake; I was in tears. When that door opened I thought: Well, this is it. Then my dad told my mom, "Open the other door," to let the wind blow through the house instead of blowing the house away.

For a few years my father and his brother farmed together, but my dad wanted to expand, to be his own boss. He started small, leasing some land, and found himself once again part of a community of people helping each other. There were two other farmers who were nearby neighbors, a pair of brothers who had a big farm, and they would exchange labor with my father. "I'd like to use your hired hands to help me on the farm," they said, "and you can use my hired hands when you need to."

Soon my father was leasing a lot of land. We had been comfortable during the time we lived in Louisiana, but after we moved to Texas I suppose you could say we were "well-off."

There were fewer French-speaking people in Texas, but soon we began to meet all the people who had come from Louisiana, and we could use our language and have our social functions again, the same as we had in Lake Charles. Wherever we've gone, we've always kept the music and cooking and social functions going, up to now.

Soon my father was a big farmer. He was growing a lot of rice, which is what that part of Texas is about—rice and oil. We had as many as 30 hired hands, including 6 or 7 men who lived in at the farm, in a bunkhouse my father built for them.

We didn't get to know the hired men personally, not to the point where we'd hang around with them. They had their things to do and we had ours; they went out and did their work, and came back and went to the bunkhouse. They were a mixture of people: some were black, Creole, white, a few were Mexican (oddly enough, there weren't many Mexicans in that part of Texas then). People ask me if the men used to sing work songs as they worked. They never sang work songs, but they did sing blues. It was loneliness, probably, from being away from their families. After work, I'd hear them singing songs, playing harmonica.

All those men, including the day laborers, had to be fed, so Mom and all the other farm women needed a lot of help to cook for 20, 30 people during the growing season. When my dad was working with his brother, my mom and her sister would cook together. They would hire other women to come in, and (unfortunately for my older sisters) daughters had to help, too. They had to cook a big meal for everybody, three times a day. We had one worktable, and a round dinner table big enough for nine people. When we had to feed all the hired men, we used a long table with benches because you could seat more people that way. My mother started cooking in Beaumont with a wood stove, and then she got a kerosene stove, too, because she needed two stoves to cook for that many men. Although she used the kerosene stove during the summer, and to cook for a crowd, she still preferred the old wood burner. She said it had a more even heat—and on a kerosene stove, if you're in the middle of making a cake and you run out of kerosene, that smelly fume comes out and gets into the cake, and you have to throw the cake away.

Breakfast was very early in the morning. The workday was from sunup to sundown; we didn't look at the clock, we just went with the sun. For breakfast, we had eggs. My mom always made either biscuits or hotcakes. In summertime, when she didn't want to heat up the oven, she would make a skillet biscuit, just one big biscuit, called *un dobro*, like the dobro guitar. Cook one side, flip it, and cook until done. Then either cut or break pieces from it.

My mom called her hotcakes "crepes." Her crepes were neither like the hotcakes of today nor like the French crepes. They were about four inches across, and she always used a little oil or lard in the bottom of the pan, which made the crepes form a little crust around the edge that would curl up, like a crisp brown ring. We put butter and syrup on them. When we didn't have any syrup, she would make some by browning the sugar, adding water to it, and cooking it until it thickened. It was real tasty with a little butter in it, or a little vanilla to give it flavor. It tasted better than a lot of syrups on the market today.

Sometimes we had bacon, too, but not every day, because people made their own bacon and it was precious. We ate rice as a cereal, mixed with milk. We had grits, or we could break up corn bread and eat it with milk as a cereal. (I still do.)

Dinner, at noon, was our main meal. Unless the men were working within a mile of the house, we had to bring the food to them and feed them from the back of a pickup truck; otherwise, too much time would be lost. The food was very, very hot, and it was never very far to go. When they saw the truck coming, the men would line up ready to eat. Each man had his own plate, all prepared and packed. Often my mom would put the whole pot in the back of the truck and go with it to the field. The men would come by with their plates, like a buffet—although not as elegant.

There were red beans and rice, and we always had meat for the working men: big pieces of beef, either short ribs or stews. Half the time it was chicken or pork, a vegetable, and bread. It was a balanced meal, because we raised our own corn, any vegetable you wanted, and most of our own meat. And rice—

rice was always there, and we loved it. We ate it cold. But in case some of the men might not like rice, mom also made bread, boiled potatoes, and corn bread. The men loved the corn bread.

For dessert, my mom would make bread pudding, gingerbread, ginger cookies, tea cookies, and muffins. On weekends she had the time to prepare a good meal for the whole family for a sit-down dinner.

The men had a 30- to 40-minute lunch break, and a rest period of about an hour. If it was too hot, especially during the month of August (the hottest month in Louisiana and Texas), they would get under the vehicles, or by the side of the vehicles, where there was shade, and lie down and relax for a while, maybe an hour, maybe two. It could really be murder out there in those fields. However, when my dad could see bad weather coming (you could look out across the plain and see that it was going to rain by nightfall), he would say, "When you guys are finished with your meal, let's get back to work," and they just followed through.

Supper was late in the day, because my dad worked in the field until sundown. We ate at sundown, whenever that was—it could be as late as nine o'clock at night in June. We always ate supper together as a family. We cheated sometimes; we took off with one of mom's rolls because we often got hungry when we had to wait for my dad. If he wasn't home by a certain time, that meant he was working overtime in the fields, and my mom would go ahead and feed the family.

When you're farming, the seasons are different to you than to city people: Thanksgiving, for instance, was not celebrated in the same way. Whether or not it was a national holiday, it didn't really matter to the farmers, because they had to work. It was a time of year when they could not take a day off. They had to get everything turned over before the rainy season came.

Winter was very slow, though. They had very few men working during the winter months. Most of the men would go home to their families. Some of the younger guys wanted to hang around, although they weren't charged for staying in the bunkhouse, they were there on their own. So winters I could concentrate on school, but I spent a lot of my summers cooking.

We learned to cook by watching Mom. She started teaching us when we were very young. First came washing dishes, and then washing vegetables and going out to the truck patch. I was eight or nine years old when I started; my sister Agnes was a very good cook because she started a lot younger than the rest of us: she was the oldest child and Mom needed her. I really knew how to cook when I was still quite young, but I kept saying I didn't so I wouldn't have to—but finally I had no choice. It's funny, my mom would cook all the food that is now known as "Cajun/Creole cooking," but it didn't mean that much to us at that time because that was just our way of life. We never imagined that one day it would become trendy or popular.

Around the age of 11 or 12 I started watching what Mom and big sister were doing, because if they had to go help in the field, you might have to do the cooking. I started cooking a little at about 10 or 11: I would get the rice ready. The first main meal I cooked for the family was at about age 14. I was scared stiff, because it had to be edible, with eight people sitting there expecting a good meal. My mom said it was good. I remember one of the meals I cooked was pinto beans and rice, and the beans were a little too watery. Then my mom boiled them very rapidly to thicken them a little, so I learned from that.

I didn't cook every day, but after a while I had my day to do the cooking. The hardest thing for me was making biscuits. We made biscuits from scratch, and I learned from watching Mom. She never measured anything. My biscuits were hard—not enough shortening or baking powder. I had some traumatic experiences. I had to cook meat and, being a youngster, listening to the radio or letting my mind wander, I scorched it.

With all the men working, I no longer had to work in the fields—until World War II broke out when I was 13. Within a few months, there was a man shortage. The women, even the wives with all their other chores, would help in the fields, and so would the children.

I couldn't do the heavier chores, but there was still a lot that women, girls, and young boys could do to take the place of a man. We could rip open the fertilizer sacks and the rice sacks so that when the planters arrived for refills, they wouldn't have to waste the time or manpower to do it. I learned to drive a tractor. When the men came in at night to bring the tractors in and drive them into the shed, I'd say, "Okay, I'm going to take a run." I'd go and meet my brother, saying, "Willie, Willie, let me drive." And he let me. He didn't care. I would take it and drive it around in the barnyard, while my dad was still in the fields. I wouldn't do it when Pop was around.

One day I heard my dad saying, "I need another man. I need a man on that tractor and I don't have time to do it."

And I said, "I can drive the tractor."

He said, "No, you can't drive the tractor."

I answered, "But I did. I've been driving it in the yard, in the barn. Do you want me to do it?"

He looked at me, saying, "Naw. You can't. I can't trust you on it."

My brother said, "She can do it."

"Can she? Are you sure?" my dad asked. "Then you watch her. I'll put her with you."

The tractors would follow each other in different parts of the field doing different things. Some would plant, some would cover, some would roll. So my father let me drive, covering or rolling.

But he wouldn't let me plant. Planting was very difficult. You had a tractor that was pulling a planting machine, which would plant several rows at once, over an area about 20 feet wide. The machines would drop the rice seedlings down, and another tractor would follow, rolling over and covering the seedlings. The guy in the planting tractor would start out making a wide square in the field, then he would go in and make smaller and smaller squares, filling in the big square. You had to know what you were doing, or you might leave a big 15- or 20-foot area that you missed. You had to have a good eye, too. When the planting tractor had made a certain number of rounds, another tractor would follow with the fertilizer. The planting tractor never got out of that square, the machine never left its route.

My father had taken into the family a young man named Benjamin Semien, whom he did not legally adopt, but who became, informally, our adopted brother. He and Willie said they were going to a dance one night. I asked to go, but they said no. I asked "Why not?" but they wouldn't explain. So they went . . . and the dance happened not to be in Beaumont at all. It was in Lake Charles, 65 miles away. They borrowed Mom's car and drove all that way, and after the dance, and the party after the dance, they didn't get back until four in the morning. And poor Willie had to be in the field at sunup, because during planting, it's a seven-day workweek, no days off until the work is all done.

Any other time it wouldn't have mattered, but if you're planting you've got to follow the line. And Willie was so sleepy. I was on the seed truck opening the sacks, and as I watched him, I said, "No, he's not going right. God, he's not making a square anymore—he's just going!" But I was too far away from him to holler at him and wake him up.

Then he shook his head awake, and he turned around, going, "Jesus, where is it?" Even at a distance you could tell he was searching for that line.

So I ran out to him, saying, "Are you sleepy?"

And he said, "Yeah, I'm so sleepy I can't see."

"Do you want me to plant?" I asked.

"No!" he said. "I can follow that line better than you."

"I've seen what you guys are doing; I can do it," I said.

"No."

"But Willie, you missed an area over there," I said.

"No, I caught up my line."

"No, you didn't," I said. "You caught up but you left a big hole in the middle. Okay, we have a bet. When the rice comes up, you're going to have this big triangle that you didn't cover."

When the rice came up, I couldn't wait to go out there and see this big dry piece of land with nothing on it. It was shaped like a triangle—and Willie said, "You win."

When my father saw it, he didn't know when it happened, or who was planting that day. Nobody told him. Since I wasn't a planter, I was cleared—and Willie and Benjamin stayed in good grace with my mom and dad. I kept that secret for years and years.

SUMMER ON THE FARM

GRANDMA'S CREPES

All my grandparents passed on when I was very young. My mother learned this recipe from her mother, and handed it on, in turn, to us. It makes thin, sweet breakfast pancakes, rather than the classic French crepes that are stuffed with all manner of things. The pancakes can be sprinkled with a little powdered sugar, or served with a syrup or fresh fruit.

Makes about 18 pancakes

1 cup flour
1½ teaspoons granulated
    sugar
1½ teaspoons powdered
    sugar
1¼ teaspoons baking
    powder

½ teaspoon salt
2 eggs, lightly beaten
1 cup milk
½ cup water
  Butter or oil

Combine dry ingredients. Stir in eggs, milk, and the water. Beat to mix well, but do not overbeat. Let batter stand at least 20 minutes, better yet 1–2 hours. (Batter may also be refrigerated overnight.)

Heat a crepe pan or small skillet (4–6 inches diameter) over medium heat until it is hot but not smoking. Film it lightly with butter or oil (for instance, rub the end of a stick of butter over it). Stir batter again, and pour about ¼ cup batter into the skillet. Gently tilt the pan to spread batter evenly. Fry about 1 minute, until crepe is lightly browned on the bottom and sides. With a spatula, flip the crepe over and cook about 1 minute longer to brown the other side. As soon as crepe is done, remove it from the pan and keep it warm (in a low oven, or tented with foil). Grease the pan again and continue making crepes until all the batter is used.

MAMA'S HOMEMADE SYRUP

Serve over waffles, pancakes, or (of course) Grandma's Crepes.

Makes about 1 cup

1   cup sugar
½   cup plus 2 tablespoons
     water

1   tablespoon butter
½   teaspoon vanilla or ¼
     teaspoon maple flavor

Cook sugar in a cast-iron skillet over low heat until all the sugar crystals are melted. Remove from heat. Carefully add the water: liquid may spatter slightly as a crackly caramel forms on the surface. Stir to mix well. Return to low heat and cook, stirring constantly, until the caramel dissolves again and mixture forms a smooth syrup. (This will take no more than 10 minutes.) If syrup thickens too much, stir in a little more water by tablespoonfuls. Stir in butter and flavoring and blend well. If some hard caramel crystals are still visible, pour the syrup into a bowl or gravy boat. (Most crystals will remain in the skillet.) Serve syrup hot (you can reheat it in a microwave).

BUTTERMILK BISCUITS

Biscuits were nothing special to us. They were like toast is to most people. We had them almost every day, especially with eggs. My mom would make big drop biscuits the size of your fist, which we called "fist biscuits." I prefer to make rolled biscuits. These are very easy to make and quick to bake—they just *taste* special.

Makes 1 dozen

2　cups flour
1　tablespoon baking
　　powder
½　teaspoon salt
⅛　teaspoon baking soda

3　tablespoons shortening
1　cup buttermilk (see
　　Appendix)
2　tablespoons melted butter

Preheat oven to 450 degrees. Combine dry ingredients. Blend in shortening with a fork or pastry blender until mixture develops a texture like coarse cornmeal. (A food processor may be used, if desired.) Add buttermilk slowly and stir well until dough forms a large ball, without overmixing. With floured hands, knead dough lightly a few minutes, until it is bouncy. On a well-floured board, roll out dough into a rough square or rectangle ½ inch thick. (In hot weather, if dough is too sticky to handle easily, chill it about 10 minutes before rolling it out.) Cut out biscuits with a biscuit cutter or inverted drinking glass and place them on a cookie sheet ½ inch apart. Brush with the melted butter. Bake 12–15 minutes, or just until lightly browned. Serve hot or warm.

CHICKEN AND DUMPLINGS

Nothing could be more comforting and fulfilling than tender dumplings and falling-off-the-bone chicken.

Serves 6

CHICKEN STEW:
4-pound chicken, cut into serving pieces
3   cups water
Scant 2 cups strong chicken broth (or a 14½-ounce can)
1   teaspoon salt
¼   teaspoon white pepper
⅛   teaspoon cayenne
1   clove garlic, minced (about 1 teaspoon)
1½ ribs celery
1   large onion, halved

2   tablespoons chopped parsley

DUMPLINGS:
2   cups flour
1   tablespoon baking powder
½   teaspoon salt
¼   teaspoon baking soda
3   tablespoons shortening
1   cup buttermilk (see Appendix)
3   tablespoons flour mixed with ⅓ cup water

To make chicken stew: Place chicken in a 4-quart Dutch oven with the water, broth, salt, white pepper, and cayenne. Bring to a boil and skim foam for a minute or two. Reduce heat to a simmer and add garlic, celery, onion, and parsley. Cover and simmer gently 1¼ hours before adding dumplings.

To make dumplings: Sift flour, baking powder, salt, and baking soda together. With a fork or pastry blender (or in a food processor), work the shortening into the flour mixture until the texture is that of cornmeal. Rapidly stir in buttermilk. Form dough into a ball and with floured hands knead it on a floured board a few seconds, until bouncy. Roll out dough into a square or rectangle ½ inch thick and cut it into 1½-inch squares. Drop into the hot chicken stew when chicken is nearly done, cover the pot again, and simmer 15 minutes.

With a slotted spoon, remove chicken and dumplings to a platter or serving dish. Off heat, stir the flour paste into the broth left in the pot. Return to low heat and simmer a few minutes, stirring constantly, until thickened to a gravy. Pour the gravy over the chicken and dumplings and serve immediately.

~~~~~~~~~~~~~~~~

ALICE PATILLA'S OXTAIL STEW

This recipe comes from my first cousin. I try to have oxtails as often as possible; they're really a delicacy. We used to have them more often than now, as I'm on the road so much. They do take a long time to cook.

To minimize fat, cook oxtails a day ahead, chill, and skim off congealed fat before reheating. Serve them with rice and a vegetable.

Serves 4

Heaping ¼ cup (4–5 tablespoons) roux (page 20)
3½–4 pounds oxtails, cut into 2- to 3-inch sections
Salt, black pepper, and cayenne to taste

About ¼ cup oil
1 medium onion, chopped
½ of a medium bell pepper, chopped
2 cloves garlic, chopped
2 teaspoons salt
1 teaspoon black pepper
1 teaspoon cayenne

Let roux come to room temperature. Meanwhile, wash oxtail sections and pat dry. Cut off as much exterior fat as possible, and season to taste.

Film a large, heavy skillet or Dutch oven with the oil, add the oxtails, and brown on all sides over medium-high heat, stirring frequently to keep meat from sticking and turning to brown evenly. (You may have to work in batches.) Add a small amount of water to moisten (about ½ cup), and keep turning meat over until it is fully browned. Stir in onion, bell pepper, garlic, and seasonings. Cook about 1 minute to soften. Add just enough water to cover and bring to a boil. Reduce heat, cover the pan, and simmer about 45 minutes.

Bring back to a boil for 1 minute, remove pan from heat, and stir in 2–3 tablespoons roux. Return pan to low to medium heat and, as liquid bubbles gently, gradually stir in additional roux until liquid thickens to a thin gravy. Over low heat continue simmering, stirring occasionally, until meat is very tender. This will take 2–3 hours total cooking time. During the final half hour, occasionally tilt the pot and with a large metal spoon skim excess fat from the surface of the cooking liquid. (If desired, chill several hours in the refrigerator to congeal the fat; lift it off and reheat the oxtails.) Serve hot.

About Pork Backbones

Even before the era of supermarket meat cases, you couldn't get backbone from butchers in all parts of the country; it was a specialty mainly of Louisiana and Texas, and a favorite of those who raised their own hogs. The backbone cut is the whole, unsplit spine of the pig (the bony center of the saddle cut, including some fatback and some rind), cut out separately with some meat left on it. This cut has almost disappeared because a butcher who provides a backbone cut loses the high-priced, popular center loin chops and roasts.

Country-style spareribs (also called "baby back ribs," or "farmer-style ribs") make an excellent substitute for backbone, as do the slightly tougher pork neckbones.

Although especially delicious, these cuts render more fat into the cooking liquid than is considered healthful for those who labor behind desks rather than plows, so it's best to start backbone stews (or, for that matter, any dish involving stewed ribs) several hours or a day in advance; when the stews are refrigerated 2 hours or more, the fat will congeal into a thick layer on top and can be lifted easily and discarded.

‹‹‹‹‹‹‹‹‹‹‹‹

PORK BACKBONE STEW

When we had a stew, we used roux instead of adding flour to thicken it, so our stews had a distinctive taste. We just liked the taste of roux, so I suppose that's why my mom did it that way. You can serve the plain stew and have vegetables or a salad on the side, or you can add carrots, turnips, new potatoes, little sweet onions, and/or sweet peas. The turnips will definitely give the stew a different taste, a real outstanding taste. The carrots and other vegetables will add flavor to it, too. By varying the vegetables, each time you'll have a whole new stew. Serve it over rice, or with French bread to mop up the sauce.

Serves 4-5

¾ **cup roux (page 20)**	½ **cup minced fresh parsley**
4-5 **pounds pork backbones, neckbones, or country-style spareribs (baby back ribs), cut into pieces about 3 inches long**	**Optional vegetables (use any one or any combination for a total of 3-4 pounds):**
1 **teaspoon salt**	**Carrots, pared and thickly sliced**
½ **teaspoon white or black pepper**	**Turnips, pared and cut into bite-size chunks**
¼ **cup oil**	**Whole small new potatoes ("creamers") or quartered larger boiling potatoes, peeled**
2 **cloves garlic, chopped**	
½ **cup chopped onion**	
⅓ **cup chopped bell pepper**	**Pearl onions, blanched and peeled (see Appendix)**
½ **cup chopped celery (optional)**	**Green peas**
⅓-½ **cup chopped green onions**	

    Let roux come to room temperature. Meanwhile, season the meat with the salt and pepper. In a large flameproof casserole, heat the oil and brown the meat on all sides, working in batches if necessary. Add the garlic, onion, bell pepper, and celery. Stir a few minutes over high heat until vegetables soften. Add enough water to cover the meat. Bring to a boil.

    Reduce heat, cover, and simmer about 30 minutes. Return briefly to a boil, then remove pot from heat and stir in a spoonful of roux. Place pot over low heat, and as liquid simmers continue stirring in roux by tablespoonfuls until liquid thickens to the consistency of a stew. Simmer uncovered about 1 hour longer, until you can separate the bone with a fork. If possible, refrigerate overnight so that fat can be removed, then reheat before proceeding; otherwise, tilt the pot and with a large metal spoon carefully skim excess fat from the surface of the liquid. (There will be quite a lot.) Add the green onions and parsley and simmer a few more minutes to soften them. Serve over rice.

To include optional vegetables: Add carrots, turnips, and/or quartered large potatoes about 30 minutes before stew is done (adjust timing according to how large and mature the vegetables are). Add pearl onions to the stew for the last 20 minutes of cooking. If using small new potatoes, add them to the stew for the last 20 minutes of cooking. Stew may then be refrigerated overnight, if desired, and reheated the next day.

Shortly before serving, add green onions, parsley, and peas (if using) and simmer about 7 minutes longer.

〰〰〰〰〰〰〰〰

MUSTARD GREENS WITH
HAM HOCK OR SALT PORK

For this dish, you can use Chinese mustard—that's the type with the big smooth leaf—or the type with irregular leaves that's called curly mustard. Be sure to put in the stalks, because that's where most of the vitamins are, and most of the taste as well. The ham hock or salt pork (see Appendix) can be cooked a day or two in advance and refrigerated until ready to use. Ham hock adds a smoky taste and chewy texture; salt pork adds a salty taste and tender texture.

Serves 3–4

½ **pound ham hock or ham
  ends or ¼ pound salt
  pork**
3 **bunches mustard greens**

¼ **cup oil or bacon fat**
½ **teaspoon salt**
½ **teaspoon cayenne**
½ **teaspoon black pepper**

If using ham hock, cover it with water, bring to a boil, reduce heat, and cook gently, uncovered, until completely tender when pierced by a fork (1–2 hours for tight-skinned ham hock, or about a half hour for loose-skinned hock or ham ends). Drain and set aside, reserving the cooking water to use with the greens. When hock is cool enough to handle, cut the meat into bite-size pieces or slices. Reserve. If using salt pork, boil about 10 minutes or until the skin is tender. (Discard the cooking water from salt pork.) Rinse salt pork well, slice it into thin, inch-square pieces, and set aside.

Place greens in a large pot and soak about 10 minutes in lukewarm water. Drain and then wash the greens very well, leaf by leaf, under a lot of running water, rinsing them and letting them drain at least 3 times. (This is necessary in order to rid the greens of sand, bugs, and bad spots.) Chop the stalk ends into inch-long pieces and place them in a large saucepan with a lid. (If using homegrown greens, do not use stalks of any plants that have bolted, as they will be tough and bitter.) Tear or chop the leafy parts into 4-inch pieces and add them to the saucepan. Add 1 cup water (if using ham hock, use its cooking water) and bring it to a gentle boil. Add the oil or bacon fat, salt, peppers, and the reserved ham hock or salt pork. Reduce heat, cover, and simmer gently until the stems of the greens are tender to the touch with a fork. The greens take very little time to cook—30 minutes for tender young mustard greens to 40 minutes for tougher greens. Serve hot.

BEETS ÉTOUFFÉE

Here, fresh beets are cut into shoestrings. If you prefer to shred them quickly in a food processor, decrease the cooking time to about 10 minutes.

Serves 3–4

1 teaspoon butter	¾ cup water
¼ of a small red or yellow onion, chopped	⅛ teaspoon salt
	½ teaspoon sugar
3 medium beets, pared and cut into shoestrings (about 2½ cups)	½ teaspoon vinegar

In a 10-inch skillet or wide saucepan, melt the butter over medium heat and add onion. Sauté until onion softens. Stir in beets. Add the water, salt, sugar, and vinegar. Simmer covered until beets are tender (about 20 minutes).

About Okra

My mother had her own truck patch, and she had all the vegetables that you can grow in Louisiana and Texas. Okra was done after the hottest weather was just about gone. The pods are sticky, but it's the leaves that kill you. When my mother used to send us out to pick okra, she told us to wear long-sleeve shirts and gloves and just pick off the pods, don't touch the leaves, they're too rough. And as youngsters we'd say, "Oh, what do we need long sleeves for, we know better." And I'd go to the okra patch and when I got back, I'd be itching and scratching and actually swelling. When those leaves touch your bare arms, it's like somebody's sticking you with a bunch of little needles. I had to take a bath and get all that stuff off and I had to rub down with lamb tallow or Vaseline. That was one of the things I hated: "Go and pick okra" was like telling me, "Go get stung by bees."

Fresh okra is best, but you can have okra all year round by using frozen okra. I find now that okra is good to help build blood. My brother-in-law was very ill a few years ago and blood transfusions are against his religion. The doctors told him to eat okra, to help build his blood.

Okra oozes thin, translucent strings (like spiderwebs) as it cooks. Some people refer to the stringing of okra as "roping." If you cook it long enough, it quits stringing. Adding a little salt while frying it will help stop the stringing, too. When the stringing stops, you can add other ingredients to okra. You can cook okra with shrimps, with prawns, or with chicken, or with a combination of these ingredients. You can add smoked sausages to give it that extra flavor, that smoky Creole cooking flavor.

〰〰〰〰〰〰〰

OKRA ÉTOUFFÉE

Serves 4–6

2 **pounds fresh okra**
¼ **cup oil**
Salt to taste
¼ **cup white or yellow chopped onion**
¼ **cup chopped bell pepper**
2 **cloves garlic, chopped**
½ **pound smoked sausage (page 122 or store-bought), cut into inch-long slices (optional)**

2 **medium-large fresh tomatoes (about 8 ounces each), peeled (see Appendix) and coarsely chopped (preferable), or 16-ounce can tomatoes**
1 **teaspoon cayenne (or to taste)**
½ **teaspoon black pepper**
1¼ **cups water**
Cooked rice

Cut the okra into slices ½–1 inch thick, discarding the heads and the tough tails. Film a large skillet thinly with the oil and add the okra. Salt lightly and sauté over low to medium heat, stirring constantly, until the okra has almost stopped stringing (about 20 minutes). Add the onion, bell pepper, and garlic. Sauté, stirring occasionally, until vegetables soften. Add the sausage, tomatoes, cayenne, and pepper.

Gradually stir in enough of the water to make a liquid the consistency of a thick soup. Continue to simmer over low heat about 30 minutes. Correct seasonings and serve over rice.

Okra With Chicken: Cut a frying chicken into serving pieces and season with salt and cayenne to taste. Heat 2 tablespoons oil in a skillet, add the chicken pieces, and brown them well on all sides, working in batches if necessary. Meanwhile, cook okra as above, using a large, deep skillet or flameproof casserole. When the okra has cooked about 30 minutes, add the chicken pieces, partly cover the pan, and continue cooking until chicken is cooked through (about 20 minutes longer). Optional sausage may be added with the chicken. Serve over rice. Serves 4–6 as a main dish.

Okra With Seafood: When okra has cooked 30 minutes, add 1½ pounds shrimps or prawns (peeled, deveined, and rinsed), or 2 Dungeness crabs (cleaned, rinsed, cracked, and cut into pieces), or 6 cleaned, cut-up blue crabs. If desired, add sausages with the seafood. Cover the pan to seal the flavor in and simmer until seafood is cooked through (no more than 15 more minutes). Serve with rice. Serves 4–6 as a main dish.

OKRA AND TOMATOES

Serves 6–8

2 pounds fresh okra	¾ teaspoon cayenne
½ cup oil	¼ teaspoon black pepper
1 teaspoon salt (or to taste)	2 large, ripe tomatoes,
¾ cup chopped onion	peeled (see Appendix)
½ cup chopped bell pepper	and diced
1½ tablespoons chopped garlic	4½ cups chicken broth or water

Cut the okra into slices ½ inch thick, discarding the heads and tough tails. In a heavy 10-inch or 12-inch skillet, warm the oil. Drop in the okra slices and stir well. Cook over moderate heat, stirring frequently. When okra starts to brown (or when it begins to stick to the bottom of the skillet), reduce heat and scrape the skillet with a wooden spoon (leaving in the browned bits for flavor). Sprinkle okra with the salt and continue frying over low heat, stirring often, until it stops stringing. When no more strings appear, stir in onion, bell pepper, garlic, cayenne, and pepper. Sauté 5 minutes. Add tomatoes. Cook until tomatoes are soft (about 5 minutes). Stir in broth or water, bring to a boil over high heat, reduce heat, and simmer uncovered 20 minutes.

FRESH LIMA BEANS

Cooking times in this recipe are suited to large, mature, fresh lima beans (rather than baby limas or frozen beans), so shorten the time if your beans are tender.

Serves 4

1 cup fresh lima beans
3 cups water
  Salt to taste
  About 1 teaspoon bacon
    fat (or to taste)

Black or white pepper and
  cayenne to taste
About ½ teaspoon sugar (or
  to taste) (optional)

In a 2-quart saucepan, combine beans and the water. Salt lightly and bring to a boil. Reduce heat to medium to maintain a slow boil and cook until beans are slightly softened but not yet tender (about 30 minutes), stirring occasionally. If water evaporates too quickly, add some more. Add bacon fat and, tasting carefully, stir in pepper, cayenne, and additional salt to taste. Continue simmering, and after a minute or two taste again and add sugar if desired. Slowly boil the mixture until it thickens and beans are tender (15–30 minutes longer).

FRESH CORN MAQUECHOUX
(Mrs. Lewis's Stewed Corn and Tomatoes)

My mom used to make this when we were kids and that's how I learned to make it. It's only made with fresh corn on the cob. I'm sure it's been around a long time. Maquechoux (pronounced mock-SHOO) looks like it's a French word, but it's not Parisian French, so it must be Louisiana patois. The corn is cooked very gently, so that it steams in the liquid from the tomatoes. (On an electric stove, use the "warm" setting.) You've got to include the sugar—it makes all the difference in the world.

Although maquechoux is best when the corn is freshly picked and sweet, of course, it can also rescue those disappointing supermarket ears. (When nobody is looking, break off a kernel in the store and nibble it raw, to discover whether the corn is sweet or has gone starchy.)

Serves 4–6

6 **ears tender fresh corn**	1 **tablespoon sugar (or more, for starchy corn)**
1 **or 2 medium fresh or canned tomatoes, peeled (see Appendix), finely chopped**	1 **teaspoon salt**
	1 **teaspoon cayenne (or to taste)**
3 **tablespoons finely chopped yellow or white onion**	½ **teaspoon black pepper**
½ **of a medium clove garlic, minced**	¼ **cup oil**

Shuck the corn. With a sharp knife, shave the kernels from the cobs into a large bowl, using a sawing motion; do not penetrate into the cobs. Then scrape the cobs again with the dull edge of the knife in order to milk them of their juices.

Add tomatoes, onion, garlic, sugar, and seasonings to the corn. In a heavy 4-quart saucepan or Dutch oven, heat the oil until it is warm, not hot. Stir in the corn mixture until all the ingredients are well coated with the oil. Cover the pot and cook over the lowest possible heat about 20 minutes, uncovering only to stir frequently with a wooden spoon. (This prevents corn from sticking to the bottom, forming a paste, and burning.) Taste carefully; if corn is not sweet, stir in a little more sugar and simmer a few seconds longer to melt it. When corn is cooked through, serve immediately.

〰〰〰〰〰〰〰

CORN BREAD

Serves 4–8

1 cup cornmeal	1 cup milk or buttermilk
¾ cup flour	3 tablespoons oil or melted butter
2½ teaspoons baking powder	
¾ teaspoon salt	1 egg, lightly beaten
¼ teaspoon baking soda	1½ teaspoons oil or butter

Preheat oven to 425 degrees. Mix together all ingredients except the 1½ teaspoons oil. Grease an 8-inch square baking pan or a 10-inch cast-iron skillet with the 1½ teaspoons oil and heat in the oven until it is quite hot. Pour the batter into the hot oil and smooth it with a knife to make an even surface. Bake until a knife inserted in the center comes out clean (15–20 minutes).

〰〰〰〰〰〰〰

SWEET PATTY PAN
SQUASH DESSERT

This dessert is made with the small, flat squashes (also known as cymling) when they're in season, cooked so that they taste like apple pie. When making the biscuits, roll the dough out thin (¼ inch).

Serves 4–6

1   **pound pattypan or scallop
    summer squashes
    (yellow or green)**
½   **cup sugar**
3   **tablespoons butter**

½   **teaspoon cinnamon**
¼   **teaspoon nutmeg
    Freshly made Buttermilk
    Biscuits (page 91) or
    biscuits from a mix, 1
    per person (optional)**

Preheat oven to 350 degrees. Peel the squash and slice ¼ inch thick.
Place slices in a saucepan, cover with water, and bring to a boil over
high heat. Reduce heat and boil gently until squash is tender but not
mushy (about 5 minutes). Drain and return squash to the saucepan.
Add sugar, butter, cinnamon, and nutmeg. Simmer 5 minutes, stirring
to combine well. Pour squash mixture into an 8-inch pie pan and bake
20 minutes. Raise temperature to 400 degrees and bake 10 minutes
longer. Serve warm as a dessert, "as is" or spooned over hot biscuits.

~~~~~~~~~~~~~~~~~

THELMA'S BERRY DUMPLINGS

This warm dessert is quick, simple, and very comforting. The
dumpling batter doesn't require a "fine hand with pastry," just room-
temperature butter, a bowl, a wooden spoon, and 5 minutes' free time.

Serves 4–6

BERRY MIXTURE:
2½ **cups blackberries or
    boysenberries (fresh or
    frozen without sugar)**

DUMPLING DOUGH:
4   **tablespoons (½ stick)
    butter, at room
    temperature**

2½ **cups water**
½   **cup sugar**
2   **tablespoons butter**
½   **teaspoon cinnamon**

¼   **cup shortening (or
    additional butter), at
    room temperature**
½   **cup sugar**

1	egg	1	teaspoon baking powder
1	tablespoon milk	¼	teaspoon baking soda
2	cups flour		Pinch of salt

Before starting to make the dough, place all berry mixture ingredients in a large, wide saucepan (preferably coated with enamel or porcelain). Bring to a boil, reduce heat, and simmer uncovered 20 minutes (stirring occasionally) until mixture turns syrupy.

To make dumplings: Cream butter, shortening, and sugar together in a large bowl, beating with a wooden spoon until fluffy. Blend in egg and beat briefly until fluffy. Stir in milk. Add flour, baking powder, soda, and salt. Blend thoroughly. (If dough remains dry, stir in 1 additional tablespoon milk.) Gather dough into a ball and with floured hands knead it about 30 seconds. On a well-floured board, roll out dough into a rough rectangle about ⅓ inch thick. Cut dough lengthwise and crosswise to form pieces about 1½ inches square. Drop 4 or 5 squares into the simmering berry syrup and cook 3 minutes on each side. Test by tasting a corner of a dumpling; it should be slightly moist but not doughy. As dumplings are done, remove them to a casserole dish. Continue the process until all the dough has been cooked. Pour the berry syrup over the dumplings in the casserole. Serve hot or warm.

THELMA'S PEACH COBBLER

The dough for the crust is similar to the dough for the Berry Dumplings above.

Serves 6–8

5   cups fresh peaches (or 2 bags frozen sliced peaches without syrup, 16 ounces each)
1   cup sugar
⅓   cup butter
1   teaspoon nutmeg
1   teaspoon cinnamon
1   tablespoon cornstarch dissolved in 2 tablespoons water

SWEET COBBLER CRUST:
1   cup (2 sticks) butter at room temperature (or ½ cup each butter and shortening)
1   cup sugar
2   eggs
2   tablespoons milk
2   teaspoons vanilla
1   teaspoon baking powder
¼   teaspoon baking soda
¼   teaspoon salt
4   cups flour

Preheat oven to 350 degrees. To peel fresh peaches, drop them into boiling water; boil until skins start to split (about 30 seconds). Drain, peel, pit, and slice them. Place peaches in a nonreactive saucepan of at least 2-quart capacity. Add 1 cup sugar, ⅓ cup butter, the nutmeg, and cinnamon. Bring to a boil. Stir in cornstarch paste. Reduce heat to medium and cook 5 minutes. Remove from heat.

To make the crust: Cream together 1 cup butter and sugar until fluffy (by hand, or in a food processor). Beat in the eggs, then stir in milk and vanilla. Stir in baking powder, soda, and salt. Beat 2–3 minutes (or process 30 seconds). Little by little, beat in the flour until well mixed. With floured hands, shape dough into 2 balls. On a floured board, lightly roll out each ball of dough, working from the center to the edges, until each ball is large enough to fit a 9″ × 13″ baking pan (or equivalent). Do not stretch the dough. Place 1 crust in the pan, pour in the filling, and lay the top crust over it. Cut several small slits in the top crust to vent it. Bake until light brown (about 30 minutes).

4

A Country Boucherie

W hether they were living in Louisiana or Texas, the way Louisiana people dealt with butchering their livestock was to have a big party called a *boucherie*. There would be seven or ten families in the group, and they would take turns butchering their animals and holding the *boucherie* at their houses. One day they would butcher at your house, one or two of your cattle or pigs, and everybody got a piece of the meat. Then it would rotate; you would go to somebody else's *boucherie* and get a big fresh piece of meat from their animals. Everybody got their share.

They did this several times a year, in autumn and spring. They could do it in any month except July and August, when it was too hot and the meat would spoil before you could get it all preserved.

When my father decided to slaughter a hog, he used to put the hog in a separate pen, one with a floor made of boards so the hog couldn't dig into its own waste. And he fed that hog differently, fed it better than the other hogs that weren't on the line for slaughter. (We did the same for chickens, too, although we didn't have a *boucherie* with chickens. We put the chickens in a pen with mesh flooring for a few weeks, and we knew that the chickens would be completely cleaned out before they were slaughtered.) That's how they were protected.

A *boucherie* was a treat. For beef, they butchered a calf of a year to a year and a half years old, not the veal type, but what they now call "baby beef." Since hogs don't furnish as much meat as cattle, there were fewer people for the pork *boucherie* and more people for the beef, but often they didn't kill just one pig, they butchered three, four, or five of them. The men took care of slaughtering the animals, bleeding them and cutting them up, bringing the women the meat to cook. And those women cooked all day long.

Oh, it was a heavy day of cooking at a *boucherie*. Pots were all over. The kitchen wasn't large enough, so they used big black pots outdoors over a hardwood fire. From the hog they would always make both *boudin noir* (blood sausage) and *boudin blanc* (white sausage). That was for all to eat who were there, and if there was any left, everybody got a piece to take home for the kids. Those parts that you couldn't smoke, corn, or can, like the organs, would go into a big pot of soup, a *bouilli*, for all the people at the *boucherie*. All the meat was distributed by the end of the day.

After we finished cooking the soup, the boudins, and the meat, we would cook down the fat to make lard for oil, grease, and shortening. We put the lard in gallon-size aluminum buckets. I think the person who held the *boucherie* would keep the most, and what was left was divided among the others. Everyone would bring their own little cans for the leftover lard, and they would take it home.

Finally, late, late in the afternoon, almost in the evening, they made the cracklings. In the same pot they had used to cook down the lard, they cooked the cracklings, frying the pieces of solid fat that were left over from making lard. The cracklings were a snack, a delicacy, and they were always the last thing cooked because by then the women had to start preparing the evening meal.

The work of preserving the meat continued after the *boucherie.* The person who held the *boucherie* would take most of the leftover meat and can it, because there was no refrigeration. Each house had an icebox (literally, an insulated metal box filled with chunks of ice you bought from the iceman), but there were no refrigerators or freezers. You could keep a couple of pieces of meat in the icebox for a couple of days, but no longer. After a *boucherie,* people would cook the leftover meat and put it up in jars.

Making bacon was left up to each person at the *boucherie.* Each person might get a piece of pork belly to go and smoke at his own home. If anyone had a large smokehouse, he would smoke as much as he could: Each family's bacon had a string on it, and the bacon was hung in the smokehouse like stockings hanging on Christmas Eve. Although all the meat was cut up about the same size, everybody knew which piece was theirs; you didn't have to write names on them. And of course, after the bacon was cooked and eaten everyone would save the bacon grease to cook with. Nothing usable was ever thrown away.

People didn't age their beef, but they made beef tasso *(tasseaux)* to preserve some of it. Nowadays, when people refer to "tasso," they usually mean peppered Cajun hams made from the loin of pork, but our tasso was made from air-dried beef. They might call it beef jerky today, but the taste isn't the same as jerky. They would cut the beef into strips, season it real well, and hang it to dry in the sun. It was no longer that hot in autumn, but it was warm enough to dry the tasso.

My mom made homemade smoked pork sausages, too, as well as boudin. To stuff sausages into the casings, she used the very end of a young calf's horn. My dad would saw off the sharp end, not the big end, and cure it. Then Mom would cook it in the oven for a while and then clean it carefully inside, and sand the outside with some kind of sandpaper. When they were finished with the horn, it was as smooth as a marble floor, so there were no snags inside to hold any particles of meat. Mom would insert the smaller end of the horn into a piece of casing (or sometimes she slid the casing over the tip of the horn), and push the seasoned meat through into the casing, using two or three fingers, squeezing and pushing, squeezing and pushing, until the meat filled the whole piece of casing.

Sometimes she used the very sharp end of a type of pumpkin we grew, called a *couchaque*. It had a long pointy end, similar to a cow horn, and people would dry it in the sun and use it for a sausage stuffer.

At that time people would smoke their sausages three days, at least, to make sure they were well cured. Mom would keep out just enough that would safely last without refrigeration, and the rest she canned in pork lard: She heated the lard very, very hot. The jars for the canned sausages had to be washed very clean, rinsed several times, and heated in the oven to sterilize them. She always kept the jars very hot until she filled them. After arranging the sausages in the jars, in pieces, she poured the hot lard over the sausages to the top. When it cooled, she sealed the jars. That meat would last a long time. Sometimes she would lose a jar, but usually she didn't, because she knew just how to do it.

You had to can the meat, too, if you wanted to preserve it. People would can pieces of meat in oil or lard, same as the sausages.

They also made salt pork, well cured in brine, as another way of preserving the meat of the pork belly. The saltier it was, the better it kept. Of course, you didn't say, "I'll leave this here for three months and use it then." As soon as it was cured, you started using it, a little bit today, another little bit tomorrow, until it was all gone. The salt pork was kept in brine, usually in the coolest room—not in the kitchen. My dad used the coolest compartments in the barn. There was always a heavy cover over the brine (held on with a big rock, or a few bricks) to make sure the animals couldn't get to it.

In the late 1930s, they started making refrigerators, and in the early '40s my dad bought one. Those refrigerators were the same size as the little freezers they have now; you weren't able to keep a lot of things, but you could keep a little meat and other food in there longer than you could in an icebox. The process of butchering and preserving meats stayed almost the same. They put the pork belly in the brine, but having refrigeration meant you could take the salt pork out of the brine sooner, put more salt on it, and keep it in the refrigerator for a few days.

Today, with freezers and refrigerators in the homes, and large community meat lockers in rural areas, a *boucherie* is more of a social event, like a big barbecue, rather than a way to get together with the neighbors to use up a lot of meat all at once.

If you'd like to see a *boucherie*, see Les Blank's films about Creole and Cajun life, *Dry Wood* and *Spend It All. Spend It All* shows one held in Eunice, Louisiana, at the house of Marc and Ann Savoy. Marc is not only a fantastic accordion player himself, but he has single-handedly revived the art of making the Cajun style diatonic push-button accordion. His wife, Ann, is the author of *Cajun Music: A Reflection of a People;* Volume I came out in 1984 and she's working on Volume II now. She's also the coordinator for a series of concerts (broadcast over the radio), cosponsored by the city of Eunice and the National Park Service, held every week at the historic Liberty Theater in Eunice. Each show includes music from two bands, one Cajun, the other Creole or black.

In fact, the last *boucherie* I attended was also at Marc and Ann's, just a few years ago—at that time, there was a film crew on hand. Scottish musician Aly Bain, a member of the hot Celtic music group the Boys of the Lough, was making a British television documentary called *Aly Meets the Cajuns*, which has since been broadcast all over the world. I had just done a show at the Audubon Zoo in New Orleans, and I went from there to spend a week in southwestern Louisiana, where the kind of music I play really began. After doing Ann's radio show with Wayne Toups, I played for an outdoor dance on the opening night of the Acadian Festival in Eunice. There was a big crowd, and those in charge tried to get the area in front of the stage roped off so people wouldn't dance—but they got rid of the ropes and danced anyway! Marc and Ann held their *boucherie* in the same week, in the middle of all these activities. It really felt wonderful to see so much interest in our music and our traditions, and to take part in all the events.

AN AUTUMN *BOUCHERIE*

HOG'S HEAD CHEESE
(Souse)

Hog's head cheese, souse, or headcheese, is eaten as an hors d'oeuvre. It's good at parties or as a snack at home. It's not a cheese, but a rich meat spread. Serve it on crackers of your choice, with No-Name Hot Sauce—and ooh, la la! Ask the butcher to chop the head into 6 pieces to make it easier to fit into a pot and to cut the cooking time. If you want to make a smaller quantity, some butchers will sell you a few pieces of a cut-up hog's head.

Headcheese is an important part of the Cajun-Creole heritage, arising from the *boucherie* tradition of using every part of the pig. Although it takes some time to cook, the homemade version is a world apart from the processed "headcheese" of the supermarket deli case, and is well worth the effort.

When my husband, Ray G, makes souse, he includes most of the fat from the head; this adaptation is a good deal leaner, with a fat content similar to that of a French country-style pork pâté—which in fact this dish very much resembles. (As lagniappe, you can make lard from the fat trimmings and meat stock from the broth.)

Makes about 3 pounds (to serve about 20)

1	hog's head (about 12 pounds) sawed into 6 pieces	1	large yellow or white onion (about 9 ounces)
2-3	teaspoons salt (or to taste)	2	bunches green onions
1	teaspoon black pepper (or to taste)	½	bunch parsley (stalks and leaves)
¼-½	teaspoon cayenne (or to taste)	¼	cup oil

Remove the tongue and eyes from the hog's head; discard the eyes. Wash hog's head and tongue thoroughly and pull out any bristles and hair follicles. (A needlenose pliers works well.) Place the pieces in a very large pot (or 2 pots), cover them with water, and bring to a boil. Skim foam for a few minutes until most of the foaming subsides. Add salt generously, reduce heat, and simmer until head is very tender and meat is falling off the bones (about 90 minutes from the boil), skimming the broth from time to time. Remove the meat and bones from the pot and let cool. Reserve the broth.

Cut off and discard the ears. Cut off the large slabs of exterior fat from the hog's head pieces and reserve separately from the meat. (You will have about 2 pounds of pure fat, which you can use to make Homemade Lard, page 116.) Then bone the pieces of the head. Carefully pick over each piece, using fingers and/or a boning knife to get every scrap of meat (along with some of the surrounding fat), including meat hidden in the hollows between the bones. Include the fatty pieces with streaks of pale-colored meat in them. (Do not, however, include the bubbly-textured, pink meat that's embedded in gristle.) Skin the tongue and include its meat. If present, the brain may be included, if desired. Cut all meat into chunks and pick over again with fingers, discarding small bones, bone chips, cartilage, and gristle. There will be about 3 pounds of meat, including fatty pieces. Grind the meat in a meat grinder set to a coarse "chili grind," or pulse in a food processor until shredded but not pasty. (Do not overprocess.) The resulting mixture should be 30%–40% fat. If mixture is lean, grind some of the reserved fat and add it to the meat. (If desired, remaining fat may be made into lard; see page 116.)

Season the ground meat carefully to taste with salt, pepper, and cayenne, kneading in the seasonings and feeling through the meat again to remove any remaining lumps of gristle, bone, cartilage, or tough fat nuggets. Reserve ground meat.

Chop the onion fine (about ¼-inch pieces). Mince the green onions as fine as possible (using a food processor, or mini-chopper, if available); you should get about 2 cups. Mince the parsley very fine (with food processor, mini-chopper, or a clean coffee grinder, if available), to obtain about ½ cup, packed.

In a large, heavy saucepan, heat the oil, and over medium heat sauté onion, green onions, and parsley until tender, stirring frequently. Stir the ground meat into the mixture. Pour in enough of the reserved cooking liquid (1–1½ cups) to make a mushy mixture that's approximately as thick as a very thick spaghetti sauce. (Remaining cooking liquid may be discarded, or saved to make Pork Stock, page 116.) Heat together until bubbling and simmer about 5 minutes to blend flavors. (If you find you've added too much liquid, drain meat briefly in a sieve.) Taste again and correct seasonings, keeping in mind that when the mixture has been chilled it will taste less salty.

Place mixture in a rectangular baking dish (about 7″ × 11″). Let cool, then refrigerate until jelled. To serve, cut the pâté into thin slices or 2-inch cubes. Serve with crackers and No-Name Hot Sauce.

〰〰〰〰〰〰〰〰

NO-NAME HOT SAUCE

This spicy table sauce made with fresh green peppers resembles Mexican *salsa picante.*

Makes about 2½ cups

1-4 **fresh hot peppers (cayenne, jalapeño, or serrano)**	**About ¼ cup minced fresh parsley or cilantro (leaf coriander, or Chinese parsley) (optional)**
2 **medium tomatoes, quartered**	
1 **small center-stalk celery rib (without leaves), chopped**	1-2 **green onions, minced (optional)**
About ¼ cup minced bell pepper (optional)	**Salt and cayenne to taste**

Trim and seed the hot peppers, mince them very small, and place in a bowl. Chop tomatoes into small squares and add them, with their juices, to the peppers. Mix in celery (and bell pepper, parsley or cilantro, and/or green onions, if you like). Carefully add a little salt just to bring out the flavor. If mixture is not hot enough, add more hot peppers or some cayenne, to taste.

HOG'S HEAD LAGNIAPPE: STOCK AND LARD

Pork Stock (from hog's head broth):   Combine leftover hog's head broth in a stockpot with 2 large onions, quartered; 2–3 large carrots, pared and coarsely sliced; 1 rib celery with leaves; 3 sprigs parsley; 1 clove garlic; 1 bay leaf. Bring to a boil, reduce heat to medium, and keep at a light boil until liquid reduces by about a third. Reduce heat and simmer uncovered until liquid reduces to about half and a meaty flavor develops (about 1 hour). Strain and let cool to tepid, then cover and refrigerate overnight. Skim and discard congealed fat. Store stock in refrigerator for immediate use, or freeze up to 6 months. Use in pork stews and braises in place of water or canned meat stock. Makes about 8 cups.

Homemade Lard: Coarsely chop 2 pounds pork fat, and grind coarsely in a meat grinder or pulse to shreds in a food processor. Place fat in a cast-iron skillet (or other heavy, ovenproof pan) and pour 1 cup cold water over it. (If using fat that hasn't already been boiled, let soak at room temperature overnight before proceeding.) Preheat oven to 225 degrees. Place pan on the stovetop and cook over medium heat until the fat starts to sizzle (about 5 minutes). Place in the oven and bake until all water has evaporated, leaving liquid fat and crisp cracklings (about 2 hours). Remove from oven, let cool briefly, and strain into a heatproof bowl, pressing on the solids to extract all the liquid fat. (If you like cracklings, return solids to the skillet, salt them to taste, and fry them over medium heat until they are crisp; drain on paper towels and serve warm as finger food or on salad.)

Pour the lard into a container large enough to hold it easily, lightly cover with aluminum foil, and let cool to room temperature before sealing and chilling. Lard will keep about 2 months refrigerated, 6 months or longer in the freezer. Use homemade lard to replace hydrogenated lard (for example, in Latin American cooking and pie crusts) or in place of oil in pork dishes. It will have a much finer, meatier flavor than packaged lard. Makes about 2 cups.

About Barbecue

You get a different taste in your meat by barbecuing, especially with wood. Not pine—it produces a black smoke rather than heat and it makes food taste like resin. So you need hardwoods like oak, or briquettes. Barbecue on low heat at first and bring heat into the process later. You need a heavy cover to keep the smoke and heat in your meat; otherwise, it will take longer and the meat will dry out and it won't taste barbecued. If you only have an open pit, you can use some type of Dutch oven to cover your meat. (Turn the Dutch oven upside down over the meat.) Because of the smoke, barbecued food is more filling than baked foods. It's a fact. My father brought our attention to that. He said when you eat smoked foods, you get satisfaction a lot sooner than you do from food cooked indoors, and it stays with you longer.

Note: There are two kinds of sauce for barbecue. In Texas, they are called "mopping sauce" and "sopping sauce." The mopping sauce is a basting sauce, which keeps meats moist while they're on the barbecue, and adds a depth-charge of cooked-in flavor. Use it on chicken, ribs, chops, whatever you're grilling. The tomato-based barbecue sauce will burn if it's used as a baste. You can paint a little of it on the meat just during the last few minutes on the grill. Then serve the barbecue sauce in a bowl, along with the cooked meat, so your guests can use as much as they want.

RUSSELL'S BARBECUE BASTING SAUCE

I learned to make this basting sauce from my brother-in-law Russell Thomas, of Lake Charles. It is well worth the few minutes it takes, lending barbecued meats a deep-down tang.

Makes about 1½ cups

¾ cup white or cider vinegar
½ cup water
2 tablespoons oil or
     margarine
1 teaspoon chopped garlic
     (or ½ teaspoon garlic
     powder)

1 teaspoon Worcestershire
     sauce
½ teaspoon salt
½ teaspoon cayenne
½ teaspoon black pepper
½ teaspoon onion powder
⅛ teaspoon dried thyme
     leaves, crumbled

Combine all ingredients in a saucepan. Heat gently 10 minutes to blend. Brush on meat before and during grilling.

〰〰〰〰〰

IDA'S BARBECUE SAUCE

Lightly baste barbecuing meat or poultry with this sauce just during the last few minutes of cooking, and serve remaining sauce as an accompaniment to the cooked meat.

Makes 1½ cups

¼ cup olive or vegetable oil
1½ cups chopped onion
4 teaspoons minced fresh
     garlic (about 4 large
     cloves)
1 cup tomato sauce
1 cup water
¼ cup ketchup

1 tablespoon red wine
     vinegar
1 tablespoon brown sugar
¾ teaspoon salt
¾ teaspoon cayenne (or to
     taste)
½ teaspoon dry mustard
¼ teaspoon black pepper
⅛ teaspoon nutmeg

Heat the oil in a saucepan (preferably stainless steel or enamel-coated). Add onion and garlic and cook over low heat, stirring occasionally, until softened (about 5 minutes). Blend in tomato sauce, the water, ketchup, and vinegar. Continue cooking slowly until mixture bubbles. Add remaining ingredients and simmer 10–15 minutes, stirring frequently. Taste carefully and correct seasonings. Sauce may be used as is, or it may be strained or pureed to form a smooth sauce, if preferred.

∿∿∿∿∿∿∿∿∿∿∿

MARC SAVOY'S BARBECUE SAUCE

People often ask whether there's a difference between Creole and Cajun cooking. Marc Savoy, a superb accordionist from Eunice, Louisiana (in the heart of the "Cajun prairie"), and an equally superb cook, provides his slow-cooked barbecue sauce recipe, which is similar to mine in ingredients, but finally different in taste and texture. He starts the sauce early, then uses the rendered oil in place of a basting sauce. (However, nobody will throw you in jail for using Russell's Basting Sauce with Marc's Barbecue Sauce.)

Makes about 3 cups

1 cup oil

2 cans tomato sauce, 8 ounces each

1½ pounds onions (2 grapefruit-size, or 3 large), chopped

1 large green bell pepper, chopped

4 large cloves garlic, chopped

¼ of a lemon, seeded and thinly sliced (including rind)

1 heaping tablespoon brown sugar

2 heaping tablespoons prepared yellow mustard

2 heaping tablespoons Worcestershire sauce

1 teaspoon cayenne
Dash each salt and black pepper
Thickly sliced homemade-style white bread

Combine all ingredients except bread in a very heavy, nonreactive pot. Cook over medium-low heat, stirring occasionally, until oil has separated from sauce and sauce is very thick (about 2 hours). Pour off the oil into a bowl and use it to baste the meat, once meat is half-cooked. Eat the remaining sauce spread on the bread.

<<<<<<<<<<<<<<<<<<<

BOUILLI
(Beef Soup)

Bouilli is a rich, hearty soup that includes beef "spare parts" of varying tastes and textures, all cooked spoon-tender. The soup's flavor improves markedly when it's cooked in advance and reheated. Serve *bouilli* on mounds of rice, as a substantial first course or a main dish.

Serves 8–10 as a soup course

2	slices beef shank	2	teaspoons salt
½	pound lean beef stew meat	1	bay leaf
½	pound beef heart	*1	medium kidney
3½	quarts thin (uncondensed) meat stock or water (or a combination)	⅓	cup chopped green onions
½	cup chopped yellow onion	⅓	cup chopped parsley
⅓	cup chopped celery		14½-ounce can stewed tomatoes, chopped if whole
2	cloves garlic, finely chopped	2	cups rich meat stock (or a 14½-ounce can clear beef broth)
			Cayenne to taste
			Cooked rice

*Note: Kidney-haters can substitute calf or pork liver: Blanch it separately in lightly boiling water 5 minutes, then cut it up and add it to the soup.

In a large stockpot combine beef shank, stew meat, heart, and thin meat stock or water. Bring to a boil. Reduce heat to moderate so that the liquid bubbles gently. Skim foam and particles for about 15 minutes or until foaming subsides. Add yellow onion, celery, garlic, salt, and bay leaf. Simmer 45 minutes.

Remove meat from the liquid with a slotted spoon and, when cool enough to handle, cut it into small pieces. Remove skin and fat from the heart, and gristle from the shanks. Return all the meat to the broth, along with the shank bones. (The cook may eat the marrows or reserve them for another use.) Continue simmering meat and broth.

Meanwhile, cut kidney into pieces about 1½ inches square. Remove the central cord of fatty tissue and the attached gristle. Place pieces in water to cover, bring to a boil, reduce heat to moderate, and cook kidney 15 minutes. Drain and rinse the kidney (discarding the broth) and add the meat to the soup pot. Stir in green onions, parsley, tomatoes, rich meat stock or canned broth, and cayenne. Taste and correct seasonings. Cook over moderate heat so that soup lightly bubbles until all the meat is fork-tender (about 2 hours). (Ideally, soup should be refrigerated overnight, or for up to 4 days. Skim fat and reheat.) Remove the bay leaf and bones, and serve soup very hot over mounds of rice.

About Sausages

The following recipes for smoked farm-style sausages and unsmoked boudin both call for casings. Sausage casings are available from well-stocked butcher shops (whether routinely or by special order) and by mail (see Appendix). If casing and smoking the sausages is impractical, however, you can use the Smoked Sausages recipe to make unsmoked, uncased country breakfast patties. After correcting the seasonings, wrap the meat and let it rest overnight (or up to 2 days) in the refrigerator to develop flavor. Form the meat into patties about the size of thin hamburgers, and fry as breakfast sausages. Wrap any remaining patties individually and freeze them until needed. (Meat can also be formed into a long loaf like a salami, wrapped tightly and frozen, then sliced as needed.)

If necessary, you can make sausages using a food processor instead of a grinder, with some loss of texture: Cut meat into small chunks and pulse it; do not overprocess it. If you have no sausage stuffer, substitute a pastry bag with a wide metal tip or a funnel with a wide bottom. Affix the casing to the tip with a rubber band and stuff the mixture into it by hand or with any rounded implement (such as a dowel or wooden spoon handle) that will fit.

wwwwwwwwww

SMOKED SAUSAGES

Serve these deliciously smoky sausages at breakfast, or use in jambalaya, gumbo, and étouffées. They can also be smothered with tomatoes and onions as a main dish, or used to flavor vegetable dishes or beans.

Makes 8½ pounds smoked sausages
or about 45 breakfast patties

8½ pounds pork (25%–30% fat), coarsely ground ("chili grind"), preferably at room temperature

¼ cup plus 1½ tablespoons salt

¼ cup plus 1½ teaspoons crushed dried red pepper (for very spicy Louisiana link-style sausage; use much less for mild sausage)

1½ tablespoons garlic powder

1 tablespoon white pepper Pork sausage casings OR (for sausage patties) 4¼ teaspoons powdered sage (or to taste)

Combine all ingredients except casings in a large roasting pan and mix well. Knead 3–4 minutes; include sage if making uncased breakfast sausage patties. Let stand 20 minutes at room temperature to allow flavor to develop. Pinch off a small piece of the mixture, form into a tiny patty, fry it to taste the seasonings, and correct seasonings as needed.

Cut the sausage casings into 2½- to 3-foot lengths. Using a sausage-stuffing attachment on the meat grinder or mixer (or see "About Sausages," above, for improvised methods), fill each casing until it's firm but not packed. It may be more convenient to fill the casing to only 8 inches, tie it but not cut it, and continue, so that you have strings of sausages instead of a single giant. Tie the ends. Either smoke the sausages the same day or refrigerate them and smoke them the next day.

To smoke the sausages, use a smokehouse, if possible (see Appendix for alternatives). Using a hardwood like oak, start a very low, smoky fire with no open flame. (Do not use charcoal lighter or briquettes.) Drape sausages over a wooden dowel (an iron rod is liable to get too hot and break the sausages). Hang the sausages 4–5 feet above the fire. Tend the coals to keep the smoke going, rather than a real fire; if fire flares up, slowly sprinkle water or dirt on the coals until flames die down. Smoke the sausages at a temperature between 170 and 250 degrees (measured by inserting an instant-reading thermometer in any air vent) at least 8 hours. If you can, smoke them the next day as well. Wrap all the sausages tightly. Reserve as many sausages as you will use during the next week, and store the rest in the freezer.

To serve smoked sausages as a meat course, cook in a small amount of water (about enough to come halfway up the sausage) until heated through.

BOUDIN

Boudin, a delicious light sausage, is usually served as an hors d'oeuvre. It also makes a great sandwich on French rolls.

Makes about 9 pounds of sausages

4 pounds boneless pork jowls (pork cheeks) or, if unavailable, 2 pounds pork belly with its skin, or 2 pounds fatback with its skin
3 pounds boneless pork butt
2 pounds pork livers
1 teaspoon salt
5 cups uncooked rice

4 tablespoons cayenne
¾ tablespoon black pepper
¾ tablespoon salt
1 teaspoon garlic powder
3 cups finely chopped green onions
1 cup minced fresh parsley
Pork casings

Combine the meats in a large Dutch oven or 2 large pots with water to cover. Add 1 teaspoon salt (divided evenly if using 2 pots). Bring to a boil and boil over medium heat until meat is fairly tender. (Remove liver after 5–7 minutes; remaining meat will take about 1 hour.) Remove meat from broth and let cool, reserving the broth.

While meat cools, cook the rice (see page 30). Grind the meat coarsely and gradually add the cayenne, black pepper, ¾ tablespoon salt, and the garlic powder to it, tasting as you go until meat is seasoned to taste. Add about 1¾ cups of the reserved broth a little at a time until meat is well moistened, saving the remaining broth. Add cooked rice, green onions, and parsley and blend in well. Correct seasonings. Cut casings about 12 inches long. Stuff meat mixture into casings and tie off ends. (See "About Sausages," pages 121–122, for alternate methods.)

Heat remaining broth until it is hot but not boiling. Carefully lay a few pieces of boudin in the broth and heat about 5 minutes, never letting the broth come to a boil. Remove boudin from the broth and serve immediately, or let cool to room temperature.

Boudin not used the day it is made can be wrapped well and frozen for later use. Reheat it in a microwave until warm, or wrap in foil and warm in a 350-degree oven until hot.

CREOLE LIVER AND ONIONS

Soaking liver in milk takes away the gaminess.

Serves 4

1 **pound calf or beef liver**	3 **tablespoons flour**
1 **cup milk**	2 **tablespoons oil**
½ **teaspoon salt**	2 **tablespoons butter**
⅛ **teaspoon cayenne**	1 **cup sliced onions**
⅛ **teaspoon garlic powder**	2 **tablespoons water**

Trim any tough ligaments from the edges of the liver. Soak liver in the milk about 15 minutes. Drain liver and pat dry with paper towels. Mix the salt, cayenne, and garlic powder and rub into both sides of liver. Coat both sides lightly with the flour. In a large skillet, heat the oil over moderate heat. Add the liver. Brown 1 minute per side and immediately remove from heat.

In a smaller skillet, melt the butter and sauté the onions until golden brown. Pour onions over the liver. Add the water. Cover and return skillet to low heat. Simmer 10 minutes (for thickly cut liver) or until liver is done to your taste. (Time will vary according to the thickness of the liver and preference of the cook. If liver is thin or if pinkish liver is preferred, simmer very briefly just to heat through.)

~~~~~~~~~~~~~~~~~~

CHAUDIN
(Ponce with Rice Stuffing)

Chaudin (pronounced show-DAN) was a special treat when my mother made it for us. Ponce (or pounce, or paunce) is actually the stomach of a pig. It is shaped like a kidney. It is the stomach lining that gives this dressing a distinctive taste. When cooked, the stuffed ponce will be like bread, with a brown crust and a lighter filling. You can use this as an entrée or as a rice dressing to go with roast fowl. Some of the family also make a chaudin stuffed only with meat, to serve as a main dish.

Serves 4

PONCE:
1   whole pork stomach
      (ponce), about 1 pound
1   quart water mixed with 1
      tablespoon vinegar
½   teaspoon salt
¼   teaspoon black pepper

STUFFING:
      About 1 tablespoon oil
1   pound ground pork
¾   teaspoon salt
½   teaspoon black pepper
½–1   teaspoon cayenne

¼   teaspoon dried sage,
      crumbled
¼   cup chopped yellow or
      white onion
¼   cup chopped bell pepper
¼   cup chopped parsley
2   tablespoons chopped
      garlic
½   cup meat broth or water
¼   cup chopped green onions
1   cup cooked white rice
1   egg, beaten
1   tablespoon oil or melted
      butter

Soak the ponce in the water and vinegar overnight in the refrigerator, if there is time (or at least 20 minutes). Wash the ponce very well. Using a dull knife, scrape off any fat and jelly. (Fat may also be removed, very carefully, with a sharp knife, taking care not to puncture the skin.) Turn ponce inside out and scrape the inside. Turn it right-side out again, so that the lighter-colored side is on the outside. Pat it dry with a paper towel, sprinkle it with ½ teaspoon salt and ¼ teaspoon pepper, and rub the seasonings in. Set it aside.

To make the stuffing: Barely film the bottom of a skillet with about 1 tablespoon oil (because ground pork has a lot of fat already). Season the ground pork with ¾ teaspoon salt, ½ teaspoon pepper, the cayenne, and sage, and add it to the skillet. Brown the pork over medium heat, stirring frequently. Add onion, bell pepper, parsley, and garlic. Cook 5 minutes to soften vegetables. If pork has rendered an excessive amount of fat, drain mixture briefly in a strainer and return it to the skillet. Add meat broth or water and green onions and simmer over low heat 3 minutes. Remove from heat. Add the rice and stir well. Let cool to no hotter than lukewarm. When cool, stir in egg.

With a large, strong needle (ideally, a sailmaker's needle or trussing needle) and quilting thread (or thin white cooking string, like that used for trussing turkeys), sew up all openings in the ponce except one opening through which the dressing will be stuffed. Stuff the ponce (but not too tightly) and sew up the final opening. (Any leftover dressing can be reserved and served as a side dish at another meal: Place it in a baking pan and bake 10–15 minutes at 350 degrees.)

Choose a deep cast-iron pot with a tight-fitting cover or a Dutch oven (or a similar deep, heavy casserole) just large enough to hold the ponce snugly without actually touching it. Film the pot with 1 tablespoon oil or melted butter, heat it slightly, and carefully place the ponce in the pot. Gently brown the ponce on all sides. Add 1 cup water, cover tightly, and simmer 2½–3 hours, turning the ponce every half hour with a spatula in one hand, a large spoon in the other. Regulate heat so that liquid maintains a constant simmer. If water evaporates too quickly, add ½ cup water at a time, as necessary. Repeat until ponce is cooked through and fork-tender. Remove ponce from the pan; reserve the cooking liquid and keep it warm. When cool enough to handle, cut ponce into ½-inch-thick slices, and pour gravy over them.

All-Meat Chaudin: For the meat component of the dressing, use ¾ pound ground pork, ½ pound ground beef, and ¼ pound ground veal. After adding the onion mixture to the skillet, sprinkle the skillet contents with 2 tablespoons flour and sauté, stirring constantly, until vegetables are softened and flour starts to brown. Proceed as above, but omit the rice.

PINTO BEANS (OR RED BEANS)

Creoles are known for cooking red beans, pinto beans, and lima beans (these are all dried beans). Pinto beans are my favorite. I basically do pinto beans and red beans the same way. Don't soak beans before you boil them, because soaking weakens the taste. The beans go well with steak or fried chicken as a side dish. You can serve them over rice, or just eat them with bread, corn bread, or crackers.

In New Orleans, beans and rice are a standard Monday night main dish. To serve this recipe as a main dish for 4 or 5 people, increase the amount of meat to about 1 pound, including ham hock and/or any smoked sausages you have on hand.

Serves 4–6 as a side dish

½	**pound dried pinto beans (or red beans)**	¼	**cup chopped green onions**
¼	**cup chopped yellow or white onion**	3	**tablespoons minced fresh parsley**
1	**teaspoon salt**	1-2	**fresh hot peppers (cayenne, serrano, or jalapeño), seeded and minced (or 1 teaspoon dried cayenne if no fresh peppers are available)**
6-7	**cups water**		
¼	**teaspoon each black pepper and white pepper (or ½ teaspoon of either one)**		
¼	**cup bacon fat**	1	**bay leaf**
¼	**pound salt pork, ham hock, or a leftover end of a ham**	¼	**teaspoon baking soda***

Pick over the beans by running a few of them through your hands at a time and removing anything that isn't a bean. Wash beans well in a colander. In a deep pot, combine beans, onion, salt, and 6–7 cups water to cover. Bring to a boil. Reduce heat. Add black and white pepper and bacon fat. Simmer uncovered at least 1 hour, stirring occasionally. Add more water if liquid evaporates too quickly.

Meanwhile, prepare salt pork or ham hock (see Appendix). Blanch salt pork in boiling water to cover about 5 minutes; drain, rinse, and cut into thin inch-square slices. To use ham hock, drop into boiling water, reduce heat, and simmer until partly tender (about 1 hour). Cut meat into bite-size pieces. The end of a ham needs no special preparation, except cutting up.

After beans have cooked about 1 hour, add meat and the remaining ingredients. Simmer uncovered, stirring frequently, scooping from the bottom of the pot to make sure beans don't stick and burn. Add more water if beans dry out too quickly. Simmer until a bean flattens when you barely touch it (about 1 hour longer). If the liquid has failed to thicken, increase the heat and boil rapidly until the consistency of a thin gravy. If consistency is too thick, add ½ cup water and simmer 15 minutes longer. Remove bay leaf before serving.

*Note: The baking soda counteracts the notorious side effect of beans.

COLE SLAW

Cabbage was always an autumn vegetable for us. We never had it in the heat of summer; it was easier to digest in cold weather.

Serves 6

⅔ cup mayonnaise
½ teaspoon sugar
¼ teaspoon salt (or to taste)
⅛ teaspoon white pepper

⅛ teaspoon dry mustard
½ teaspoon vinegar
4 cups shredded cabbage
½ cup shredded carrots

Combine mayonnaise, sugar, seasonings, and vinegar, stirring well. Stir in cabbage and carrots. Chill until ready to serve.

CREOLE VINAIGRETTE
(French Salad Dressing)

Toss your favorite salad ingredients with this dressing.

Makes 2 cups

1¼ cups vegetable oil
½ cup wine vinegar
¼ cup water
¼ cup minced onion (use a sweet variety if available)
2 tablespoons chopped red bell pepper
2 cloves garlic, minced or put through a garlic press
1 tablespoon dried sweet basil, crumbled (or 3 tablespoons fresh, chopped)
1½ teaspoons Worcestershire sauce
½ teaspoon sugar
½ teaspoon salt
¼ teaspoon freshly ground black pepper
¼ teaspoon cayenne

Combine ingredients in a quart jar. Cover and shake vigorously. Refrigerate 1-2 hours and shake again before dressing salad. If refrigerated long enough for the oil to congeal on top, remove from refrigerator about 2 hours before serving.

~~~~~~~~~~~~~~~~~~

CORNICHONS DES TOMATES VERTES
(Thelma's Chowchow)

My mother always made chowchow, a sort of relish, from a mixture of cucumbers, green tomatoes, and green cayenne peppers. We added the chowchow to the food after it was cooked, kind of like Tabasco sauce. My sister-in-law Thelma makes this fiery, vinegar-free version, meant to be served within a few days; it's a wonderful addition to a barbecue. For a milder rendition, substitute slightly piquant chiles (such as Anaheims or Tam jalapeños) for the very hot ones.

For gardeners, chowchow is a tasty way to use up green tomatoes and the last burst of hot peppers before frost kills the plants—but city dwellers can also fix chowchow as a way to cope with the hard green supermarket tomatoes of winter.

Makes 3 cups

1 cup fresh hot peppers (serranos, cayennes, summer-grown jalapeños), trimmed, seeded, and chopped
½ cup chopped onion
½ cup chopped bell pepper

½ cup peeled, chopped cucumber (preferably pickling cucumber)
1 medium-size green tomato (or slightly red, but still crunchy), chopped
1 teaspoon prepared mustard
Salt

Combine all ingredients in a heavy saucepan and sprinkle a little salt on them to help draw out their water. Simmer uncovered over low heat until tender (about 30 minutes). Spoon the mixture into a jar, let cool, seal, and refrigerate several hours or days.

~~~~~~~~~~~~~~

WARM BEET AND POTATO SALAD

Serves 8–12

8 medium beets
5 medium red-skinned boiling potatoes
2 teaspoons salt
½ teaspoon black pepper

¼ cup white or cider vinegar
2½ tablespoons oil
⅔ cup chopped onion (preferably a sweet onion)

In separate saucepans, cover beets and potatoes with water, bring to a boil, and boil until tender when pricked with a fork (30–60 minutes for beets, depending on their age, and 25–40 minutes for potatoes). Drain and let cool until vegetables can be handled. Peel beets and potatoes, cut into chunks or slices, and combine them in a serving bowl. Sprinkle with salt and pepper. Combine vinegar and oil in a small saucepan and bring to a boil over high heat. Add onion, reduce heat, and simmer 1 minute to wilt. Pour mixture over the beets and potatoes and mix well. Serve warm.

~~~~~~~~~~~~~~~~~~~~

PIECRUST

Piecrusts can be made in advance and frozen before baking. To use a frozen piecrust, fill it and bake it without defrosting, increasing the baking time until crust is golden brown.

Makes two 9-inch piecrusts

2 cups flour	4 tablespoons (½ stick) cold butter (or additional shortening)
½ teaspoon salt	
½ cup shortening	
	4-6 tablespoons ice water

Combine flour, salt, shortening, and butter. Blend well until the mixture looks like a coarse meal. (This can be done in a food processor, with a pastry blender, or by rubbing the shortening in well with fingers.) Blend in ice water a tablespoon at a time until the dough clots into little balls. Gather dough into a large ball and turn it onto a floured board. Cut dough in half and roll out each half (using a light side-to-side motion) until dough is slightly larger than a 9-inch pie pan. Fold each piece of dough lightly in half and transfer to pie pan; unfold dough and press the edges to the side of the pan with a fork, or make ridges by pinching along the edge of the pie with thumb and index finger. Trim off any overhangs and use the trims to patch splits, cracks, or gaps (if any) in the crust.

To bake the crusts before filling them, poke many small holes in the center and sides with a fork. Bake at 450 degrees 6 minutes before adding a fruit filling that will be baked at length; bake 10–12 minutes (or until edges are brown and center is solid) for a custard pie that will be baked only briefly.

〰〰〰〰〰〰〰〰

PUMPKIN PIE

Makes one 9-inch pie

2 cups cooked, pureed pumpkin (or a 16-ounce can pumpkin)
½ cup sugar (or to taste)
1 teaspoon cinnamon
½ teaspoon ground ginger
¼ teaspoon freshly grated nutmeg (optional)
¼ teaspoon salt

3 eggs, lightly beaten
1 cup evaporated milk
¾ cup whole milk
    9-inch piecrust, unbaked (page 132)
1 cup heavy cream, whipped, or 1 cup crème fraîche or sour cream

Preheat oven to 450 degrees. Combine pumpkin, some of the sugar, the spices, and salt. Taste and add remaining sugar gradually until mixture is as sweet as desired. Add eggs and both types of milk. Stir to blend well. Pour into the piecrust and bake 10 minutes. Reduce heat to 325 degrees and continue baking until a knife inserted into the pie comes out clean (about 40 minutes longer). Let cool several hours. Serve with whipped cream, crème fraîche or sour cream.

5

Creole Courtship

World War II brought a manpower shortage to all the farms; all the boys were going into the service. Now my father *had* to let me drive the tractor, and use me as a substitute for one of the men. Finally he had me driving the planter.

One day, our neighbor, Mr. Pipkin, asked my dad for an extra man to help on his farm. All the farmers were their own weathermen in those days. They could tell, somehow, when the rain was coming.

"I don't have an extra man," my dad told Mr. Pipkin, "but my daughter has been working in the field and she drives a tractor. As long as my son-in-law is working with you—I want Ida to work in the same field with him—I'll let my daughter come and work for you for a day."

Mr. Pipkin promised that he'd put me in the same field with my brother-in-law. Then my dad said to him, "Now, I'm letting my daughter go and help you, and I don't want any of those men using foul language in her presence." And Mr. Pipkin promised.

I didn't want to go. I didn't mind working for my dad, but for some reason, I didn't want to work for anyone else.

Mr. Pipkin arranged to pick me up in his truck, and he was the worst driver in the world. He'd pass every day in front of our door, and we always laughed at his driving. He couldn't get his truck going for love or money. Every time he'd get his truck going, it would conk out. And while he was driving, he'd keep beeping the horn—we used to call him "the beeper"! We could hear him cursing, too, when his truck stalled. My dad knew that he cursed a lot; that's why he had Mr. Pipkin promise that nobody would use foul language in my presence.

So I got in Mr. Pipkin's truck, and of course he couldn't get it started. And he said, "God da . . . ! Excuse me, Ida. Excuse me." And he would start off again, and he couldn't shift very well, and I was laughing so I had to turn my head the other way so he wouldn't see. And the truck stopped again, and he'd say "God da . . . ! Excuse me, Ida."

When I finished working for Mr. Pipkin, he paid me a man's pay. Not a kid's pay, but a man's pay, because he felt I'd done a man's job. He was really a very nice man.

So it's hard to say just why I didn't want to work for him, or what I would rather have been doing on a Saturday. What was there to do? Nothing. They didn't let teenage girls play with teenage boys very often. As young kids, it was okay, but when you became a teenager they didn't let you climb trees, you didn't wrestle with boys, and you didn't play with the boys. You could, however, play baseball with the guys sometimes.

But I'd rather have spent the day playing the Victrola, winding, cranking, playing my sister's records (because I didn't have any of my own). And she'd say, "Don't you play my records!" because those 78 rpm records were easily broken. If you dropped one, forget it!

My sister mostly had rhythm and blues records, and a few country western. Sometimes, though, she would listen to our mom's Cajun records even though that wasn't really her kind of music. At night, my mom would sit by the fire, while my dad smoked a cigarette, and turn on the Victrola and play Cajun music and relax.

On Saturday nights they'd go to the fais-dodo, the *la la*. ("La la" meant that the songs would be in French.) A fais-dodo (pronounced feh doe DOE) is a big dance. The literal translation of fais-dodo is "to put to sleep"—but that doesn't mean they were dull parties; they were very lively parties. The whole family would go, children and all, and the name may have come from the fact that there was always a place for the kids to go to sleep after supper, a room they called *la salle des enfants*, the children's room. Of course, the kids wanted to listen to the music and peek through the doors, but they had to stay in their own room and play together until they went to sleep.

After the kids went to sleep, the grown-ups would party all night long, and on into the next day sometimes. In fact, I've heard my parents mention another meaning of "fais-dodo"— that the party would go on so long that some people would fall asleep in their chairs—sort of a "bop till you drop."

To stay awake, they'd make chicory coffee, and it was *so-o-o-o* strong. They'd buy the beans and they would brown them and grind them with chicory. The strength of the coffee came from how dark they roasted it. They always drank it *au lait*, with sugar and milk, although a few people were brave enough to drink that real strong coffee black, and I think that's how demitasse coffee came about. They didn't have the demitasse cups, but when someone asked for a demitasse, they poured them half a cup.

People sometimes ask me about the song "Jambalaya," and whether we had "jambalaya, crawfish pie, and filé gumbo" at our fais-dodos. Well, I don't remember any crawfish pies. I do remember meat pies, sweet potato pies, jambalaya, filé gumbo, and of course boudin, but by the time I was born nobody I know of was making crawfish pie at home. (I know they still make it in restaurants.) My relatives make crawfish bisque, they make stuffed crawfish, they make crawfish étouffée (page 61)—but not crawfish pie. (If you want to experiment, though, you could try making crawfish pie using the Cane River Meat Pie dough on pages 21–22 stuffed with peeled crawfish tails in a spicy cream gravy, like the pasta sauce on page 210.)

Most often, though, people just had little parties at their houses. They'd invite their closest friends and relatives, make some gumbo or boudin, and play the music. We called our area "the triangle," because in that triangle-shaped region between Beaumont, Orange, and Port Arthur, there were a lot of Louisiana-born people who had brought their records with them, and some of them were amateur musicians who played Cajun music. When my mom's two brothers came to visit, that was definitely a party—because they played accordion!

They'd clear out the biggest room (usually the living room) for a dance area, putting the couches and tables in the bedrooms, leaving just the chairs. Some of the neighbors had real nice barns, and they would use their barns for parties—but it would be pretty dusty, and the floors were very rough for dancing. Parties were better in the house.

And they would dance the evening away. If there was no one to baby-sit for the younger ones, they'd bring their kids. We'd ask our parents, "Can we go, too?" Well, they loved it, loved to take us along.

At the house parties they played Cajun music and zydeco, and folks danced the Cajun dances. There was no zydeco music on records yet, but the local musicians would play it at parties. It was all acoustic, and I used to feel sorry for those men. I sat there and watched one musician, an accordionist, and that poor guy was so drenched with sweat, I think you could have wrung water out of his shirt. It was so hot, and there was no air conditioning. There were fans—but how's a fan going to cool a room filled with 30, 40 people dancing?

As kids, we had to sit around and watch. We wanted to dance, too, but they'd make us go to the *salle des enfants*. And that wasn't fun—if you couldn't dance, what fun could you have?

Even when I was old enough to dance, if there weren't any youngsters my age I didn't go out on the dance floor. After a while, the other families started bringing their youngsters to meet the other girls or guys of the same age, and then we were allowed to dance when the floor wasn't too crowded.

I learned to dance by watching the adults—and dancing with my sister. At 15 I was starting to get interested in boys, but there was a shortage of boys because of the war. All the boys went into the service as soon as they were 18, and I didn't like the 14-, 15-year-old guys—they were kids. They talked like kids, acted like kids, and I thought, "Uhh-uhh, these are just kids."

But at that age, you went around with school friends, and you had a boyfriend at school.

There were a lot of school activities: school plays, football games, basketball games, baseball games, girls' softball. Because it was a country school, they played more outdoor basketball and baseball than indoor sports. I was usually on the girls' basketball team; it was hard work, hard play, fun. And we'd go to the games when the guys from our school went to another school to play, and we did a lot of yelling and screaming. I think maybe that's when I lost my voice. I think I injured my vocal cords. Since then I've had vocal nodes removed twice—but I was always raspy.

They had school dances, too. My sister went to the senior dances, and even if you weren't a senior you could go as a guest, so I went with her. Then you had the junior dances, and I would go to them, too. It was girl meet boy and boy meet girl—you didn't have to have a date or a partner.

And we'd go to church hall dances. We danced the slow dances, and a few waltzes, and, of course, the jitterbug, where you'd kick your feet up in those bobby-sox days. They'd have a band made up of local musicians, mainly beginners, and when the band was taking a break they played records to keep it going. They played a lot of R&B and some country western, but they weren't playing any Cajun music or zydeco at those church functions.

It was at one of those church hall dances that I met Ray Guillory (knicknamed "Ray G"), my future husband. Actually, it wasn't the first time. My parents and Ray G's parents were youngsters together; my dad and Ray's father had known each other for years and had gone to night school together, and they used to gamble together, playing poker late into the night at each other's houses. I can't remember whether we moved to Texas first or they moved first, but all the Louisiana people in our area would meet at church, so our parents ran into each other again. I met Ray when my parents visited his parents. My sister Hazel was friends with Ray's sisters, and I tagged along, too. I didn't even notice Ray, although (or maybe because) we're the same age. The girls just visited with the girls.

By the time I met Ray again at the church dance, when we were both 15, he wanted to dance with me. He danced very little, but he tried, because I liked dancing. I liked the jitterbug, and when some of the other guys who liked the jitterbug would ask me to dance, Ray decided, "Well, I can dance, too." He wasn't a very good dancer; he wouldn't ask me to do the jitterbug dances, he definitely wouldn't do anything except the slow, slow dances, the more romantic ones. I think that dancing the slower dances with me was one way of keeping me near. He wanted to talk with me, wanted to entertain me for the evening. When other guys would ask me to dance, sometimes he would say, "I don't think you should dance next time." He was very quiet, and he sat there and watched the others dance the fast dances. It did strike me that he was sort of romantic, because he was so quiet, but I wasn't really interested in him as a boyfriend at that time.

Years later, Ray told me he never liked to dance, because he didn't know how to dance as well as others. And I said, "But you have to learn. How're you going to learn if you don't watch someone dance and try to dance by the rhythm?" But he still doesn't like to dance. He only does the slow dances; he likes to waltz, and he does something that's not exactly a two-step, but a slow Texas-style version of it; maybe it's the Texas shuffle.

Your 16th birthday was your "coming out." You were not allowed to have a boyfriend come to your house to court until you were "sweet 16." That was the one birthday for which parents always held a really big celebration, whether for a girl or for a boy. They would have the party at home, usually on a Sunday afternoon, so you could use the yard if the house wasn't big enough for all the people. They had soda pop, lemonade, and ice cream for the teenagers. It was so nice outdoors. If it was in the winter, they had to have it indoors, and you couldn't have as many people there. I was one of the unfortunates; I was born in January. Willie was the lucky one—born in summer, he had a big, big celebration for his 16th birthday.

A few months after my 16th birthday, the war ended. Everybody was so happy; wherever you went, people were blowing horns, and they'd just grab and dance with each other and turn round and round and round. My dad went out and just shot his gun in the air.

My parents wouldn't let us go downtown because it was crazy. They were probably right: You can get hurt when people get excited. But you could hear horns for miles around. It took two or three days before it really eased off, and even then it didn't ease off entirely.

That was the summer I started seeing boys more often. When a boy started coming to court you, he had to go to your parents first and ask if he could visit. There were certain times and certain days of the week they would let him visit, and a certain time to leave—but he wasn't told to leave. If he was told to leave once, he'd never be told again. It was very embarrassing to the boy if he had to have the time pointed out to him. Most visits were on Sundays, and we were always chaperoned, so if we were having mixed company, our parents would be sitting on the porch in their swings or rocking chairs, smoking or drinking coffee all day.

If we didn't act like ladies while courting, we were punished. My mom punished me once so that I'll never forget it. I'd been punished more than once before then, but this was really heavy. I was 16 or 17, and I was trying to act adult. One young man had gotten my parents' permission to come visit me this particular evening, and for some reason (maybe I was tired that day), I wasn't interested in his company. I felt he should be a close friend of my brother, and not my friend. And I did not excuse myself—I just slipped out of the room and went to bed, leaving him sitting alone with my brother.

My mother asked me what had happened, and I told her truthfully. She said, "He didn't come to see your brother, he came to see you! And you did not excuse yourself. For that you're going to be punished. You're not going anywhere for a month." And she stuck to that month. Two weeks later there was a dance I wanted to go to, some big band that I wanted to see. Mom said, "No, you're not going anywhere." My sister begged her, my sister-in-law begged her, but she'd only say, "No way!"

I thought, "Oh boy, if I'm going to be grown up, I've got to act grown up. I have to learn how to act responsibly, like an adult." I think from that day on, I was too nice! I wanted to stay up with everybody who came to court, including my sister's boyfriend.

Even at 16 or 17, you were still considered too young to go out with boys. The boy could visit you at the house, but you couldn't go out to a movie or to a dance with him alone. If a group of people were going out together—two girls and two guys—fine, the more the merrier. When friends of my parents had children who were going to a movie or a Sunday afternoon dance, we could go with them, because they were being chaperoned by their parents; our parents trusted each other, and exchanged chaperoning us. Or I could go out with my big brother (until he started courting, and didn't have time for me anymore). But two kids couldn't go out alone.

When I'd go with a boy to an afternoon movie, Mom would drop us off, and pick us up when it ended—but 99 percent of the time a sister or brother would go along too.

For parties, my chaperone was my sister Hazel. She wasn't strict to the point where you couldn't hold hands—but you had better not leave that room or that hall. If she had let me wander off, she would probably have been in more trouble than me.

Of course, you'd feel like a baby after you learned that there were girls and boys who were going out at 16 without a chaperone—but those were the rules, period. So I was chaperoned until I was more than 18 years old. My first date alone with a guy was when I was 19.

Admittedly, chaperoned children don't learn nearly as much about the outside world as those who are not chaperoned—but really, I didn't miss anything. We went to carnivals, rodeos, movies, dances. My generation was a lot easier to entertain when we were children. There's a lot more trouble that kids can get into today than when we were coming up. We didn't have a problem with drugs because we didn't even know they existed.

My parents may have been particularly strict with us because my eldest sister had married much too young, back in Louisiana. She was only 15. A few days after the wedding, my dad called all the kids together and he said, "I let your sister start courting too young and then she was ready to marry. I don't want any of you to come and ask me or your mom to get married under the age of 18 years old. Don't ask, because you're not going to get my blessing." And of course that was important, to get your parents' blessing. And we all said, "Nope. Nope, we won't marry young." As a result, the strictness didn't come as a shock to us, or even a surprise.

Some parents actually tried to arrange their children's marriages. More often, they tried to associate a daughter with the son of someone they knew, or vice versa, and hope it would lead to something. They felt that if they knew the parents, and they were good parents, then the child had to be a good kid. (A child can go wrong, but they didn't realize that at that time.) They didn't want you to know they were doing it, but you could sort of feel it. Parents do the same thing today.

Once a couple decided they wanted to get married, they had to ask their parents' permission to become engaged. Of course, the guy and girl were always ready to get married right away, but if the parents thought that they had not courted long enough to know each other's ways and temperaments, they would insist that the youngsters court longer—until they had been engaged for a while. The youngsters usually felt that four or five months was enough. Sometimes the couple would come back again and ask to get married sooner, and the parents would compromise. They would announce the marriage in church only when the wedding date was approaching.

As Catholics, we had to arrange the wedding with the priest, and I think we had to announce it in church two or three Sundays before the wedding was to take place. Sometimes people would marry out of the faith, and in almost all these situations, the couple would take the girl's faith. If the daughter was Catholic, the parents would say, "Okay, you can marry my daughter, but she has to keep her faith," and they would try to get the young man to convert. Then he had to go to religion classes for several weeks, and when the priest thought the boy understood enough of the religion, he'd give him the chance to back out. Once the guy was ready to make the transition, he became a Catholic, and then the couple were married in the church.

You wouldn't serve gumbo at weddings—this was an occasion for a better meal. You might have pork roast or beef roast, potato salad, green salads, vegetables (red beans, peas, green beans), bread, and cake with wine.

At this stage of my life I wasn't thinking about getting married any time soon. I did plan to get married and have some children some day, although I always said, "I don't want to have as many as my mama had. That's a large family and it's a lot of responsibility." I fantasized about being a wife, a housewife, but first, from the time I was in eighth or ninth grade, I wanted to become a nurse. When I told my father my ambition, he said, "I think that's a good idea." When the other kids would tell him whatever they wanted to be, Pop would say, "I think that's a good idea." He would never say, "No, I think you should be a doctor and I think you should be a lawyer . . ." So long as you were going to go out there and get your education, you could make up your own mind.

He certainly didn't press any of us to farm, because that's a very hard life and he knew it. There are many difficulties, especially in the South, because of the weather. A storm could take your crop and blow it completely away. However, Pop did say, "If you become a farmer, be a good one. You see what I'm doing, you see how I'm doing it? Take a lesson from that and you'll see what it's all about."

None of us actually wanted to be a farmer. Willie did farm for a few years after he got married, sharecropping, but he didn't do it for very long. It's hard work. And since we rented our land, none of us was going to get stuck with the family farm, thank God.

. In fact, by now it was obvious that even my father was getting fed up with farming. Then, soon after the war ended, my sister Hazel got married. Her husband was in the service, and a few months after their marriage she moved to California, where her husband was stationed on Treasure Island, a naval base in San Francisco Bay. Hazel's move to the San Francisco Bay Area changed the whole way of life for the rest of my family.

FAIS-DODOS, DANCES, WEDDINGS: A PARTY ANYTIME

PORK RÔTI
(Baked Pork Loin)

This was a favorite dish at weddings and other great occasions.

Serves 4

1	pork loin roast, with bones, 3-4 pounds	1	teaspoon garlic powder
1½	teaspoons salt	½	cup chopped bell pepper
1	teaspoon black pepper	3-4	cloves garlic, chopped
1	teaspoon cayenne	¼	cup water (or as needed)

Preheat oven to 350 degrees. If pork is thickly covered with fat, trim off all but a thin layer (⅛–¼ inch). In a small bowl, mix salt, black pepper, cayenne, and garlic powder. Separately, mix bell pepper and chopped garlic. Make several small slits in the meat. Fill the slits with a total of 1 teaspoon of the seasoning mixture and 1 teaspoon of the bell pepper mixture (reserving the rest). Rub the outside of the roast with remaining mixed seasoning. Place roast on a rack in a roasting pan with a cover (see Cookware in the Appendix if you don't have a covered roasting pan). Pour ¼ cup water into the bottom of the pan and add reserved bell pepper mixture. If possible, let roast stand 1 hour or so at room temperature to absorb seasonings.

Roast, covered, 2 hours, basting with pan liquid every 15–20 minutes. Replenish the water as it evaporates. Uncover the roast and brown 30 minutes longer. Remove from oven. Let stand briefly before carving.

BOULETTES AND GRAVY
(Big, Spicy Meatballs)

These meatballs are large enough that preparing them goes quickly. They're tasty as a main course or a buffet dish. Serve over rice, of course.

Serves 4

1 pound lean ground beef	2 slices bread, moistened with water
½ pound ground pork	
1 egg, lightly beaten	½ cup flour
¼ cup chopped bell pepper	1 tablespoon oil
1 teaspoon salt	1 cup water
1 teaspoon cayenne	½ cup chopped parsley
1 teaspoon garlic powder	½ cup chopped green onions
½ teaspoon black pepper	Cooked rice
½ teaspoon white pepper	

Mix together meats, egg, bell pepper, and spices. Break moistened bread into pieces and knead into meat mixture. Divide mixture into 12 pieces and shape each piece into a meatball. Roll meatballs in the flour to coat well. Heat the oil in a large skillet. Over medium heat, brown meatballs on all sides. Pour off excess fat. Add 1 cup water. Bring to a boil. Add parsley and green onions and cover the skillet. Simmer 20–30 minutes. Uncover and check the liquid; if too thin, continue cooking, uncovered, until liquid thickens to a gravy. Serve hot or warm over rice.

About Jambalaya

You can make all kinds of jambalaya. You can make chicken jambalaya, you can make sparerib jambalaya (with the little tiny spareribs), you can make seafood jambalaya. You can make bean jambalaya—what they call "poor man's jambalaya." You can include chopped ham, chicken, seafood, crab, shrimps or prawns, or sausage, or any combination of the above. That's why its called "jambalaya," because all the ingredients are jammed together.

You can use all of the above ingredients at one time, but then you don't have a distinct taste, you've got a mixed taste. So if you're going to do a chicken jambalaya, you use primarily chicken. I always add sausages to my chicken jambalaya because they go well with it. Jambalaya is something you make to your own taste. Be sure to add as much cayenne as you can take. Once cayenne gets in your system it makes you sweat, and it's good for your circulation and digestive system. You can't go wrong with the red pepper.

CHICKEN AND SAUSAGE JAMBALAYA

Serves 4–5

8 cups cooked rice (preferably pearl rice; see page 30)

2 tablespoons oil
3-pound chicken, cut into serving pieces

¼ cup chopped yellow onion

¼ cup chopped green onions

¼ cup chopped celery

¼ cup chopped bell pepper

¼ cup chopped parsley

2 cloves garlic, chopped

1 pound smoked sausages (page 122 or store-bought), sliced into about 1-inch lengths

1 pound fresh tomatoes, peeled (see Appendix) (or a 16-ounce can whole tomatoes), coarsely chopped

8-ounce can stewed tomatoes

1½ cups chicken broth (or more as needed)

1½ teaspoons salt

1½ teaspoons cayenne (or to taste)

½ teaspoon black pepper

½ teaspoon sugar

¼ teaspoon powdered dried thyme

1 bay leaf

Allow cooked rice to cool completely, and break up any lumps. (If the rice is hot when you stir it into the jambalaya, it will become mushy. You want your rice to be grain-for-grain, so that the jambalaya will separate easily with a fork.)

Heat the oil in a large Dutch oven and lightly brown the chicken on all sides. Remove chicken from pan with a slotted spoon and reserve. In the same pan, sauté the onions, celery, bell pepper, parsley, and garlic. Add sliced sausages and brown 5 minutes. Then add the browned chicken and remaining ingredients. Bring just to a boil, reduce heat immediately to a simmer, and cook uncovered until chicken is thoroughly done (about 25 minutes). Stir occasionally and make sure there is always enough liquid. (Add more water or broth if liquid evaporates too quickly.)

Taste carefully and correct seasonings; mixture should be spicy. Remove the bay leaf, and if desired, remove chicken, let cool slightly, bone it, and return it to the Dutch oven. Tilt the pan and with a large metal spoon and skim any excess fat. Then, with a large serving spoon, stir in the rice by spoonfuls, until the mixture is moist and thick but neither soupy nor dry. Taste again and correct seasonings. Warm together over low heat, stirring frequently, and serve.

Sparerib and Sausage Jambalaya: Replace chicken with 3–4 pounds spareribs; if possible, have the butcher cut them in about 1-inch lengths. Begin as for Chicken Jambalaya; fresh and canned tomatoes may be omitted if preferred. Simmer spareribs until very tender (about 40 minutes for small, cut-up ribs, up to 75 minutes for larger pieces); remove bay leaf and spareribs from the pan. When cool enough to handle, remove meat from bones, and reserve. Skim fat from pan liquid; if there is time, refrigerate liquid an hour or two (or overnight) to make skimming more thorough, then return liquid to a simmer before proceeding. Return boneless meat to the Dutch oven and simmer until hot, then add rice as above, correct seasonings, and warm to serving temperature. Serves 4–5.

FRIED CHICKEN

The secret to this chicken is the baking powder in the flour that coats the chicken. It makes it crisp. If you can get a little crunch out of it, then you know you're eating fried chicken and not baked chicken. That's Southern fried chicken . . . Creole fried chicken!

Serves 4

1 **fryer chicken, 2½–3 pounds, cut into serving pieces (or 15–20 chicken wings)**
2 **teaspoons salt**
2 **teaspoons cayenne (less if unaccustomed to spicy food)**

1 **teaspoon garlic powder**
2 **eggs beaten with 2 tablespoons water**
1 **cup flour**
1 **teaspoon baking powder**
  About 3 cups oil or shortening for deep-frying

Pat chicken dry. Mix salt, cayenne, and garlic powder; season all the chicken pieces evenly with the mixture. Place chicken in a large bowl. Beat egg mixture well and pour over chicken. Stir to coat each piece. Combine the flour and baking powder in a medium-size brown paper bag and mix well. Place chicken in the bag a piece at a time and shake the bag lightly until each piece is coated with the flour mixture. Set chicken pieces aside on waxed paper.

Heat the oil or shortening in a 10-inch or 12-inch skillet or a deep fryer until it reaches 350 degrees. Chicken will be fried in 2 or 3 batches. First fry the meaty parts (breasts, legs, thighs) together, then the bony parts (back, wings), which will take less time. Place the pieces of chicken in skillet or deep fryer, leaving room for the oil to bubble around each piece. If meat is not covered with oil, turn over after 1 side is browned and brown the other side. Cook until done (about 20 minutes for the meaty pieces, 15 minutes for the bony pieces). Regulate the heat so that it stays between 350 and 380 degrees. Drain chicken on paper towels as it is done. If serving immediately, tent with foil to keep warm until all the chicken is done. Fried chicken can be served hot or at room temperature.

FRESH STRING BEANS STEAMED WITH BACON OR HAM

Any time you cook vegetables in a lot of water, you're losing a lot of flavor because it gets boiled up. These beans are steamed in just a little water, rather than boiled.

Serves 4

3 cups fresh string beans (about ½ pound)
¾ cup water
2 tablespoons oil or bacon fat
½ pound lean ham or very lean bacon slab ends, chopped in ¼-inch dice

¼ cup chopped yellow onion
1 teaspoon salt
½–1 teaspoon cayenne (or to taste)
½ teaspoon black pepper

Trim the beans, discarding tough tips, string them if necessary, and slice them or break them into pieces 1–1½ inches long. In a saucepan, combine beans with remaining ingredients. Bring to a boil, cover the pan, and reduce heat to a simmer. Cook about 20 minutes from the first boil, or until beans are as crisp tender or as soft as you like them.

MACARONI SALAD

Serves 8

8 cups water
2 teaspoons salt
1 tablespoon oil
2 cups salad macaroni
¾ cup chopped celery
3 hard-cooked eggs, grated
¼ cup mayonnaise
3 tablespoons drained
    pickle relish
3 tablespoons sandwich
    spread (mayonnaise-
    based)

2 tablespoons chopped
    pimiento or red bell
    pepper
2 tablespoons minced fresh
    onion
¾ teaspoon salt
⅛ teaspoon garlic powder
⅛ teaspoon white pepper

In a large pot, combine the water, 2 teaspoons salt, and the oil. Bring to a rapid boil. Stir in macaroni and slowly return to a boil; boil steadily, stirring occasionally to prevent sticking, until pasta is tender (about 10 minutes). Drain macaroni, rinse with cold running water, and let cool. In a large bowl, combine remaining ingredients until well blended. Add the macaroni. Mix well and chill.

〰〰〰〰〰

PIG IN THE BLANKET
(Sweet Potato Turnovers)

We call these "pig in the blanket," but in other parts of America that refers to hot dogs in a crust. If you want, you can use the same sweet potato filling in a regular piecrust (see page 132), put strips of dough over the top, and bake until the piecrust is done. Another variation is to use canned or fresh figs or apples for the filling. Slowly cook the fruit with sugar and butter until it's tender, so that it is like a preserve.

As with Cane River Meat Pies (page 21), novice pastry-rollers may get fewer pies out of the dough than experts. The filling may be halved if desired, or the dough may be doubled.

Makes about 16 turnovers

FILLING:

4 medium yams or yellow sweet potatoes (about 1¾ pounds)
1 cup sugar (or to taste)
½ cup (1 stick) butter
1¼ teaspoons cinnamon
¾ teaspoon nutmeg
¼ teaspoon ground allspice
1 egg, well beaten

SWEET TURNOVER DOUGH:

2½ cups all-purpose flour
1 cup sugar
½ teaspoon baking powder
Dash of salt
½ cup shortening, at room temperature
2 eggs, well beaten
2 tablespoons milk

To make filling: Pare yams or sweet potatoes and cut into quarters. Place in a large saucepan and add enough water to cover. Bring to a boil, reduce heat, and simmer until tender when pricked with a fork (about 20 minutes). Drain potatoes and mash well. You should have about 4 cups. Add half the sugar plus butter and spices and blend well. Gradually stir in additional sugar, tasting, until mixture is as sweet as desired. When mixture has cooled, blend in egg and set aside.

To make dough: Sift flour, sugar, baking powder, and salt together into a large bowl. Blend in shortening, breaking up with fingers. Blend in eggs and milk. (This can be done with a wooden spoon.) Knead until well blended. Cover with plastic wrap and refrigerate 30 minutes.

Preheat oven to 350 degrees. Divide the dough into quarters, and keep the part you're not using in the refrigerator until you're ready for it. Pick off small handfuls of the dough and roll each piece on a well-floured board to a circle the size of a coffee saucer, about ¼ inch thick and 5½ inches across. Spoon yam filling onto half of each circle. Fold the other half over and press the edges of the dough together with a fork to seal. Lift from the board with spatula and place on a cookie sheet. Continue until all the dough or all the filling is used up. Bake 20 minutes. Remove from oven and let cool uncovered. Serve at room temperature.

LEMON CUSTARD PIE

The lemon juice in this pie has to be fresh-squeezed, not frozen.

Makes one 9-inch pie

1   **baked 9-inch piecrust (see page 132)**

FILLING:
3   **eggs, separated**
⅔   **cup sugar**
½   **cup plus 3 tablespoons flour**
2   **cups whole milk**

⅓   **cup plus 2 tablespoons fresh lemon juice (see Appendix)**
1   **tablespoon butter**

MERINGUE:
2   **egg whites (from separated eggs, above)**
¼   **cup sugar**

Preheat oven to 450 degrees. To make the filling: Remove the white spot from the egg yolks. In a large bowl or in a food processor, combine egg yolks and ⅔ cup sugar. (Reserve 2 whites for meringue, below.) Cream well. Add the flour gradually, blending well after each addition. Add the milk a little at a time, blending well. Pour the mixture into a 2-quart saucepan and cook over low heat, stirring absolutely constantly, until mixture thickens, making sure to scrape the bottom of the pan. (If lumps start to form, use a flat-bottomed metal whisk to break them up.) When mixture is thick, remove from heat and stir in the lemon juice, then butter. When butter melts, fill piecrust with this mixture, pouring it through a mesh strainer if any lumps remain.

To make meringue: Beat egg whites until stiff peaks form. Add ¼ cup sugar and beat until well blended. Spread meringue over the pie filling and bake until lightly browned (5–10 minutes).

LEMONADE

Serves 6–8

5 medium lemons (for 1¼ cups juice)
8 cups water

1½ cups sugar
Ice cubes

Roll the lemons on the counter until softened (or microwave or parboil 1 minute). Halve lemons, squeeze on a juicer, and pour the juice into a large pitcher, reserving the lemon shells. Add the water and sugar to the juice. Cut each half-lemon shell in half again, add to the lemonade mixture, and let stand at room temperature 30 minutes. Remove the lemon shells (if left in much longer, the oil from the peel will make the lemonade too bitter). Serve over ice.

Coming to California
with a Truck Full of Rice

"**D**ad, I want you to take a vacation," Hazel would say whenever she wrote or called from California. "I want you to come and see us. You might like it here."

The timing couldn't have been better. That last year in Texas my dad had been badly disappointed by the weather, and lost a lot of his crop. A storm blew in at harvest time, and the wind and rain smashed the rice down so that it couldn't be harvested. In farming, one bad year can set you back five years.

My father went to visit Hazel in 1946, and he didn't just like it, he loved it. As soon as he got a taste of the California weather he realized he wanted to leave the South, where it's very cold or very hot, but not much in between. Spring never lasted long enough, and after summer, all of a sudden the winter would come. He had been living with those weather conditions too long; you could get rich in one year and go broke the next. He wanted to find a job where he could punch a time clock, work regular hours, and go home at night and forget about it.

And the job opportunities were great in California. If he couldn't get a job in the city, he thought, he could always get a job farming in Sacramento or Marysville in the Sacramento Valley area. Northern California has cool, rainy winters, but it's not too cold, icy, or windy.

When he came back, he told my mom, "I think you should visit California." So she went to visit Hazel, and she liked it, too. Her problem with the South was that she had high blood pressure and couldn't stand the heat. She was very happy with the weather in California, and felt that moving there would be a blessing. She picked out a house in San Francisco's Bernal Heights district, and my dad sent her the money to buy it. I don't recall my mom ever making a decision as big as buying a home before then, but since my sister was there, my dad felt that Hazel would guide her in making the deal. He had done well enough over the years that he didn't have to worry about money right away. In fact, when Mom bought the house, she bought it outright, in cash. (We just sold it last year!) We had never owned our home before.

I had mixed emotions about moving to San Francisco. Once again I had to leave so many friends behind. On the other hand, while I didn't know much about California (I had read about it in school, of course), I wanted to see what city living was like. I asked my sister, "Is this house inside the city limits?" She said it was, but at that time, Bernal Heights was actually very near the edge of the city.

It was in 1947, and I was 18, in my last year of high school, when we moved to California. There were five of us youngsters and our parents. Packing up was very difficult. Pop sold all the farming equipment, and sold it so fast, he didn't really get as much money as he could have.

We traveled in two trucks and a car. We had a big, two-ton truck and a little pickup truck with a trailer. You'd be surprised how quickly you can fill up a truck. We left our old work clothes behind, but we brought our better clothes. We took just a minimum of furniture (because our new house was partly furnished), but my mom brought some things she couldn't part with: her pots and pans, a lot of her canned goods, and those homemade mattresses of hers. And on top of that, my dad had to bring his rice.

As a farmer, he had always reserved a certain amount of rice for the family to eat from one season to another. "I don't know if I'll be able to get rice in California," he must have thought. "I've heard they plant rice out there, but certainly not in San Francisco, and I don't know how far away I'll have to go to get any. And here I have this crop, so I'm going to take some of it with me."

He'd heard that California had state agricultural agents stationed at the borders to keep people from bringing grain into the state, so he wrote to Sacramento, the capital. He told them that he was a rice farmer moving to California, and wanted to bring a certain amount of cleaned, polished rice with him for eating purposes. They sent him back a letter of permission.

Driving to California was quite an experience. I had seen hills in Louisiana and in Texas I had seen knolls, but I had never before seen such large mountains as I did when we were in Arizona. When we came down through those mountains, and you could look down and see the valley, I couldn't believe it. It was just fascinating, fantastic, breathtaking.

When we got to the inspection station at the California border, they wanted us to unload everything, and they asked my dad if we were carrying any agricultural products. He told them he was carrying rice, and had permission to bring it in. When they saw all the sacks of rice, they said, "You can't bring all this in," but my dad showed them the letter of permission. And that kept us from having to unload the whole truck; the agents must have thought, "Ehh, he's got his game together, we'll let him go."

As we got into California we started seeing flatlands and then, all of a sudden, mountains again. I thought, "Oh my God, I hope we're not going to be in between the mountains like this." I'd heard that San Francisco was hilly, and I was used to flatness.

When we finally arrived at our house, I didn't care for it too much at first. We had always lived way out in the country, on all the land we needed to go get lost on—and here we were in little matchboxes, all stuck together. Even the houses that were not flat up against each other were only 15 feet apart. The good thing was that everything was more convenient—you could jump on a streetcar or bus and go downtown, or have someone drive you downtown in ten minutes—but the price you paid was the noise. The streetcars, the traffic, the horns honking! You don't hear all that in the country.

Coming to California was like starting all over again, being born again. Here we were in a whole different environment, a whole new state. Actually I felt like I was in a new country.

During World War II and right afterward, jobs at the war plants were plentiful here, and a lot of people moved out from the South. Before we arrived, we were not really aware that there were so many Louisianians who had come to the Bay Area during the war. My dad went to work right away. He went to the unemployment office to find out what he could do. When he told them his background, they said, "Well, as a farmer, you know a lot about cattle. We'll send you to this meat-packing company as a butcher's helper. I'm sure you'll fit in well." And he did. There he was, working with the meat, cutting up the beef, just like he did at home. He worked at only two different meat-packing companies, in all, until he retired.

After a while, we began to adjust. Bernal Heights was a mixed neighborhood, mostly white and Mexican. It wasn't that strange for us because we'd never lived in a segregated neighborhood; at home, we always had neighbors of different nationalities. We started meeting our neighbors, and the youngsters in the neighborhood. Once we started school in San Francisco, we had friends from all over the world who lived here.

High school was a bit different in San Francisco. For one thing there were some compulsory courses I was supposed to have taken already. The courses you had to take depended on what you wanted to do when you graduated. To go into nursing I should have taken certain courses in the 10th and 11th grade, but since I hadn't, I just took the easy way out and went for a general education diploma.

The schoolwork wasn't any harder than it had been in Texas. I didn't feel I had an abundance of homework to do— maybe because now I didn't have all those chores. There were no chores to do here. Nothing. What was there to do except wash the dishes, help Mom clean the house, and wash clothes? Didn't have any chickens, nor any pigs to attend to. And I didn't miss them! I did miss the space to go out and walk in the yard. All I could do was step onto the front porch, and then I was on the street.

The backyard wasn't very big either. I would go out the back door and down the stairs, and within 25 feet I would be at the end of the yard. My mom still had enough land in the back to plant string beans, carrots (she loved carrots), a few beets, green onions, parsley, and mustard. She always had a little space for mustard. She tried okra once, but it doesn't work out here. For okra, it has to be really hot.

She had to change her cooking a little after moving here. You couldn't find filé for gumbo anywhere on the shelves here at that time. When my mom would take a trip to Louisiana, she would bring back the filé, or her relatives would visit and bring it in what we call a flask: "Here's a whole bunch for you." As for really good smoked sausage, even now it has to be brought from Louisiana, unless you make it yourself.

California stopped seeming like another country once we started school and began to meet the other kids. At first I felt like a little frog, sitting on a log: I knew nobody at school. Then, the way kids do, I started meeting classmates: "What's your name? You're new to this class," they would say. They asked where I was from, and tell me where they were from. In one of my classes I met two girls who lived not too far away from us—and they were from Louisiana. My smile brightened up, because I knew that we all spoke the same language, whether they spoke French or not. (In fact, they didn't speak French very well, but once you knew they were originally French-speaking, you knew about everything.)

I asked them if they liked it here; they said, "Yeah, I mean, it's home now, so you get used to it." And then I started feeling I could belong to this place.

I met my girl friend's cousin, John Semien, at her parents' home. He turned out to be a cousin of our adopted brother, Benjamin Semien, as well. John Semien played accordion, the little diatonic Cajun accordion, and I told my parents about it. "Let us know when he comes to visit again," they said. "We'd like to come and hear him play." After my parents heard him play, they decided, "Well, maybe he'll come and play a party for us." And that's how the parties started. The parties went from house to house, because we had started reaching out to the Texas and Louisiana people of our Creole background, people who knew about the music. In those days, if you played zydeco for anybody else, they thought you were crazy: "What is that chink-a-chank?" they'd ask, referring to the accordion. Let's face it, accordion was a dormant instrument for many years.

The house parties continued, and soon the Louisiana people in San Francisco started getting together on a larger scale. It started out with my dad's generation. They would ask John Semien (who was still the only Louisiana accordionist we knew here) if he could play on a particular date. Then my dad and some of his friends from Louisiana would put up the money to rent a small hall, and they spread the word around. They asked people who came to the dances to chip in to pay for the hall rent and the music, and to bring their own bottles. They always had cold drinks there for the youngsters, but the older people would bring whatever they liked. They set up the table, and friends would call out, "Oh, come over to my table and have a drink with me." It was a time for visiting, for dancing, and for just having a good time together.

After a while, in the late 1940s, my dad and some of his friends decided they would get together a membership social club. I think there were 30 to 40 members. They didn't sell tickets, but there was a small admission, a dollar or two to help pay for the hall and the band. If the admissions didn't cover the expenses, they would mention from the stage that they needed a little more, and people just came up to the stage and donated money.

They were definitely dress-up occasions. The women wore nice dresses, never pants, and the men always dressed well in a sport jacket and trousers or a suit. The younger women wanted to wear their "ballerinas"—the longish ballerina dresses that were in style at the time. There was quite a mixture of age groups there; two or three generations would come.

Parents who had teenage children brought them to introduce them to the people from their own cultural background. It wasn't that they were trying to arrange or push weddings; or maybe they were, but gently: "Oh, my friend has such a good-looking son, you really should meet him."

The dancing was mostly partner dancing: waltzes and two-steps. Of course, the youngsters didn't always like those dances, because we wanted to do the bobby-sox thing, the jitterbug, where you start out with your partner and before you knew it you were swinging out, separated. But the older people, my parents' generation, would dance as couples all through whatever dance it was.

In both the two-step and the waltz, people from Louisiana will dance in a forward direction, then they'll turn around and they'll go a little in a sideways direction; in other words, you're using all of your body, going in different directions. It's strenuous. You turn around often, giving the man a chance to do the backing up for a little bit, and then you turn around and go in another direction. A woman may be doing a lot of backing up, but not for the whole evening: "Turn around and go in another direction, please. This will make me drunk."

No matter how crowded the dance floor got at those socials, couples would hardly ever bump into each other, or step on other couples' feet. The male partner always watched out for the other dancers. Each man looked out for the space where he could take his partner. When the dance floor was crowded, you had your little space there, and when somebody else moved, you moved into that space so you wouldn't feel like you were standing still. Now and then there was a little bump here or there—but they watched out for that. That's a good dancer, somebody who's watching for everybody else's space as well as his own.

When somebody didn't look where he was going, didn't guide his partner, they used to call it "wild dancing." Everybody wants to dance in front of the bandstand, of course, but you still have to guide your partner into a certain area. Suppose you're dancing and some lady with high heels steps on your foot? That's like taking a spike and driving it through your foot! So "wild dancers" weren't very popular at our socials.

The youngest people at the socials didn't dance much, but they learned the steps by watching their parents. Some of them couldn't have been more than 14 or 15. Usually the father of these children would say, "Come on, I'll teach you our dance," and that's how they would learn. Or the mother would take the lead with her daughter, saying, "Okay, I'll dance the guy's way and you learn how to dance the lady's way." Women still dance together at Louisiana functions. Girls used to dance together because boys of 15, 16 years old were really shy in those days; they were often too embarrassed to ask a girl to dance. After they got to know you well, they would feel, "Well, gee, we're on the same level—so do you want to dance?" It was cute to see them try. (Of course, today at 12, 13, 10, 11, 6 years old, they'll say, "Let's dance!")

Even while the Louisiana people were forming their community again at those dances, my mom was taking trips back and forth to Texas twice a year, visiting relatives and bringing back 45s and LPs—because she couldn't find any Cajun records here, and she missed them! She brought back anything she could put her hands on—Joe Falcon's music, Belton Richards . . . Some of the records were no good when she arrived here with them, because they were warped by the hot sun while she was traveling. She didn't fly; my dad used to go with her, and they drove—and it was difficult to keep those records cool on the long trip.

In 1948, my mom brought an accordion home for the boys. It was the first one we ever had. "I brought this accordion here because this music is dying," she said. "I don't think you should let it die, because we've been carrying it on through my two brothers all this time. I want you boys to keep this music alive, keep it in the family, keep it going." I had no interest at that time in playing, because girls were not allowed. The accordion was not a very ladylike instrument. And when you were told what was right, what was wrong, you didn't have to make a decision, it was made for you and you just followed through.

Although we had an accordion at home, my brothers were just playing around with it until my youngest brother, Al (his stage name today is Al Rapone), decided to pick it up. He was into music, playing guitar and getting together small bands. "We're going to be musicians," he said. "We're going to have a band and we're going to play all over." Al was just 14 or 15, too young to have a band, but he and the kids used to get together and play music anyway.

After he picked up the accordion, I did too. I watched him and I whispered, "I can do that." I thought it seemed so easy—but it wasn't. I just fooled around with it. I came up with a few melodies and then threw it back in the closet. I was hiding while playing, actually.

I wasn't much into zydeco music, anyway. I liked the blues, but you didn't hear that much of it over the radio. I liked country and western because that's what I heard most of on the airwaves. I wasn't much into jazz, either, but I started liking it because you like what you hear. You like what's around you. And I used to listen to pop music. Would you believe, playing zydeco now, that I used to listen to Perry Como all the time? Andy Williams, Frankie Laine, all those guys—I had albums. I used to go out and buy albums by pop singers, and the kids would ask, "You like that music?" They liked R&B, but I was into pop music!

I was no longer chaperoned on every date. Although I was still socializing mainly within the Creole community here, my mom could see that in the Bay Area things were not the same as in Louisiana or Texas. Our parents were intelligent enough to recognize that we'd had a strong upbringing. And guys are not crazy; they can respect that. So she let us go out together. We went to movies, basketball and football games, or tried roller skating and ice skating. (I never could conquer either one. Ice skates—forget it. I got off of them the first time I got on!) We would go picnicking in the country. We used to go boat riding on the Bay. We'd go to dances (but not to nightclubs!). And the girls would have slumber parties. We used to have five, six, seven, or eight girls sleeping in one room.

A few times guys asked me to go out, and my parents said, "No, you can't go." They didn't like them. I remember once , a guy came over and my parents said, "I don't think this guy can come back."

I thought, "It's best not to let my dad get upset about it, so I'll leave this alone." I just told my dad, "Well, I didn't like the guy anyway." Later on I wondered if I would have rebelled had I liked the guy.

My dad finally explained, "You don't know these people, and I don't know their family." And that was the answer to that. "It's okay if you're going out together with girls and boys you meet at school from families I know," he said, "but we don't know him and we don't know his family." They were serious about that. So I said, "Oh well, I won't fight it. They're right because, if I don't know what his family's like, then I don't really know what he's like." My parents did their job well. I don't regret it at all.

As a result, I didn't have a steady boyfriend. We were mainly going out as a group, girls and boys. Once in a while I'd get a call from a boy from Louisiana whom my family knew well, and we'd go out to a movie or a dance or a party with some of his friends—but nothing serious. I guess I was looking for a person of my background, but there weren't many young boys. Most of them were still in the service.

After I graduated from high school I started working in hospitals as a nurse's aide, and doing part-time clerical work. My brother Willie was already married; he'd gone back to Texas and gotten married just after we came to California. He lived in Texas for two years, sharecropping, and then he and his wife Thelma moved back to California. I was now the oldest child in the house.

At this point Ray Guillory reappeared. The last time I'd seen him, in Texas, we were just acquaintances as far as I was concerned, but he admitted to me later that he kept saying to himself, "I'm going to meet this girl again. I'm going to take her out."

This was around 1948, and Ray was in the Air Force, working in the ammunition department. He came through San Francisco for embarkation, on a two-day furlough before shipping out to the Far East. He knew we were in California, and he called and said, "I'm going overseas. I'll be gone a year, and I thought I would come over and see you guys."

When he came, he said to me, "Would you like to go to a movie?"

I said, "Yeah, sure, why not?"

Then my little sister and my two little brothers chimed in, saying, "Can we go, too?"

I said, "No!"

But Ray (who's still that way) said, "Yeah, sure, you can come along if you want to."

The kids had to get Mom's permission, so I went to her and said, "Mom, I'm going to go to a movie with Ray."

The kids started yelling, "But he promised to take us! He promised to take us!" and Mom wouldn't say anything to make them stay home.

I thought, "Am I still being chaperoned? I can't believe this, 18 years old!"

So Ray took me and my sister and two brothers to a movie.

We started liking each other at that time. Ray went away, and we started writing each other every month.

When he returned to the States, he stopped by again on his way to the air base in San Antonio, where he was stationed next. I didn't really have anybody at that time, and my interest in him increased. I felt more comfortable with him than with other young men. Although Ray doesn't speak French at all, we were from the same cultural background, and we could communicate. We started to get sweet on each other, and whenever he got a furlough he'd make the trip here.

Then one day he called me from San Antonio and said, "I'm coming to California, and I'm going to be based there, and will you marry me?"

I said "What?"

He said, "Will you marry me? If you don't say yes . . ." (and listen to this option!) . . . "If you don't say yes, I won't hang up this phone. I'll just keep talking on this phone until you say yes."

I couldn't say yes right off, and he really stayed on that phone a long time. He told me he had had three beers (whether it was three glasses or three quarts, I don't know!), and he was playing a record of "Since I Lost My Baby, I Almost Lost My Mind." He's a shy guy, so he had to have a few beers and play that record before he got enough nerve to ask. And I said, "I'll tell you what, I'll give you my answer the next time you call."

I wasn't really expecting him to propose. I just wasn't serious with anyone at that time. Of course, Ray was my favorite. Probably subconsciously, I was holding back from other boys in hopes of a proposal from him. But I really wasn't that eager to get married yet. I felt very comfortable being free, not having any strings attached.

But the more I thought about it, the more I felt that he was the right guy for me, and that we were probably good for each other. I was 21 and, I thought, old enough to know right from wrong. All my girl friends were getting married; it's just that I had to make the decision a bit sooner than I wanted to.

He called three days later. And I thought, well, I can still change my mind.

Our wedding ceremony was very small, with just the family and very close friends. It couldn't have been much more than 20 or 30 people. Ray only had two weeks' leave left, because he'd used up all of his furloughs on visits to me. On the 14th day he had to be back with his company in San Antonio.

I stayed behind in San Francisco. I already owned a house; my parents taught us how to really save our money and invest, so they helped me buy a house, a two-story building in Bernal Heights that I intended to rent out. When Ray and I decided to get married, instead of renting it out I moved in. If Ray had been forced to stay in San Antonio, he wanted me to join him there, but he was in the process of transferring to Hamilton Field in San Rafael, a few miles north of San Francisco. We were lucky; he got his transfer in less than two months. At the time, servicemen were allowed to live off the base; it was just like commuting to work and coming back home. He was home every night.

He had less than a year before he was to be discharged, when the Korean War started and his time was extended another year. Luckily, since he had so little time left to serve, there was little risk they would send him to Korea.

One of the first things I got after I was married was a piano. I wanted one because I liked piano music; it sounded great to me. Of course, I'd picked up a little accordion by then, but I still wasn't interested in playing accordion—after all, how many women did you see at that time playing the accordion? Piano was much more accepted.

I started to take piano lessons, the first music lessons I'd ever had in my life. I only had piano lessons for a few weeks, and I started playing boogie-woogie when the teacher was out of the room, in front of a class of kids. She didn't like that, but I thought I knew more than her. We really didn't get along very well, and after a few lessons I said, "Forget it!" Those lessons weren't compulsory like some high school course, so I quit. Afterwards, I only played piano for myself; I never did learn to play it really well.

Ray got out of the service in 1951 and went to work at a meat-packing company. Getting married never slowed us down much. We had this big house, with a giant basement that could hold at least 100 people, so we started throwing large house parties. Our friends were younger than the group going to my dad's functions, and about 90 percent of them were from Louisiana. Although Ray hardly danced (just a couple of rounds with me, a couple with his sister), he loved to see other people have a good time.

Even after our children were born, we kept giving our parties, although not so often. Those house parties were continuous from 1949 through the early '70s. (By then, my brother Al was playing our music in different small clubs, and they were still having parties at rented halls, then the house parties began diminishing: "Why have a party at my house when we can all get together and have it at the hall—instead of getting my house all smoked up and dirty and full of paper cups and all?") But our Louisiana functions continued and were always growing larger as more and more people moved from Louisiana and "the triangle" to the San Francisco Bay Area. In fact, those dances and parties continued until I got into the music myself.

After I was married, I would go visit my mom, and the push-button accordion she brought back for my brothers was sitting there, and I picked it up and tried little melodies. Of course, I was testing my mom as well, and she wouldn't say anything. Finally, I came up with a couple of melodies and she would walk in and say, "Not bad! You're doing pretty good." And I thought, "Well, that's the okay signal."

There's still a lot of debate as to whether the Germans or the Cajuns brought the accordion to Louisiana. (The Irish claim that distinction, too.) As for the style of music, it was the Acadians, as far as I know, who brought it to Louisiana. The authentic Cajun tunes are basically waltzes and two-steps. What we're doing today is not authentic Cajun music; that's why they gave it the name "zydeco"—because of all the other influences brought into the base formed by the Cajun music. (The name actually comes from one of the earliest songs in that style, "Les Haricots Ne Sont Pas Salées" ("The Green Beans Aren't Salted"), with "Les Haricots" pronounced "zydeco" (referring to music not food).

When I started playing the accordion at my mother's house, I still wasn't taking it at all seriously. At that time, no one wanted to hear the accordion. Lawrence Welk was the most popular accordion player, and he played piano accordion. I had to teach myself to play because you couldn't take lessons on the kind of accordion I had. You could take lessons on the piano accordion, but this was a diatonic push-button, and hardly anybody played it. So if you wanted to play it, you just learned on your own. You'd find your way through and come up with a melody and then work from there.

The push-button accordion is harder to play than a piano accordion because you get different notes when you push and pull, like a harmonica. If you want a note, you need to be in the right position to push or pull, and if you're in the wrong position, you can't get that note. That's why our style of accordion is less melodic and more staccato than the styles developed on piano, or keyboard, accordions.

The push-button accordion was never designed to do professional work; the keyboard accordion was designed for that. But at that time, the only musician playing zydeco on a piano accordion was Clifton Chenier, and he hadn't recorded widely yet. After Clifton, a lot of zydeco players took up keyboard accordion, and now the younger musicians are astonished by the sound of my little accordion—by the clarity of its tone, and the sharpness of its staccato.

Back then, women simply didn't make music in public. Women sometimes sang lullabyes, or hummed as they were doing their chores, but never at the fais-dodos. At most, if there wasn't a guy to play the rub-board at a Sunday afternoon get-together, a woman might take a washboard and play rhythm. I'd heard about one Cajun woman musician: Joe Falcon's wife Cleome played drums and a little accordion. She was the only Cajun woman who recorded, and she was before my time.

It was understood that ladies did not play instruments with men: that's a man's job, you didn't see any ladies playing, so how would you feel being the first lady going on stage, the only lady with the men? It was okay for ladies to sing and play piano and violin—but not often on stage, of course. As for accordion— my mother had never seen a woman pick up an accordion and play in public. She would play little melodies, but only at home, only for us. She wouldn't play if company came.

When I began learning to play the accordion, for some reason my dad seemed to be prouder of me playing than my mom. At best she would say, "Well, that's nice. You're doing good," but my dad would say, "You should hear Ida play" when their friends would come over. "Ida, get the accordion, play for them," he'd say (and of course I refused). But Mom would never ask me to get the accordion and play; not until the '50s.

However, when I started fooling around with the instrument, playing the accordion professionally was still the farthest thing from my mind.

TO CALIFORNIA, WITH RICE

CATFISH SAUCE PIQUANT

Although catfish is traditional in Louisiana, you can substitute rock cod or lingcod. I don't use tomato paste, because too strong a tomato flavor will hide the taste of the fish. The sauce should be a light pink color. Serve this dish over rice, with a salad or vegetables on the side.

Serves 3–4

3   pounds whole catfish (or rock cod or lingcod), weighed without the head
1½ teaspoons salt
1½ teaspoons black pepper
1½ teaspoons cayenne
¼   cup oil
⅓   cup chopped celery
¼   cup chopped bell pepper
¼   cup chopped onion

¼   cup chopped parsley
¼   cup chopped green onions
2   tablespoons minced fresh garlic
½   cup water
1   cup tomatoes (preferably fresh), peeled (see Appendix) and coarsely chopped
⅓   cup flour
    Cooked rice

Wash the fish and peel the skin off (or have it done at the fish market) and cut it crosswise in slices 1–1½ inches thick. You may use the tail. Season with salt, pepper, and cayenne and set aside.

In a large skillet, heat the oil and add celery, bell pepper, onion, parsley, green onions, and garlic. Sauté over fairly high heat 5 minutes, stirring frequently. Add the water and tomatoes and simmer 10 minutes more.

Sprinkle the flour over the fish or roll each piece of fish in flour until coated lightly. Gently place the fish, piece by piece, in the sauce. Cover the pan and simmer about 10 minutes. With a spatula, turn each piece of fish over and shake pan gently to combine juices. (Do not stir, for that will break up the fish.) Simmer over the very lowest heat until the fish is cooked through (another 10 minutes). Serve immediately over rice.

Chicken Sauce Piquant: Substitute a 3-pound frying chicken, cut into serving pieces, for the fish. Season the chicken with salt, pepper, and cayenne to taste, dust with flour, and brown it on all sides in hot oil. Remove from the oil and sauté the vegetables as above. After tomatoes have simmered, return chicken to the skillet and simmer, covered, about 15 minutes; turn each piece and simmer, covered, about 10 minutes longer. Serve hot over rice.

CREOLE BAKED FISH

Any fish benefits from spicy seasoning and a lively sauce.

Serves 6

3½ pounds whole fish of choice	½ cup chopped parsley
2½ teaspoons salt (or to taste)	½ cup water
1½ teaspoons cayenne (or to taste)	¼ cup chopped celery
	¼ cup chopped bell pepper
1 teaspoon black pepper	¼ cup chopped white or yellow onion
¼ teaspoon garlic powder	2 cloves garlic, chopped
1½ teaspoons flour	2 teaspoons oil
16-ounce can stewed tomatoes, coarsely chopped	¼ teaspoon powdered dried thyme

Preheat oven to 350 degrees. Remove the head of the fish and with a small, sharp knife score both sides of the fish about 2–3 inches apart. Mix salt, cayenne, pepper, and garlic powder and rub mixture into both sides of the fish. Sprinkle with the flour. Place fish in a pan large enough to hold it easily. Combine remaining ingredients and pour them over the fish. Bake fish uncovered 30–50 minutes (about 10 minutes per inch of thickness), basting often with tomato mixture, until fish flakes easily with a fork.

~~~~~~~~~~~~~~~~~~~~~

CHICKEN FRICASSEE

I always leave the skin on the chicken in this dish. It is at its best when made with a large, flavorful chicken (baking or stewing hen, roaster, or, in California, a "Rocky"), since the broth grows richer the longer it cooks. Even when made with fryer parts, though, it's rich with down-home comfort. Serve fricassee over white rice or with corn bread. You can serve it with potatoes, but I think it's a lot better with rice.

Serves 6

	About ¾ cup roux (page 20)	¼	cup chopped parsley stems
2	tablespoons oil	1	stalk celery, chopped (with no leaves)
1	large chicken (stewing hen or roaster), about 4 pounds, cut into serving pieces (or 4 pounds chicken legs, thighs, or wings)	1	teaspoon black pepper, or to taste
		½-1½	teaspoons cayenne, to taste
1	teaspoon salt	⅓	cup chopped green onions
¼	cup chopped onion	¼	cup chopped parsley leaves
1	quart chicken broth		
*1	quart water		

*Note: If using a small frying chicken or fryer parts, replace water with chicken broth to compensate for the shorter cooking time.

Let the roux come to room temperature. Meanwhile, heat the oil in a 4-quart Dutch oven and over fairly high heat lightly brown the chicken pieces, sprinkling salt over them as they cook. Add celery and onion and sauté until softened. Add broth and the water, scraping the browned bits from the bottom of the pan as liquid comes to a boil over high heat. Reduce heat to medium-low and cook chicken at a lively simmer until nearly tender. Cooking time once liquid has come to a boil will be about 90 minutes for a stewing hen, 60 minutes for a roaster or equivalent, or 40 minutes for smallish fryer parts.

About 30 minutes before chicken is done, remove pot from the heat, and stir in a large spoonful of roux. Return to low to medium heat so that liquid bubbles gently but does not boil, and gradually add the remaining roux by spoonfuls, stirring and scraping the bottom of the pot, and allowing liquid to thicken slightly after each addition, until sauce thickens to a light gravy. Stir in chopped parsley stems, celery, pepper, and cayenne. Continue cooking until chicken is very tender. (Test by piercing with a fork.) Stir occasionally, and from time to time tilt the pot and with a large metal spoon skim fat from the surface. When chicken is almost done, taste and correct seasonings. Add the green onions and parsley leaves and simmer another 5 minutes to soften them and blend flavors.

~~~~~~~~~~~~~~~

AUNT RENA'S CABBAGE ROLLS

Aunt Rena wasn't really our aunt, but everybody called her by that name. Her stuffed cabbage can be a family main course, or can be served in a chafing dish at a potluck or buffet.

Serves 4–6 as a main dish

1 **pound ground chuck**	¼ **teaspoon black pepper**
⅓ **cup chopped onion**	1 **cup uncooked rice**
⅓ **cup chopped parsley**	3 **quarts water**
⅓ **cup chopped celery**	1 **large head of cabbage,**
6-ounce can V-8 juice	**2½–3 pounds**
1 **teaspoon salt**	1¾ **cups chicken broth (or a**
1 **teaspoon cayenne (or**	**14½-ounce can)**
crushed dried red pepper)	

Combine the meat, onion, parsley, celery, juice, salt, cayenne, and pepper. Knead well and set aside for 1–2 hours to develop flavor. Wash rice, drain, and knead into meat mixture.

In a 4-quart soup pot, heat the water to the boiling point. Set the whole cabbage in the water for a few seconds, then lift cabbage out and begin to peel off the softened outer leaves, one by one, taking care not to break or tear them. Return water to the boil and dip the cabbage again, repeating the process until all the cabbage leaves have been softened and removed.

Place 2–3 tablespoons of the meat mixture on the large end of each cabbage leaf and roll the leaf toward the small end. Place the cabbage rolls in a large pot, nestling tightly side by side, until the bottom of the pot is covered. Stack additional layers of cabbage rolls over the bottom layer. Pour in the chicken broth. Cover the pot and bring it to a simmer. (Do not boil it.) Cook until rice and meat are well cooked (about 1 hour). Serve hot.

GRILLADES AUX TOMATES
(Beef Strips with Tomatoes)

In some parts of Louisiana, *grillades* are eaten with grits for a very substantial breakfast. They're just as good at dinner, though. This recipe should be started a day ahead, so that the beef strips can absorb the spices.

Serves 4–6

1 **pound beef round**	2 **tablespoons oil**
1 **teaspoon salt**	2 **medium tomatoes, peeled**
¾ **teaspoon cayenne**	**(see Appendix) and diced**
½ **teaspoon garlic powder**	½ **cup chopped bell pepper**
¼ **teaspoon white pepper**	½ **cup chopped yellow onion**
¼ **cup flour**	

Scant 2 cups beef broth
 (or a 14½-ounce can)
½ cup water
¼ teaspoon powdered dried
 thyme

½ cup chopped parsley
¼ cup chopped green onions
Cooked rice or grits

Cut meat into ½-inch-wide strips. Season with salt, cayenne, garlic powder, and white pepper. Refrigerate overnight to absorb flavors.

Remove meat from refrigerator and let stand at room temperature 1 hour. Roll meat strips in the flour. In a large skillet, heat the oil over medium heat until very hot. Add the meat carefully and brown on both sides. Add tomatoes, bell pepper, and onion and cover the skillet. Sauté, covered, 5 minutes. Add broth, the water, and thyme. Bring to a boil, reduce heat, and simmer 30 minutes. Add parsley and green onions, cover, and simmer until meat is tender (about 1 hour longer). Serve hot over rice or grits.

SWISS STEAK WITH GRAVY

Swiss steak is a piece of beef (usually cut thinly from the round) that the butcher has run through a tenderizing machine, scoring it deeply.

Serves 4

1½ teaspoons salt
1½ teaspoons cayenne
½ teaspoon black pepper
½ teaspoon garlic powder
2¼ pounds Swiss steak

1 tablespoon oil
½ cup chopped onion
2 cups water
Cooked rice or mashed
 potatoes

Combine the salt, cayenne, pepper, and garlic powder and sprinkle over both sides of the meat. Heat the oil in a large skillet over medium heat. Carefully lay the meat in the oil. Brown both sides, add onion, and continue sautéing until onion is soft. Add the water and bring to a boil. Cover, reduce heat, and simmer until meat is tender when touched with a fork (about 1 hour). If too much liquid has evaporated and meat is not yet tender, add another ½ cup water and continue simmering until meat is done. Serve over rice or mashed potatoes.

〰〰〰〰〰〰〰〰〰〰

SMOTHERED CABBAGE
AND SPARERIBS

I cook cabbage in the water that I smothered the meat in. That has its own taste and it's good with the cabbage. Like other cabbage dishes, this hearty preparation is traditionally eaten in the colder months.

Serves 4

1½ pounds spareribs (or pork neckbones, or baby back ribs), cut into pieces	2 tablespoons oil
	2 tablespoons chopped bell pepper
1 teaspoon salt (or to taste)	1 tablespoon chopped onion
1 teaspoon cayenne	1 large cabbage, about 2½ pounds
¼ teaspoon black or white pepper (or to taste)	2 tablespoons bacon fat (optional)

Season meat to taste with the salt, cayenne, and pepper, rubbing the seasonings into the meat. Heat the oil in a large skillet or Dutch oven and brown the meat on all sides over medium-high heat. Add bell pepper and onion and sauté until wilted. Add water to cover, bring to a boil, reduce heat, and cover the pot. Simmer until meat is nearly tender (40–60 minutes, depending on size of pieces). Check occasionally to make sure water has not cooked away.

Cut cabbage into quarters, then cut each quarter crosswise. Add cabbage pieces to the spareribs. If there is not enough liquid, add ½ cup water. Bring to a boil, reduce heat, and cover. Simmer until cabbage is tender (about 20 minutes). Shortly before cabbage is done, taste carefully and correct seasonings, stir in bacon fat if using, then simmer a little longer to blend flavors.

~~~~~~~~~~~~~~~~~~~~~~~~~

TURNIPS ÉTOUFFÉE

Turnips are best in spring, when they're young and rather sweet. If only mature turnips are available, the outer layer and the core may be slightly bitter, so pare them deeply and remove the core.

Turnips have a lot of water. When they're smothered with just a little additional water, and with a little bacon fat, they come out almost like creamed turnips.

Serves 4

6 medium turnips, pared and thinly sliced	2 tablespoons bacon fat or oil
1 cup water Salt, black pepper, and cayenne to taste	1 teaspoon sugar (or to taste) ¼ pound salt pork (optional)

In a large saucepan, combine turnip slices and the water, bring to a boil, reduce heat, and simmer uncovered very slowly until they begin to get tender (about 15 minutes). Season turnips with salt, pepper, and cayenne to taste, the bacon fat or oil, and the sugar. If water is evaporating too quickly, add about ½ cup more, increase heat until liquid returns to a simmer, and reduce heat again. Continue simmering until very tender (about 15 minutes longer). Test by pricking turnips with a fork.

If using optional salt pork, while turnips are cooking drop salt pork into a separate pan of boiling water, boil about 3 minutes, drain, and rinse. Slice salt pork into thin pieces about an inch square and add to the turnips for the last 15 minutes of cooking.

Turnips with Smoked Neckbones Étouffée: For a main dish of turnips with smoked neckbones, cover 2 pounds smoked pork neckbones with water, bring to a boil, and simmer until tender (about 1 hour). Cook turnips as above (but omit salt pork). Add neckbones to the turnips for the final 15 minutes of cooking. Serves 3–4 as a main course with rice and other accompaniments.

〰〰〰〰〰〰〰

TURNIPS AND PORK RIBS ÉTOUFFÉE

Smothered turnips by themselves make a great side dish, but if you want to add meat, then you've got a main course. I think it's tastier with meat. The gravy from the meat adds a little bit of flavor to the turnips and the turnips add flavor to the meat.

Serves 4

¼ cup oil

2 pounds pork spareribs (or neckbones), cut into 3-inch lengths

3 tablespoons chopped onion

1 teaspoon salt

½ teaspoon black pepper

½ teaspoon cayenne (or to taste)

1 cup water

2 pounds medium turnips, pared and sliced ¼ inch thick

1 teaspoon sugar (or to taste)

2 tablespoons bacon fat (optional)

Heat the oil in a large skillet. Over medium heat, brown the meat. Add onion, salt, pepper, and cayenne. Stir in enough of the water to make a thin gravy. Add turnips, cover, and simmer slowly until meat is nearly tender (about 45 minutes). Stir occasionally and add more water if necessary. Add sugar to taste and cook a few minutes longer to blend flavors. Tilt the pot and with a large metal spoon skim excess fat from the surface (or refrigerate overnight, skim and reheat gently just until hot). Add bacon fat to flavor the dish, if desired; correct the seasonings and serve.

~~~~~~~~~~~~~~

CORNMEAL PANCAKES

These are a delicious breakfast with butter and syrup, but they're also a wonderful starch with dinner, just made for sopping up gravy.

Makes about a dozen 3½-inch pancakes

1 cup cornmeal	⅓ cup milk (or more if needed)
½ cup flour	
1½ teaspoons baking powder	1 egg, lightly beaten
¼ teaspoon salt	2 tablespoons melted shortening
⅛ teaspoon baking soda	Oil to grease skillet
¾ cup buttermilk	

Combine the dry ingredients in a mixing bowl. Add remaining ingredients and stir just until smooth. If the mixture is too thick, add 1 additional tablespoon milk. Heat a cast-iron skillet over medium heat until water sprinkled on it sizzles instantly and disappears in a few seconds. Brush the skillet with a little oil, and drop batter into it by tablespoonfuls. Fry the pancakes until tiny pits appear in the top and the edges are starting to brown (about 1½ minutes). Turn and brown the other side.

CARROT SALAD

This is a dish my mama started to make after we came to California.

Serves 4

5 carrots, pared	¼ cup raisins
2 apples, cored and diced	1½ tablespoons walnuts
¾ cup small marshmallows	Mayonnaise

Grate carrots using the coarse face of a grater. (Do not grate too fine or the salad will be mushy.) Combine with apples, marshmallows, raisins, and walnuts in a serving bowl and mix together. Stir mayonnaise into the mixture by spoonfuls, until it just coats the pieces.

∿∿∿∿∿∿∿∿

MABEL JOAN'S BABY LIMA BEANS WITH SMOKED HAM

Lima beans form their own creamy sauce when cooked. In my younger sister's recipe, the sauce is deliciously flavored with smoky ham and bacon fat.

Serves 6 as a side dish

2 cups (1 pound) dried baby lima beans	2 cloves garlic, chopped
8 cups water	2 tablespoons bacon fat
2 medium-size smoked ham shanks	⅛ teaspoon cayenne (or to taste)
½ cup chopped onion	⅛ teaspoon white pepper (or to taste)
⅓ cup chopped bell pepper	Salt to taste

Pick over the beans, rinse them, and place them in a large, deep pot. Add the water and ham shanks and bring to a boil. Remove from heat, cover, and let stand 30 minutes. Return pot to the heat. Add remaining ingredients. Bring to a boil over high heat, cover, and reduce heat so that beans boil slowly and gently. Cook, stirring occasionally, until shanks and beans are tender and the liquid has thickened (about 1 hour). Taste and correct seasonings. Remove shanks. Cut some or all of the meat into bite-size chunks and return meat to the pot. (If desired, most of the meat may be reserved for another use.) Cook a few minutes longer to blend flavors, and serve hot.

Lima Beans With Salt Pork: Salt pork can substitute for the ham shanks. Parboil a chunk of salt pork (see Appendix) and slice it thin before adding it to the beans.

Ida's Meatless Lima Beans: Omit ham, onion, bell pepper, and garlic. Season beans with salt, black pepper, cayenne, and about 1 teaspoon sugar, or to taste.

~~~~~~~~~~~~~~~~~~~~

SWEET POTATO PIE

Makes one 9-inch pie

9-inch piecrust, unbaked
(see page 132)
2   cups cooked, pared,
mashed yams or sweet
potatoes (2-3 medium)
½   cup sugar
4   tablespoons (½ stick) butter,
melted over low heat

1¼ teaspoons cinnamon
1   teaspoon nutmeg
½   teaspoon ground ginger
¼   teaspoon salt
¾   cup whole milk
2   eggs, lightly beaten

Preheat oven to 450 degrees. Mix together all filling ingredients except the eggs. Blend well, then fold in eggs. Pour into the unbaked pie shell. Bake 10 minutes. Reduce heat to 350 degrees and continue baking until a knife inserted into the pie comes out clean (30–35 minutes).

7

Va Pour Ça!
A Queen
Is Crowned

After I'd been married for a couple of years, I decided to go back to school to become a vocational nurse. It was only a two-year program, but after I'd been in school for four or five months I found out I was pregnant. I asked my teachers whether I could come back and keep my credits if I stayed in school until just before the delivery. They said no, I would have to start all over again. It was so discouraging that I quit.

I was happy about the pregnancy, though. Ray and I had been married two years and I thought we knew each other well enough to start a family. My gynecologist had told me, "If you're going to have children, you should have the first one by age 25." And I was 25 when I had Myrick, in September 1954.

Just after Myrick was born, my mother became very ill, and in the course of her illness she lost her sight from glaucoma. I'd go over and talk to her, and sometimes I'd pick up the accordion and play a song. Usually she wouldn't say anything, but one day while I was playing she said, "Why don't you play 'Lucille Conaille' for me?"

I said, "Are you going to sing it?" and she said, "Yeah." So from then on, I played and she sang "Lucille Conaille" ("Conniving Lucille"), and she'd laugh and say, "Well, you'll get it sooner or later." That's how I knew she had come to accept my playing accordion.

After Myrick's birth I became a full-time mother, and soon had two more kids. Ronald was born in 1956, and my daughter Ledra was born in 1958. Being a housewife wasn't really boring, because we weren't the type of people to just stay at home. For instance, before the kids were born we liked to go out camping and waterskiing at Lake Berryessa. When Myrick was born I thought, "Uh-oh, we can't take this kid out for a long time," but two weeks later we went for a weekend with some friends who lived in Sonora, California, and by the time summer came around again we resumed camping out in sleeping bags and a tent. We just took Myrick's baby mattress off the bed and brought it along.

While my children were growing, I became a lot more comfortable with cooking. I was adding Mexican food to my repertoire, some pure "American" dishes, a little of this, a little of that. San Francisco is as much of a melting pot as Louisiana. You've got nationalities you can't begin to count, and more coming all the time. You can't help but expand the kind of cooking you do.

Once the kids were all in school I got a part time job driving a school bus; I kept that job until I went into music full time. There weren't that many women bus drivers then. It was easy, though; I'd learned to drive trucks on the farm and the shifting was the same.

By 1965, we had moved into another house, in San Francisco's Oceanview district, farther away from my family, and when my youngest started grade school I began to feel a little lonely—and a little bored. Meanwhile, my musician brother Al had formed a band called the Barbary Coast Good Time Band, playing mainly Latin and rock. He wasn't playing much accordion at that time, so I asked him if I could borrow the instrument. And I started playing it.

When you're a beginner accordion player, it's like being a beginner drummer or violinist. You sound terrible! Sometimes I would pick up the accordion when the kids were doing their homework, and I thought I was being quiet, but it's not easy to be quiet with an accordion. When I would hit a wrong note, they would say, "Uh-oh, Mom!" After a while I tried not to play when the kids (or anyone else) was there, and I think I was playing better because no one was there to say, "Ooh, that doesn't sound good."

I was still listening to more pop music and jazz than Cajun music, but at some point in the late '50s my mother started bringing back Clifton Chenier's records from her trips to Texas. Clifton had just started recording; I think "Aye 'Tite Fille" was his first recording, a single for some record company in Louisiana or Texas. Up until then Cajun music was only the accordion, the violin, the rub-board, and the triangle. It was only after I heard it electrified, with drums, after Clifton Chenier (and then my brother) started playing it with amps, and I thought, "Wow! That's a whole different ball game." That's really when my interest in learning the accordion came to a peak.

I was still playing just for my family, just for fun. I played with my brother sometimes, at home, and for my mom and dad at Christmas and holidays. But when my dad would ask me to play for his friends, I would flip. "I can't do it, Dad," I would say. "I can't do it!"

By the middle '60s, Louisiana music was starting to get a lot better known. Some of us had friends who weren't from Louisiana but who heard the music at our parties—and loved it! Clifton Chenier came out and played several concerts in 1966 and 1967, and made a big impression on people. My brother Al started playing more zydeco, and when his band started playing at a small club in the Fillmore district called La Bamba, a regular crowd of people started showing up.

Other Louisiana functions were going on regularly; particularly a series of benefit dances in a school gymnasium attached to All Hallows Church in the Hunters Point section of San Francisco, near the Navy shipyards. There weren't enough church members from Louisiana to support those benefits, but the dances were open to the public, and when the priest announced from the pulpit that they were having a dance, word spread throughout the Bay Area among all the people from Louisiana and Texas. (A few years later, in the early '70s, Clifton Chenier played at All Hallows several times, drawing increasingly gigantic crowds.)

The band that provided the music for those dances was called the Louisiana Playboys, and our old friend John Semien was a member. They would always invite us to come over and listen when they rehearsed; people from Louisiana like a full house all the time. Ray wanted to go because those guys were his friends, but I didn't want to, because I thought it was just going to be guys. So Ray said, "Well, come on, their wives are gonna be there and . . ."

Ray tricked me. Once we got there, he said to me, "Play the song that you were playing the other night at home."

I answered, "Are you crazy? I'm not going to play with those guys." I still thought it wasn't ladylike to play accordion in public—and I really didn't feel I could play well enough to join them.

Ray kept urging me to sit in with the band—and I kept saying no. Meanwhile, I was listening to more music and practicing by myself at home. One evening, at a party, I finally decided to play—but only one song. It was probably "Tayo Zydeco." I had heard it on one of Clifton Chenier's albums, and I couldn't believe the guy was pumping a keyboard like that. I thought, "Oh, this is never going to work with my little accordion." Clifton played a keyboard accordion, which has four reeds for every note, while I played a push-button accordion, which has only two or three reeds. When you play a chord, you have more notes opening from a keyboard accordion.

I played only because there weren't many people there, but they liked it—and kept asking me to play again. Ray also encouraged me. I went home and started practicing more, and I finally said to myself, "Well, if they ask me again, I'll say 'Yeah.'"

One of the reasons they wanted me to sit in was that a woman accordion player was such a novelty. Every time I played one or two songs with the Playboys at those dances, the area in front of the stage would fill up with men. It was "Whoa, there's a woman playing this stuff." They had probably never seen a woman play before.

I had no desire, no need, to become a musician. I was very satisfied with my life. But for some reason, after I conquered those two or three songs, I wanted to expand my repertoire. My favorite number was "Tayo Zydeco" because it was the first song that I felt comfortable playing. It's not an easy song. If you like it, you can do it, because you've got to have it up here in your head before you can put it into your fingers. Then I played the country western song "I'm So Afraid of Losing You," by Charlie Pride; I wasn't doing a great job with it, but (as they say) I was making it through the night. Another song I did was Billy Swan's "I Can Help."

My brother invited me to join his Barbary Coast band—at least part-time. "I think you should come sit in with us at the different clubs," he said. "I'll tell you the good ones." He thought it would be better exposure for me because his band consisted entirely of professional musicians, not part-time musicians.

During the early '70s I started sitting in with my brother, and sometimes with the Playboys. By then, my youngest was in high school, so I didn't have to worry about baby-sitters.

In 1975, my cousin George Broussard decided he would promote a Mardi Gras masquerade dance at All Hallows, and try to get it into the newspapers so they could draw more people than they ever had before. He called a lot of musicians and asked them to donate their time: He invited my brother, he invited blues musicians, and he invited the Playboys. And he also invited me.

"No way!" I said. "Not with all those musicians! Are you kidding?"

My brother said, "Come on, no problem, you can do it."

My husband said, "Oh, Ida, you can do it."

So I agreed to sit in that night at the Mardi Gras dance.

There's always a king and queen of Mardi Gras, so early in the evening the schoolkids from All Hallows marched through the hall, and they had a little king and a little queen, both wearing crowns. They sat them on chairs, and the musicians played a few songs for them, and then their mothers took them home. Then the party was left to the adults.

Now it's party time, everybody's having a drink, everybody's dancing, and that's when I noticed a guy taking pictures. I didn't think anything of it until I picked up the *San Francisco Chronicle* newspaper a couple of Sundays later, and found my picture on the front cover of the Sunday magazine! The guy with the camera had been a magazine writer, Peter Levine!

Later that day, two fans (both Louisiana people) sent flowers and congratulations, and so did my sister. My sister was laughing, saying, "I don't believe this. I mean, bang, here you are on a magazine cover, and you're not a trained musician." One of my girl friends who'd gone to school in New Orleans said she never thought she'd see the day when Cajun music would be played by a woman, and west of Louisiana at that.

I read the article Peter Levine had written; he had done some thorough research on the music, about how the basis for it had come from Acadia—and then he had a whole article about this lady: Queen Ida.

"Queen Ida?" I asked myself. "Where did he get that?" And then I remembered that as the evening ended, George Broussard was introducing everybody, and he had been joking around and said, "Tonight we're going to crown you, Ida: Queen of the Zydeco Accordion and Queen of Zydeco Music." He laughed, and everybody applauded, and that was the end of it, I thought—until the article came out.

Meanwhile, calls were going to the church, and the poor cook at the priest's home gave all these messages to the priest, who finally had someone phone me and tell me about it: "People are calling, club owners, and they want to see your band." Then the priest must have gotten tired of taking messages, and they started calling me at home—owners of small Bay Area clubs—and all I could say was, "I don't have a band, I was just sitting in; I don't have a band, I was just sitting in." When my brother came over I said, "Here, you take over these phone calls."

Finally he told me, "I'm sorry, Sis, I've been telling them that we'll do it—but you're going to have to come."

I said, "No way am I going! My repertoire is about five songs."

He said, "You can do the five songs. They want to hear you, so let them hear you. But you know, you do have to learn to play more songs."

Soon after that, I started joining his band at rehearsals and performing with them regularly. But you know, I think if the audience had not been so responsive, I would've said "Forget it!" and put the accordion back in the closet at my mom's house. However, people wanted to hear me, so I had to do it.

It started as "The Barbary Coast Band, featuring Queen Ida" when I was just sitting in on two or three songs. Then it became "Queen Ida and the Barbary Coast Band," and finally Al and I changed it to "Queen Ida and the Bon Temps Zydeco Band" when we really started going out and working. (Eventually my brother Al went out on his own again, but we used to sit in with each other's bands occasionally, whenever we were both in San Francisco.)

In 1976, Tom Mazzolini, the Bay Area blues promoter (and a very nice person), said he wanted the band to play at the second annual Bay Area Blues Festival. The Monterey Jazz and Blues Festival was having a "Louisiana Day," and a lot of Louisiana and Texas musicians were in town, including the Wild Tchoupitoulas. They played the San Francisco festival, too, so it was a great afternoon. We played only a 20-minute show. (The next year, they called us back to do 45 minutes, which is unusual.) It was great exposure: there were 10,000 people there who had never heard our music before.

I was interviewed at the '76 festival and they asked me, "Where do you think zydeco music is going to go? Is it going to move on up or is it just going to sort of hang low?"

"No way!" I said (feeling very brave). "No way! The zydeco is like reggae; I can see reggae moving up and I can see zydeco moving up."

We landed a contract for our first album, *Queen Ida Plays Zydeco*, with GNP Crescendo, a Los Angeles record company that had been instrumental in keeping jazz alive when everyone else had turned their backs on it. (Since then, we've done eight albums for GNP.)

Even then, I still didn't feel that music would be a full-time career for me. I thought my brother could play the accordion better than I could, and he could get somebody else to replace him on guitar. I felt, "I helped put the music out there, now you guys can take over and I'll just come in for a cameo appearance here or there."

Al was still doing more of the singing than I was, because I didn't want to sing. Playing the accordion and singing—you have two jobs to do. And to try to have some kind of composure—that's three jobs.

When I started singing more, I had to start using more than one accordion. The diatonic accordion is very limited in keys, so I used an ADG accordion when I wanted to sing in a higher key, a GCF accordion for songs that are a little lower, and an F,

B-flat, and E-flat accordion that's even lower. They all look alike, and I have to label them so I won't pick up the wrong one!

As the repertoire expanded, just a few of our songs ("Rosa Majeur" is one) came from old ballads. The others are pretty much stories about boys and girls, love songs we've written or traditional Cajun songs (like "Jolie Blon'") we've translated. In some Cajun songs, the lyrics are sad but the music is very lively—and those songs we do not translate into English. We keep them all totally in the patois, because if you understand the words, the sad story ruins the happy music, and vice versa.

At first we played mainly around the Bay Area, and I kept my job driving the school bus. Our first record album didn't sell very well, and people still didn't know our music. When we looked for bookings, the promoters would say, "Well, we don't know the band or anything about the music, so send us a tape." But a tape is never as good as a live band, no matter who records it. When you're listening to a tape and haven't seen the band live, you can't visualize what's going on, who's playing or what they look like.

After Ledra went off to college in 1976, we started to tour more widely, but it was still tough going. All that started changing in 1978, when I met John Ullman (who runs Traditional Arts Services along with his wife, Irene Namkung). John became our agent, and he had to spend endless time on the phone explaining what zydeco music was. (These days, John and Irene don't have to make the calls anymore; they *get* the calls. We've played so many places, there's great word of mouth from one promoter to another.) John started booking us on some gigs here, some gigs there, including a tour funded by the National Endowment for the Arts, with Tracy and Eloise Schwartz, Wade and Julia Mainer, and the Golden Eagles

Mardi Gras Indians, that went from Washington State down to Santa Cruz, south of the Bay Area.

Then, in 1979, we were nominated for an award called a Bammy, a Bay Area Music Award. Taj Mahal was nominated against us in the same category, and I thought "Oh, poor Ida! We don't stand a chance against this guy"—and, of course, we didn't and he won. Afterwards, I congratulated him and asked him to autograph my program. He laughed, and gave me the autograph, and said he'd seen us play.

"You know," he said, "they would love your music in Europe. Have you ever been to Europe?"

I told him we hadn't, and he said he would talk to his agent in New York. A week later, after the agent had had a chance to look at our pictures and press material, and hear our albums, he called back and offered us a deal for a two-week tour of Europe. It would be strenuous, not luxurious. *Va pour ça!*, I decided—go for it! Just pay me and I'll go. You've got to start out at the bottom. And as many musicians have discovered, if you work in Europe for a while your chances in America improve.

Ray was very proud, very happy. But he was still working as a truck dispatcher—which was good, because with me working at my music full time (when it wasn't that popular), and with three kids to put through school, we would probably have gone on welfare otherwise. I tried to get him to change his vacation so he could go to Europe with me, but he said, "No, I don't want to go. You go ahead and I'll keep everything together here." You need that kind of cooperation if you're going to succeed in any business. Obviously Ray is not a jealous man, and I think he felt that I was in good hands, going on the road chaperoned by my two brothers, Al and Willie.

It seems I've been chaperoned all my life! Now it's my son, but the truth is, I feel a lot better traveling with the family. I don't think I would be on the road today if I had to be with five strange musicians—it would be too boring. But with my husband there, or my two brothers, or my son, then wherever I am, I'm still home.

My brother Willie went on the road with us in 1979 as our washboard player and choreographer, and stayed with us until 1988. His last three years, when we wanted a special introduction to one of our songs, Willie invented something that my guitarist, Denny Geyer, named "Zydaerobics." (John Ullman says his steps are based on the old-time buck dance, or buck-and-wing, that came out of the solo male dancing tradition of Louisiana.) Denny and Willie started doing Zydaerobics together, and we would call out, "Okay, you want to do the Zydaerobics?" and we would get the whole audience involved. After Willie left we asked Myrick to try it, but he refused. Willie's Zydaerobics is a hard act to follow. But now my son-in-law, who is Samoan, sometimes comes on and does a "Samoan Zydeco" dance!

Once we started going to Europe, we usually went twice a year for five- to seven-week tours. We traveled all over—by plane, boat, and van. The boat from Stockholm to Finland is great! There's entertainment on the boat, three rooms with different types of bands: a rock band for the young, another band for the middle-aged, and a jazz band for the old folks. And they have the best meals and games. Oh, it's fun! Unfortunately, we still play a lot of one-nighters. We've driven as far as 500 kilometers (about 350 miles) a day to do a single engagement.

It's more work than you think—and less of a free vacation. On my first tour to Europe, I would go out sightseeing and come back about three o'clock in the afternoon, just in time to take a bath and get ready for my sound check, which is usually five o'clock. I found myself so tired that I stopped sightseeing, except to go out in the morning and come back and rest, and that's how I'm able to go on and on.

The audience in Europe is very appreciative. We did a festival in Italy, and that was the place that I feared the most. A stagehand had told me, "They're going to really love your music—but this audience lets you know when they don't like it. By the third song, if they don't like it, they throw things. They throw papers, and sometimes they throw bottles and cans. But I'm not anticipating any of that for your music."

I said, "Wow! Don't tell me!" But after the third song they were applauding, screaming, dancing, and coming up to the stage. It went really well for us. Unfortunately, it didn't go well for the band after us. They were a small jazz band, and they played three songs and had to get off because the audience *did* throw things at them. I thought, "Oh gee, that stagehand was right. Lucky we made it."

When we tour in other countries we always have a road manager with us who can speak several languages. And many Europeans speak English. In French-speaking countries like Switzerland, Belgium, Canada, France, they understand my patois and I understand them—even though their accent is different, and a lot of words are pronounced differently. I did love the food in France, and in Italy. They have great steaks and pastas, super bread, wonderful sauces, and very tasty pastries. Denmark has wonderful pastries, too.

In July 1988, we were the first zydeco band to tour Japan, and in 1989 I went on a State Department–sponsored tour of Africa: Ghana, Algeria, Senegal, Côte d'Ivoire (Ivory Coast),

Togo, and the Congo Republic. I was surprised to see how modern the cities are—when you look out your airplane window, you think you're going to land in an American city, with all the tall buildings.

All but Ghana are French-speaking countries, and we understood each other very well. I spoke to them in French whenever I introduced the band or talked to them, and they loved it. In fact, one lady in Senegal liked my tune "Hey La-Bas" so much that she told me, "This is gonna be the Senegal theme song." (*La-bas* means "over there" and the "hey" is just street slang to say, "Pardon me . . ." "Hey! La-bas" means "Hey, you over there.")

We went to a workshop with some musicians in Accra, Ghana. It was a great afternoon at a beautiful restaurant by the ocean, owned by one of the teachers of drums and his wife. They played the drums, and they were teaching anybody who wanted to learn how to play the drums and how to dance to the music. It was wonderful. I played, I danced. And then I tried what they call a "talking drum." That went really well, until I got so excited I got off-beat and had to quit.

The first time we were nominated for a Grammy (as opposed to a Bammy), we were touring Germany on the evening the ceremony was held in New York. I felt great about the nomination for *Queen Ida in New Orleans;* it's an honor to be nominated for a type of music that had been so dormant so long, and to find it's now recognized by the whole music industry. I didn't think we were going to win it, though—and we didn't. Not that time.

We recorded our fourth album, *On Tour,* live in Denmark on the last night of a seven-week tour. Almost every song sounds too fast to me. But, seven weeks on the road, going home tomorrow, it's like, "Let's hurry up and finish this tour!" And that's the album that won the Grammy!

I didn't know we'd been nominated; I had to read it in the paper like everyone else. The letter arrived after the newspaper ran the story. Actually, they sent a certificate: "Congratulations, you've been nominated for the Best Ethnic/Folk Recording Album for the year of 1982."

When I received that certificate, my brother said, "We're going to this one, aren't we?" This time the ceremonies were in Los Angeles at the Shrine Auditorium, so we booked everything around that date. As we were sitting in the audience Al said to me, "That little clutch purse you're holding—do you have money in there?"

"Yeah," I said.

"Give it to me. I'll put it in my jacket pocket."

"What for?"

"When you win, you're going to throw your purse up in the air."

I said, "Yeah, sure, Al. Sure, we're going to win. Look who's in our category." I've forgotten who the other candidates were, but they were people whose music was getting played all over the air.

But sure enough, they said "And the winner is . . . Queen Ida and the Bon Temps Zydeco Band!" I thought, "I must have said that in my own mind; they didn't say it."

Then my brother punched me, saying, "We won!"

"Ohhhhhhh!" I yelled, and the purse went up in the air.

It was the greatest moment in my life, and in my career. It was unbelievable, unexplainable: no words can express the feeling. It's like the work is not all in vain.

The Grammy ceremony was televised throughout the world, and I started receiving telegrams from promoters all over Europe. The Grammy boosted the band into another category, a higher level. Now John could get more money for the band and better engagements. Suddenly, we were internationally known; promoters were more interested in hearing a Grammy winner playing this music. We've even made it to Carnegie Hall, opening for Ladysmith Black Mambazo in December 1987. Paul Simon sat in with Ladysmith, and we were able to chat for a few minutes backstage.

I started getting busier and busier, especially after we were nominated for Grammys twice more. Ray finally retired from his job and became our road manager. By 1986, I was on the road 150 to 200 days a year. We mainly do one-nighters, and those are the hardest. When you get a weeklong gig, you only have one sound check, and the guys don't have to break down everything every night. You can just take your instrument and play.

Most of the time we drive from one gig to the next. For some reason, I don't like to fly anymore—but you have to get there somehow. I would really rather be on the ground. Ray started talking about buying a bus, but I didn't want a bus. A bus is too small, and I didn't want to have to sleep on the road, or to use the bathroom with all the guys. I told him I would go with a motor home, and that the bookings had to allow me to sleep in a real bed. So we got a mobile home.

It makes cooking on the road a lot easier—but even before we got the mobile home we'd done a lot of our own cooking. It's so much nicer than having to stop and eat fast food. Whenever we can, we find a motel that has kitchenettes.

We'll always have a gumbo at least once, and the rest of the time we'll just fry some chops, steaks, or burgers. We don't have time to cook beans from scratch, but we'll get a can of beans and we'll work it up with a little salt pork or bacon, or we'll make chili out of it. And of course we'll cook our rice. We've got to have that rice. Ray likes a lot of soups; as far as he's concerned, if he makes a big pot of soup, that's a meal. And Ray always buys me hot green peppers, because he knows I love to cut them into my food. One day we were touring some part of the country where we didn't expect to see hot peppers (the Midwest, I think), and in walked Ray G, saying, "Looka this!"—and he handed me a big bag full of peppers, too many to use up before they spoiled. I ended up making pickled hot peppers in that motel kitchenette, using empty orange juice bottles instead of Mason jars, to preserve them until I got them home. (It worked, too!)

As our road manager, Ray takes care of all the hotel arrangements, routes, and bills; he drives us to the engagements, drops off the equipment, and collects the money at the end of the show. Three years ago our band had a trophy made, consisting of a little van; at the bottom was inscribed "Manager of the Year." When we presented it to him, Ray G was in shock! He was just one big smile!

My son Myrick (nicknamed Freeze) started to get involved with the band back in the summer of 1976, when we were about to go on our first tour to Texas and Louisiana. Myrick had a van, and he said, "I'll take my van to carry people and luggage and instruments." To him it was a vacation, and when the tour was over he went back to school. Afterwards, he'd go on the road with us occasionally for short periods of time between jobs and school.

For three or four years after Myrick got married he was a stay-at-home boy—but finally he said, "Well, I think I'd like to hit the road with you guys. Do you have a position open for me?" He started out as a roadie and as a second percussionist, backing up my brother Willie on rub-board. Finally he started teaching himself to play the accordion.

When Willie left the band in '88, Myrick said, "You don't have to replace Willie, I'll play the washboard and once in a while I'll sit in on the accordion." So that's what he's doing now—and when we don't have an opening act he and the band open the show for me. He's writing and arranging, too, and it's starting to happen for him on his own: His first tour as the leader of the group was in the spring of 1990, and he got good reviews. He's now working on his first solo album for GNP Crescendo.

It's a hectic life, though. As a way to get out of touring I once thought about opening a restaurant, or taking over the kitchen at one of the clubs I played in San Francisco. I even discussed the idea with one club manager. He warned me about the expenses involved, and told me to think about it carefully. My sister, who worked as a waitress for 30 some years, told me, "If you don't have someone at that cash register that you trust, and I do mean trust, your profit goes right out the door." Well, I thought about it, about all the risks, and the difficulty of overseeing a professional kitchen, and I finally decided, forget it. Then John had the idea of my writing this cookbook.

My plan now: I'm going to work as long as I can, as long as it doesn't endanger my health, but I do want to spend more time at home than I have in the past four years. Last year I spent 189 days on tour! I'd like to decrease that, and help Myrick get a start. As my mom told us, you have to keep the music going. It's been passed on from generation to generation, and now we're passing it on to Myrick. I hope he'll pass it on to his children's generation, and keep it alive. His son Daniel is 14 and into the rap stuff; all you hear when he passes by is whoop bop, whoop bop, whoop bop, whoop bop. Of course, Myrick didn't want any part of anything at that age either; I think—I hope—Daniel will find himself interested in our music somewhere down the line. I'm not sure it will be Myrick's son, but I'm sure there will be sustained interest in the music in the next generation.

My other grandchildren are all girls. Ledra's daughter Crystal, who's four, is around me all the time. She sees the accordion here at home and she likes music, she likes to dance. Her parents were playing a joke on me through the kid, and they gave her a toy accordion at Christmastime—in fact, she received two toy accordions. She picked up one of them and marched through the house playing it. Then she said, "Oh, Grandma, I'm gonna be like you, I'm gonna play zydeco."

One day her father told her, "Will you take your accordion in your room and play it in there!"

She turned around and said, "But I'm gonna be the next Queen Ida."

Laissez le bon temps rouler!

Let the good times roll!

IN CALIFORNIA AND
ON THE ROAD

CRAWFISH (OR PRAWNS) AND PASTA

This quick and delicious dish can be a first course or an entrée. It's very rich made with half-and-half, richer yet when made with cream. If crawfish meat is unavailable, prawns or shrimp make an excellent substitute.

Serves 4 as main course, 8 as appetizer

3	tablespoons butter	½	teaspoon white pepper
3	tablespoons flour	¼	teaspoon salt (or to taste)
1¼	cups whole milk	½	pound uncooked crawfish
½	cup half-and-half (or heavy cream)		meat (or prawns), peeled, deveined, and chopped bite-size
2	tablespoons chopped onion	1	tablespoon parsley
½	teaspoon cayenne	2	cups dry pasta twirls

In a heavy saucepan over low to medium heat, melt the butter and stir in the flour until well blended. Combine milk and half-and-half. Off heat, gradually stir milk mixture into flour mixture. Add onion,

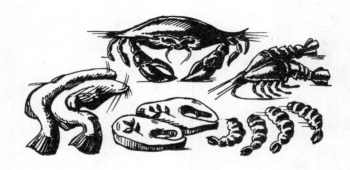

cayenne, white pepper, and salt. Return pan to low heat and simmer mixture until it thickens (about 5 minutes). Stir in crawfish or prawns and simmer 5 minutes longer. Taste carefully and correct seasonings. Add parsley.

Meanwhile, cook pasta according to package directions. Drain pasta and mix with the sauce. Serve hot or cold.

~~~~~~~~~~~~~~~~

SPICY CORN SOUP WITH BEEF

Serves 6–8

3 quarts water
2 slices of beef shank
1 teaspoon salt
2 cans creamed corn, 15 ounces each
15-ounce can whole corn kernels, drained
1 cup diced potato (or more for a thicker soup)

½ cup fresh or canned tomatoes, peeled (see Appendix) and chopped
¼ cup chopped bell pepper
1 tablespoon chopped onion
2½ teaspoons salt, or to taste
½ teaspoon cayenne (or to taste)

In a Dutch oven or deep saucepan of at least 2½-quart capacity, bring the water, beef, and 1 teaspoon salt to a boil. Reduce heat and cook so that the water is just bubbling until shanks are tender and the meat is falling off the bones (about 2 hours). Remove shanks and, if desired, cut the meat into small pieces and return it to the pot. (The cook gets to eat the marrow from the bones or to reserve it for another use.) Add remaining ingredients (stirring salt in gradually to taste) and cook until potato is tender (about 30 minutes longer). Correct seasonings, simmer briefly to blend flavors, and serve hot.

Note: If too much water evaporates during cooking, the juice from the canned corn may be added to the soup.

RAY G'S SPECIAL

Ray G's quick frittata of leftover rice and whatever meat is handy makes a light, satisfying midnight supper after a gig (whether it's my gig or yours).

Serves 2

3 slices bacon, cut into small pieces (or ½ cup ground meat, diced sausages, or diced ham)	1½ cups (packed) cooked rice
	1 tablespoon chopped green onions
1 teaspoon oil (or as needed)	¼ cup cooked peas or string beans (optional)
2 eggs, beaten	Salt and pepper to taste

In a skillet, fry meat until cooked, stirring frequently. (Film skillet with oil if using ham.) In another skillet, heat 1 teaspoon oil. Add the meat, eggs, rice, green onions, vegetables if using, and salt and pepper to taste. Stir occasionally until eggs are cooked and rice and meat are hot.

~~~~~~~~~~~~~~~~~

BARBECUED SALMON

I first tasted this dish while touring in Alaska. It's simple to make and so delicious!

Serves 4–6

1 teaspoon garlic powder	1 small whole salmon, about 3 pounds without the head (or 2–3 pounds salmon steaks)
¾ teaspoon salt	
½ teaspoon cayenne	
¼ teaspoon black pepper	1 cup sliced yellow, white, or red onion
	Lemon wedges

Start a fire in a barbecue pit and let flames burn down. Meanwhile, mix seasonings together in a small bowl and rub the mixture all over the fish on both sides. Place a large sheet of aluminum foil over the barbecue grill. Place the fish on the foil, scatter the onions over the fish, and wrap the fish with the foil. Grill the fish about 25 minutes (more or less depending on the heat of the fire). Open the foil and check doneness of the fish: Lift a small piece with a fork. Salmon is cooked when its meat flakes off easily. Serve with lemon wedges.

~~~~~~~~~~~~~~~~~

SALMON CROQUETTES

These Creole-style croquettes are similar to crab cakes.

Serves 4

15-ounce can salmon (or 1½ cups cooked salmon meat)	¾ teaspoon cayenne
1½ cups cooked, mashed potatoes (or dry bread crumbs)	½ teaspoon garlic powder
	⅓ teaspoon powdered dried thyme
¼ cup chopped green onions	¼ teaspoon black pepper
2 tablespoons chopped celery	1 egg, lightly beaten
	¼ cup cornmeal
2 tablespoons finely minced yellow onion	¼ cup flour
	2-3 cups oil for deep-frying
	Lemon wedges

In a mixing bowl, combine salmon, potatoes, chopped vegetables, and spices. Mix well, add egg, and blend thoroughly. Make patties about 2½ inches across. Mix cornmeal and flour, and roll each patty in the mixture to coat.

In a heavy skillet, heat enough oil to cover the patties. When oil reaches about 350 degrees, slip the patties into it and deep-fry them about 2½ minutes, or until golden brown. Drain briefly on paper towels and serve hot with lemon wedges.

POULET RÔTI
(Baked Chicken Casserole)

Serves 4

3¼-pound chicken, cut into serving pieces (or 3¼ pounds legs and thighs)

1   teaspoon salt

1   teaspoon garlic powder

½   teaspoon cayenne

½   teaspoon black pepper

1½ tablespoons Creole Vinaigrette (page 130), strained, plus ¼ teaspoon crumbled dried oregano leaves (or use bottled Italian dressing)

¼   of a medium bell pepper, sliced

½   celery rib, cut into ½-inch slices

½   of a carrot, quartered

⅛   of a medium-size yellow onion, sliced

Preheat oven to 350 degrees. Mix salt, garlic powder, cayenne, and black pepper and rub the mixture all over the chicken pieces. Place in an ovenproof casserole with a lid. Pour dressing over the chicken. Add remaining ingredients and cover. Bake 45 minutes, basting halfway through with the pan juices. Uncover, add ¼ cup water, and bake until chicken is cooked through (20–30 minutes longer).

~~~~~~~~~~~~~~~~

DIRTY RICE
(Browned Rice Dressing)

This spicy, flavorful version of a classic Louisiana dish differs from the more familiar renditions by using only chicken giblets (rather than including the customary ground beef), and by poaching the giblets until tender before they're fried. The poaching liquid becomes a delicious broth, and the giblet meat comes out toothsome rather than tough. The rice has to be cool when it's added to its seasoning mixture. You can use leftover rice, or can start the dish a few hours (or a day) ahead. This dressing may be used with turkey, baked chicken, barbecue, or any type of meat. It can be a stuffing for poultry, or even a main dish.

Serves 6–8

About 5 cups cooked white rice (preferably pearl rice; see page 30)

*2 pounds chicken gizzards

½ cup oil

¼ pound chicken livers, finely chopped

½ cup finely chopped parsley

½ cup chopped green onions

½ cup finely chopped bell pepper

⅓ cup finely chopped celery

¼ cup finely chopped onion

2½ teaspoons cayenne pepper (less if a mild dressing is desired)

2 teaspoons salt (or to taste)

1 teaspoon black pepper

1 teaspoon poultry seasoning

*Note: Chicken hearts can be substituted for some or all of the gizzards; for extra richness, replace some of the poaching water with chicken broth.

A few hours (or a day) ahead, cook the rice, seasoning it during cooking with a little salt. Let it cool to room temperature and break up any lumps.

Wash the chicken gizzards, place them in a 2-quart saucepan, and add just enough water to cover. (Do not fill the pan to the top.) Bring to a boil, reduce heat so that liquid bubbles gently, and cook until tender (about 1 hour). Drain, reserving all the broth. Let gizzards cool until they can be handled, then grind or chop them medium coarse and set aside.

In a large skillet, heat the oil and sauté the remaining ingredients over fairly high heat, stirring. (Add the cayenne a little at a time until dish is very spicy to your palate.) Reduce heat to low, stir in the chopped gizzard, and add about 3 cups reserved gizzard broth. Add the rice by dropping large spoonfuls of it into the broth and stirring gently until you feel you have the mixture neither packed and dry nor soupy, but just right. It should have the consistency of a moist dressing. (Any leftover rice can be reserved for another use.) Let the rice heat a few minutes over very low heat, stirring frequently, then serve.

Ray G Talks Turkey, Quail, Blackbird

"My mom used to raise turkeys just for Thanksgiving," Ray G remembers. "She had customers that wanted their turkeys raised differently or fed differently than the market turkeys. We'd have to watch our turkeys in the fall real close, close, close. We'd turn them out and they'd walk around through the fields. Some hunters would walk by and shoot at our turkeys thinking they were wild turkeys.

"We would grow black-eyed peas in between the corn. We never harvested the peas. That was feed for the quails and the doves. We never had to hunt. Back in the late '30s, we used to charge hunters one dollar a head to hunt. The hunters would kill over their limit, especially the quails and doves. They would always give us what was over their limit.

"We used to make a jambalaya with blackbirds. During the cold months, we used to take an old door and prop it up with a stick, and attach a string to it and bring it all the way back to the barn. We'd put a little grain under the door. When the area was full of blackbirds, we'd jerk the stick out. That's how we used to get our blackbirds for our jambalaya."

∿∿∿∿∿∿∿∿

RAY G'S GAME BIRD JAMBALAYA

Ray G's cooking is simpler and more mildly seasoned than mine, and his jambalaya is closer to the "perlaw" (pilau) of the mid-South than to the spicy cooking of Louisiana. Despite his mention of blackbird jambalaya, any other small, land-based bird (such as quail, dove, squab, grouse, or even Cornish game hen) will not only do as well, but will do a whole lot better. Ray prefers to serve only the breasts of the birds, on grounds the other parts are too bony to bother with. (Those parts can be used to make the broth, if desired.)

Serves 4

½ teaspoon salt
½ teaspoon cayenne (or to taste)
½ teaspoon garlic powder
2 tablespoons oil
8 breasts of quail, dove, or squab (or whole boned quails, or 2 game hens, cut into serving pieces)
½ of an onion, chopped
1 teaspoon flour

*2 cups chicken broth or game bird stock
4 cups cooked pearl rice, cooled (see page 30)
1½ cups frozen green peas (or a 12-ounce can field peas, or pigeon peas, if available)
2 tablespoons chopped parsley (optional)

*Note: For game bird stock, follow instructions for the stock used in turkey gravy (page 30), using giblets and spare parts of the game birds in place of turkey giblets.

Combine salt, cayenne, and garlic powder. Rub into all sides of the birds. In a large skillet with a cover, gently heat the oil. Add the birds and cook over very low heat, 10 minutes per side. (The birds are not browned, but steam-cooked.) Stir in onion and flour and cook until the flour is well browned. Stir in the broth, bring to a boil, reduce heat, and cover the pan. Simmer until the birds are cooked through (20–30 minutes).

Pour off all the stock into a bowl, leaving the poultry in the pan. Taste the stock and correct the seasonings. Mix the rice with the birds. A spoonful at a time, stir stock into the rice, until mixture is moist but not soggy. Stir in peas and parsley. Cook over low heat, stirring frequently, just until rice and peas are heated through and flavors are blended.

SPICY CABBAGE AND CORNED BEEF

Corned beef and cabbage is a meal in itself. I usually serve it with corn bread and butter. Sometimes I serve it with rice, spooning a little of the water from the cabbage over the cooked rice to flavor it.

Serves 6–8

1 **corned beef brisket, 3–3½**   **Black pepper and cayenne**
  pounds   **to taste**
1 **large cabbage, quartered**   **Salt (optional)**
                                 2 **tablespoons oil (optional)**

Place corned beef in a large pot with water to cover. Bring to a boil, reduce heat, and simmer uncovered until tender (about 3 hours). Remove the meat, saving the cooking liquid. When meat is cool enough to handle (while cooking the cabbage), cut it into slices.

Place cabbage quarters in a pot, add about 2 cups cooking liquid from the corned beef, and season it highly with black pepper and plenty of cayenne. Taste and add salt if necessary, and add the oil if desired. (The corned beef may have released sufficient salt and fat into the water already.) Bring liquid to a boil, cover, reduce heat. Simmer cabbage until it is tender (20–25 minutes from the boil). During the last minute or two of cooking, place a few slices of corned beef on top of the cabbage to give it extra flavor.

Use a slotted spoon to place the cabbage on a serving dish, and arrange corned beef slices around it.

STUFFED BELL PEPPER

Corn bread is a major part of the stuffing.

Serves 4

1 recipe corn bread (page 103)	2 tablespoons chopped celery
4 large bell peppers	2 tablespoons chopped parsley
¾-1 pound ground meat (chuck, or a combination of chuck and pork)	1 teaspoon salt
¼ cup chopped onion	½ teaspoon black pepper
¼ cup chopped green onions	¼ teaspoon cayenne
	¼ teaspoon white pepper
	1 teaspoon flour
	3 tablespoons tomato sauce

Bake the corn bread and let cool. Meanwhile, cut off the stem end of the bell peppers and remove the cores, seeds, and thick white veins along the sides (taking care not to cut into the meat of the pepper). Bring about 2 quarts water to a boil in a large saucepan. Drop in the peppers and boil 10 minutes, turning occasionally. Remove peppers from the water and let cool.

Preheat oven to 350 degrees. In a large skillet, brown the meat, stirring. Add onions, celery, parsley, and seasonings. Sauté 5 minutes, stirring frequently. Stir in the flour. Add tomato sauce and 1 cup water, bring to a simmer, and simmer 5 minutes. Cut off the browned edges of the corn bread and discard (or eat). Break the corn bread into pieces and add them to the meat mixture a few at a time, mashing with a fork to blend with the sauce and meat. If mixture is too dry, stir in warm water a tablespoonful at a time, until well moistened.

Fill bell peppers with the mixture. Place peppers in a casserole dish with the open sides up, and carefully pour 1 cup water around the peppers. Cover casserole with foil and bake 20 minutes. Remove the foil and bake 5 minutes longer. Serve hot.

TAMALE PIE

Here's the flavor of tamales with much less work.

Serves 4–6

**CORNMEAL MUSH
CRUST:**
1   cup cornmeal
½   teaspoon salt (or to taste)
½   teaspoon cayenne
½   teaspoon chili powder
¼   teaspoon black pepper

FILLING:
1   tablespoon oil
1   pound lean ground beef
1½ tablespoons chili powder
1   teaspoon salt

¼   teaspoon black pepper
2   jalapeño peppers (fresh or
       canned), seeded and
       minced
¼   cup chopped onion
¼   cup chopped bell pepper
       16-ounce can whole
       kernel corn, juice
       included
       2¼-ounce can sliced black
       olives
2   tablespoons tomato sauce
       Cayenne to taste

To make the crust: In a small bowl, mix cornmeal with ¾ cup cold water until it is dampened well. Bring 2 cups water to a boil in a saucepan. Gradually stir in the cornmeal mixture, a little at a time. Reduce heat to a simmer and stir in seasonings. Continue stirring over low heat until the water is absorbed and mixture becomes thick and pasty. Taste and correct seasonings. Remove from heat and let cool slightly. With a spoon, spread the mixture over the bottom and sides of a large, deep pie pan or similar-size casserole, to form a pie crust. Let cool about 10 minutes before filling.

Preheat oven to 350 degrees. To make the filling: Film a large skillet with the oil. Add meat and brown it over medium heat, stirring constantly. Stir in the seasonings and jalapeños. Sauté about 3 minutes. Add ½ cup water and remaining ingredients. Cook over low heat 15 minutes. Spread filling inside cornmeal crust. Bake 30 minutes. Serve hot.

SPICY MEAT LOAF À LA REINE

A jolt of cayenne, along with the Creole seasoning trinity (celery, bell pepper, and garlic) makes this a big change from all-American meat loaf.

Serves 6–8

3	slices bread	2½	teaspoons cayenne (less if a mild loaf is desired)
2½–3	pounds ground meat (such as beef chuck)	1½	teaspoons salt
¼	cup chopped celery	½	teaspoon black pepper
¼	cup chopped bell pepper	2	eggs, well beaten
¼	cup chopped onion		*16-ounce can stewed or whole tomatoes, drained and chopped
3	medium cloves garlic, finely chopped	½	cup water

*Note: If using tomatoes packed in pure tomato juice, the juice may replace some or all of the water in the topping for the loaf.

Preheat oven to 350 degrees. Soak bread in a little water a few seconds, then drain and squeeze out. Knead together meat, celery, bell pepper, onion, garlic, and seasonings. Knead in the bread and add eggs. Mix well. Place mixture in a 9″ × 11½″ baking dish and mold into a loaf about 2½ inches thick. Pour tomatoes over the loaf and add the water. Bake 30 minutes. Reduce heat to 325 degrees and cover with foil. Continue baking another 30 minutes, basting occasionally.

BEEF AND VEGETABLE CASSEROLE

This is sometimes called "poor man's casserole," although there is nothing especially impoverished about it. It does include a shortcut, however, in the use of canned vegetable soup. Serve it with French bread and butter.

Serves 6–8

2	tablespoons oil	2	cloves garlic, finely chopped
2	pounds lean ground chuck	6	medium potatoes, pared and sliced about ¼ inch thick
½	teaspoon salt		
¼	teaspoon black pepper		
⅛	teaspoon cayenne	2	cans vegetable soup, 10½ ounces each
½	cup chopped onion		
⅓	cup chopped bell pepper	1½	cups water

Heat the oil in a skillet. Sprinkle the meat with the salt, pepper, and cayenne, and start to brown it in the skillet, stirring constantly. When it begins to change color, add onion, bell pepper, and garlic. Fry until meat is lightly browned. Drain meat mixture in a strainer or colander. Reserve meat mixture.

Preheat oven to 400 degrees. Butter the bottom and sides of a deep casserole. Layer half the potatoes in the bottom of the casserole and add half of the meat mixture, then repeat. In a bowl, stir together the soup and the water. Pour over the meat and potatoes. Place a piece of foil loosely over the casserole and bake 30 minutes. Reduce heat to 350 degrees and continue baking until potatoes are tender (30–35 minutes longer). Serve hot.

BEETS ÉTOUFFÉE

This recipe uses fresh beets cut into shoestrings. If you prefer to shred them quickly in a food processor, decrease the cooking time to about 10 minutes.

Serves 3–4

1   teaspoon butter
¼ of a small red or yellow
    onion, chopped
3   medium beets (about 2½
    cups), pared and cut
    into shoestrings

¾ cup water
½ teaspoon sugar
½ teaspoon vinegar
⅛ teaspoon salt

In a 10-inch skillet or wide saucepan, melt the butter over medium heat and add onion. Sauté until onion softens. Stir in beets. Add the water, sugar, vinegar, and salt. Cover and simmer until beets are tender (about 20 minutes).

〰〰〰〰〰〰

PICKLED HOT GREEN PEPPERS

I no longer make chowchow, but I still like to pickle little hot peppers. They go well with stews and gumbos. You can sprinkle some of the vinegar from the hot peppers over steak or beans and rice. If you wish, you can add slices of carrots to the peppers. You can make any amount you like.

Makes about 6 pints

*About 6 pints fresh hot
peppers, about 1½ to 2 inches
long (such as jalapeños,
serranos)

About 1 quart distilled white
vinegar
About 6 pint-size Mason jars
and lids

*Note: You may substitute ½–1 cup thinly sliced pared carrots for an equal amount of peppers.

Wash peppers well (or wipe carefully) and pat dry one by one with paper towels. Heat vinegar to a full boil. Meanwhile, place the peppers in the clean jars, packing them tightly. Pour the hot vinegar into each jar, up to the top. (Unused vinegar may be poured back into the bottle for later use.) When pepper mixture is completely cooled, seal each jar with a lid.

Let pickles cure in a cool, dark place at least 2 weeks before using.

QUEEN IDA'S BREAD PUDDING

Serves 8–12

12 slices day-old bread, or
    bread ends (white,
    wheat, or egg bread)
4   eggs, lightly beaten
1½ cups whole milk
1   cup evaporated milk (or
    heavy cream, or half-
    and-half)
½   cup sugar
1   teaspoon baking powder

1   teaspoon vanilla
½   teaspoon cinnamon
½   teaspoon nutmeg
⅛   teaspoon ground cloves
3   tablespoons raisins,
    soaked in warm water 5
    minutes and drained (or
    soaked in ¼ cup rum)
⅓   cup butter, melted

Preheat oven to 350 degrees. Place bread on a cookie sheet and toast lightly, about 4 minutes a side, so it won't be too soggy. Break bread into small pieces and place in a bowl. Add eggs, whole milk, evaporated milk, sugar, baking powder, vanilla, cinnamon, nutmeg, and cloves. Drain the raisins; reserve the rum, if using, for the sauce. Stir in raisins and butter. Pour mixture into a well-greased baking dish about 11″ × 14″ × 2″ (such as a lasagna pan) and bake 20 minutes. Using a fork, test a little pudding from the center to see whether it's cooked. The custard should be very slightly browned but not dry. Let cool and slice. Serve with lemon sauce or hard sauce.

LEMON SAUCE FOR
BREAD PUDDING

A double boiler is used in this recipe so that the egg yolk will thicken the mixture without turning into scrambled eggs. (See Cookware in Appendix for substitutes.)

Makes about 1 cup

½ cup sugar	4 tablespoons (½ stick) butter, cut into pieces
1 egg yolk (white spot removed)	1½ tablespoons fresh lemon juice (see Appendix)
1½ teaspoons cornstarch	
Pinch of salt	

Half-fill the lower half of a double boiler with water and bring to a boil. Meanwhile, cream together sugar and egg yolk (in a food processor, or beating in a bowl with a wooden spoon). Add cornstarch and salt and blend well. Add 1¼ cups water a little at a time, blending after each addition, until all water is absorbed.

Pour mixture into the upper half of the double boiler and stir constantly and strongly over low to medium heat, scraping the bottom of the pot, until mixture begins to thicken. (If egg starts to scramble, remove the top half of the double boiler for a moment and stir fiercely to cool the mixture, then return it to reduced heat.) Add the butter and lemon juice and continue stirring until butter melts and mixture is creamy (about 10 minutes more). If there are any lumps, force sauce through a strainer. Serve hot or warm.

Hard Sauce: Substitute ¼ cup brandy, whiskey, or rum for the lemon juice.

BANANA PUDDING

Serves 4–6 (or more)

½ cup flour
½ cup sugar plus ¼ cup
⅛ teaspoon salt
4 eggs, separated
1⅓ cups milk

1 cup half-and-half (or light cream)
½ teaspoon vanilla
   11- or 12-ounce box vanilla wafers
   3 or 4 ripe bananas

In a heavy saucepan (1½ quarts or larger), combine flour, ½ cup sugar, and salt. In a bowl, lightly beat together egg yolks, milk, and half-and-half. (Reserve egg whites.) Stir liquid mixture into flour mixture, blend well, and stir in vanilla. Cook uncovered over medium heat, stirring constantly, until mixture thickens. If any lumps form, break them up with a flat-bottomed wire whisk (or force custard through a strainer when done).

Preheat oven to 425 degrees. Spread a layer of vanilla wafers on the bottom of a 1½- to 2-quart ovenproof casserole. Cover the wafers with ⅓ of the custard mixture. Peel bananas and slice them, and place ⅓ of the banana slices over the custard. Twice more, repeat layering the wafers, custard, and banana slices, to make 3 layers. Beat ½ cup of the reserved egg white until stiff peaks form. Add ¼ cup sugar and beat until very stiff and glossy (about 15 seconds). Spoon meringue on top of the pudding and smooth it to cover the entire surface. Bake about 5 minutes to lightly brown the top of the meringue. Serve warm or chilled.

8

New Healthy Recipes

In days gone by, folks worked 14-hour days on the farm and burned up all of the calories found in traditional Creole food. Realistically, no one gets that kind of workout from their job nowadays (although I certainly do when I'm on stage!). As we head into the next century everyone is realizing (and Ray G and I are no exception) that we have to change the way we eat in order to stay healthy. We hope that you and your family and friends will enjoy these lowfat alternatives to some of the most popular Creole dishes, and that you all stay healthy and keep on zydeco dancing!

BARBECUED SALMON

4–6 servings

1	teaspoon garlic powder	2½	pounds salmon steaks
¾	teaspoon salt	1	cup sliced yellow, white,
½	teaspoon cayenne		or red onion
¼	teaspoon black pepper		Lemon wedges

Start a fire in a barbecue pit and let flames burn down. Meanwhile, mix seasonings together in a small bowl and rub the mixture all over the fish on both sides. Place a large sheet of aluminum foil over the barbecue grill. Place the fish on the foil, scatter the onions over the fish, and wrap the fish with the foil. Grill the fish about 25 minutes (more or less depending on the heat of the fire). Open the foil and check doneness of the fish: lift a small piece with a fork; salmon is cooked when its meat flakes off easily. Serve with lemon wedges.

Each serving provides:

242 calories; 33.8 g protein; 10.78 g fat; 94 mg cholesterol; 0 mg carbohydrate; 1 g dietary fiber; 2 mg calcium; 1.35 mg iron; 74 mg sodium

〰〰〰〰〰〰〰〰

BEETS ÉTOUFFÉE

Serves 3–4

	Nonstick vegetable oil cooking spray	¾	cup water
⅓	cup chopped red or yellow onion	⅛	teaspoon salt
		½	teaspoon sugar
3	large beets, pared and cut into shoestrings (about 2½ cups)	½	teaspoon vinegar

Place a 10-inch skillet over medium heat and spray evenly with nonstick vegetable oil cooking spray. Add the onion and sauté until onion softens. Stir in beets. Add the water, salt, sugar, and vinegar. Simmer covered until beets are tender (about 20 minutes).

Each serving provides:

25 calories; 0.75 g protein; 0.02 g fat; 0 mg cholesterol; 5.6 g carbohydrate; 1.9 g dietary fiber; 11 mg calcium; 0.39 mg iron; 92 mg sodium

~~~~~~~~~~~~~~~~

BLACK-EYED PEAS

Serves 6–8

3	cups dried black-eyed peas	1/2 green bell pepper, seeded and chopped
1	cup diced smoked turkey	
3	cloves garlic, chopped	1 1/2 teaspoons salt, or to taste
2	jalapeño peppers, trimmed, seeded, and chopped	1/4 teaspoon black pepper
1	onion, chopped	8 cups water

Combine all ingredients in a 4-quart Dutch oven or heavy saucepan. Bring to a boil, cover, reduce heat, and simmer until peas are tender (about 1 hour). Check liquid from time to time, adding more water if liquid is evaporating too quickly. When peas are done, check liquid again. If it is too thin, increase heat to moderate, uncover pan, and cook until liquid thickens.

Each serving provides:

124 calories; 9.76 g protein; 2.35 g fat; 15 mg cholesterol; 16.8 g carbohydrate; 10 g dietary fiber; 26 mg calcium; 1.41 mg iron; 806 mg sodium

BOULETTES AND GRAVY
(BIG, SPICY MEATBALLS)

Serves 4

1½ pounds ground turkey breast meat
2 egg whites, lightly beaten
¼ cup chopped green bell pepper
1 teaspoon salt
1 teaspoon cayenne
1 teaspoon garlic powder
½ teaspoon black pepper
½ teaspoon white pepper
2 slices bread, moistened with water
Nonstick vegetable oil cooking spray
1 cup water
½ cup chopped fresh parsley
½ cup chopped green onions

Mix together turkey, egg whites, bell pepper, and spices. Break moistened bread into pieces and knead into meat mixture. Divide mixture into 12 pieces and shape each piece into a meat ball. Spray a nonstick skillet with nonstick vegetable oil cooking spray and place over medium heat. Add meatballs and brown on all sides. Add 1 cup water. Increase heat and bring to a boil. Add parsley and green onions and cover the skillet. Simmer 20 minutes. Uncover and check the liquid; if too thin, continue cooking, uncovered, until liquid thickens to a gravy. Serve hot or warm over rice.

Each serving provides:

458 calories; 85.37 g protein; 5.1 g fat; 204 mg cholesterol;
11.3 g carbohydrate; 1.01 g dietary fiber; 82 mg calcium;
3.94 mg iron; 891 mg sodium

CHICKEN AND TURKEY SAUSAGE GUMBO

Serves 5–6

1 (2-pound) chicken, cut into serving pieces, skin and fat removed	1 bay leaf
Vegetable oil cooking spray	1 large green bell pepper, seeded and chopped
1 tablespoon cayenne (or to taste)	1 cup celery, chopped
1½ teaspoons black pepper	1 large yellow onion, chopped
1½ teaspoons salt	1 bunch green onions, chopped
9 cups fat-free, reduced sodium chicken broth	1 cup fresh parsley leaves, chopped
2⅓ cups roux flour (see recipe on page 241)	About 1½ teaspoons filé powder (optional)
¾ pound smoked turkey sausage cut into ⅓-inch slices	

Remove the skin and fat from the chicken pieces and discard. Spray a broiler pan with vegetable oil cooking spray and turn on the broiler. Place the chicken pieces in the broiler pan in a single layer. Combine the cayenne and black peppers with the salt, mixing well. Season the chicken pieces lightly with the mixture (reserve remaining seasoning). Broil the chicken 5 minutes per side, turning only once. Set chicken aside.

Place a large (5-quart) Dutch oven over high heat. Add the chicken broth and bring to a boil; reduce heat to a simmer. Add the roux flour in batches, stirring with a whisk if need be to prevent big lumps. The liquid will thicken slightly. To the broth and roux flour add the turkey sausages, chicken, remaining seasoning mixture, bay leaf, green bell pepper, celery, and yellow onion, and simmer, covered, 20 minutes. Adjust heat to maintain a steady simmer; do not boil. Add the green onions and parsley and continue to simmer until the chicken is cooked through (about 15 to 20 minutes). Taste carefully and correct seasonings if needed. If liquid has gotten too thick, stir in a little water or broth. Serve gumbo hot over a mound of rice.

To make this a "gumbo filé," sprinkle a little filé powder (about ¼ teaspoon) into each person's empty gumbo bowl, then spoon in the gumbo and rice and stir together.

Each serving provides:

378 calories; 26 g protein; 7.1 g fat; 73 mg cholesterol; 44.1 g carbohydrate; * dietary fiber; * calcium; * iron; 1037 mg sodium

* = data unavailable

~~~~~~~~~~~~~~~

CHICKEN AND TURKEY SAUSAGE JAMBALAYA

Serves 4–5

Nonstick vegetable oil cooking spray

1 pound chicken breast halves, skinned and boned, cut into 1½-inch strips

½ pound smoked turkey sausage, sliced into 1-inch lengths

1 cup chopped yellow onion

1 bunch chopped green onions

½ cup chopped celery

½ cup chopped bell pepper

¼ cup chopped parsley

2 cloves garlic, chopped

1 pound fresh tomatoes, coarsely chopped

8-ounce can stewed tomatoes

1½ cups fat-free, reduced sodium chicken broth

1 teaspoon salt

1½ teaspoons cayenne (or to taste)

½ teaspoon black pepper

½ teaspoon sugar

¼ teaspoon powdered dried thyme

1 bay leaf

6 cups cooked rice

Spray the inside of a large pot with nonstick vegetable oil cooking spray. Place the skillet over high heat. Add the chicken and brown. Add the sausage and continue to cook, stirring frequently, for 5 minutes. Add the yellow and green onion, celery, bell pepper, parsley, garlic, fresh and stewed tomatoes, and stir well. Add the chicken broth, salt, cayenne, black pepper, sugar, thyme, and bay leaf; stir well. Bring just to a boil, reduce heat immediately to a simmer, and cook uncovered until chicken is thoroughly done (about 15 minutes). Stir occasionally and make sure there is always enough liquid (add more water or broth if liquid evaporates too quickly). Taste carefully and correct seasonings; mixture should be spicy. Remove the bay leaf. With a large serving spoon, stir in the rice by spoonfuls, until the mixture is moist and thick but neither soupy nor dry. Taste again and correct seasonings. Warm together over low heat, stirring frequently, and serve.

Each serving provides:

391 calories; 25.4 g protein; 4.5 g fat; 54 mg cholesterol; 59.93 mg carbohydrate; * dietary fiber; * calcium; * iron; 1001 mg sodium

* = data unavailable

〜〜〜〜〜〜〜〜〜〜

COLE SLAW

Serves 6

2/3	cup fat-free mayonnaise	1/8	teaspoon dry mustard
1/2	teaspoon sugar	1/2	teaspoon vinegar
1/4	teaspoon salt (or to taste)	4	cups shredded cabbage
1/8	teaspoon white pepper	1/2	cup shredded carrots

Combine mayonnaise, sugar, seasonings, and vinegar, stirring well. Stir in cabbage and carrots. Chill until ready to serve.

Each serving provides:

25 calories; 0.77 g protein; 0.1 g fat; 0 mg cholesterol; 6 g carbohydrate; 1.24 g dietary fiber; 26 mg calcium; 0.34 mg iron; 225 mg sodium

〜〜〜〜〜〜〜〜〜〜

CREOLE BAKED SNAPPER

Serves 6

2½ pounds whole snapper
2½ teaspoons salt (or to taste)
1½ teaspoons cayenne (or to taste)
1 teaspoon black pepper
¼ teaspoon garlic powder
1½ teaspoons flour
  Nonstick vegetable oil cooking spray
  16-ounce can stewed tomatoes, coarsely chopped

½ cup chopped parsley
½ cup water
¼ cup chopped celery
¼ cup chopped bell pepper
¼ cup chopped white or yellow onion
2 cloves garlic, chopped
¼ teaspoon powdered dried thyme

Preheat oven to 350 degrees. Remove the head of the fish and with a small, sharp knife score both sides of the fish about 2–3 inches apart. Mix salt, cayenne, pepper, and garlic powder and rub mixture into both sides of the fish. Sprinkle with flour. Spray a baking dish with nonstick vegetable oil cooking spray; place the fish in the dish (large enough to hold the fish easily). Combine remaining ingredients and pour them over the fish. Bake fish uncovered 30–50 minutes (about 10 minutes per inch of thickness), basting often with tomato mixture, until fish flakes easily with a fork.

Each serving provides:

218 calories; 36.8 g protein; 3.7 g fat; 64 mg cholesterol; 7.3 g carbohydrate; 1.34 g dietary fiber; 39 mg calcium; 1.1 mg iron; 1043 mg sodium

FRESH CORN MAQUECHOUX

Serves 4–6

6 ears tender fresh corn
2 fresh tomatoes, finely chopped
3 tablespoons finely chopped yellow or white onion
1 clove garlic, minced
1 tablespoon sugar (or more, for starchy corn)
1 teaspoon salt
1 teaspoon cayenne (or to taste)
1/2 teaspoon black pepper Nonstick vegetable oil cooking spray

Shuck the corn. With a sharp knife, shave the kernels from the cobs into a large bowl, using a sawing motion; do not penetrate into the cobs. Then scrape the cobs again with the dull edge of the knife in order to milk them of their juices.

Add tomatoes, onion, garlic, sugar, salt, cayenne, and black pepper to the corn. Heat a heavy 4-quart saucepan over medium-low; spray in an even layer of nonstick vegetable oil cooking spray; stir in the corn mixture. Cover the pot and cook over the lowest possible heat about 20 minutes, uncovering only to stir frequently with a wooden spoon. (This prevents corn from sticking to the bottom, forming a paste, and burning.) Taste carefully; if corn is not sweet, stir in a little more sugar and simmer a few seconds longer to melt it. When corn is cooked through, serve immediately.

Each serving provides:

106 calories; 3.47 g protein; 1.2 g fat; 0 mg cholesterol; 23.5 g carbohydrate; 4.17 g dietary fiber; 10 mg calcium; 0.8 mg iron; 372 mg sodium

FRESH STRING BEANS STEAMED WITH TURKEY HAM

Serves 4

3   **cups fresh string beans (about ½ pound)**
     Water to fill bottom of steamer
3   **slices bacon, cut into cubes**
½   **pound turkey ham, chopped in ¼-inch dice**

¼   **cup chopped yellow onion**
½   **teaspoon salt**
½–1   **teaspoon cayenne (or to taste)**
½   **teaspoon black pepper**

Trim the beans, discarding tough tips, string them if necessary, and slice them or break them into pieces 1–1½ inches long. Fill the bottom of a steamer with water, add the bacon, and bring to a boil, making sure there is not enough water to boil up through the holes in the bottom of the steamer basket. Combine the string beans, turkey ham, onion, salt, cayenne, and black pepper together and place them in the steamer basket. Cover and steam for 7–10 minutes, or until the beans are as crisp, tender, or soft as you like them. Check to be sure there is enough water in the steamer basket to last through the cooking of the bean mixture. Discard the bacon and water left in the bottom of the steamer pot. The bean mixture will have a hickory-smoke flavor from the bacon.

Each serving provides:

115 calories; 12.68 g protein; 3.3 g fat; 32 mg cholesterol;
8.6 g carbohydrate; 3.54 g dietary fiber; 55 mg calcium;
2.95 mg iron; 835 mg sodium

OKRA ÉTOUFFÉE

Serves 4–6

2	pounds fresh okra
	Nonstick vegetable oil
	   cooking spray
		¼	pound smoked turkey
			   sausage, cut into 1-inch
			   long slices

¼	teaspoon salt	2	fresh tomatoes, coarsely

¼	cup chopped white or
	   yellow onion
			chopped, or 1 (16-ounce)
			   can tomatoes

¼	cup chopped green bell
	   pepper
		1	teaspoon cayenne (or to
			   taste)

2	cloves garlic, chopped	½	teaspoon black pepper
		1¼	cups water

Cut the okra into slices ½–1 inch thick, discarding the heads and the tough tails. Film a large skillet with the nonstick vegetable oil cooking spray and add the okra. Salt lightly and sauté over low to medium heat, stirring constantly, until the okra has almost stopped "stringing" (giving off thin, translucent strings as it cooks), approximately 20 minutes. Add the onion, bell pepper, and garlic. Sauté, stirring occasionally, until vegetables soften. Add the sausage, tomatoes, cayenne, and pepper. Gradually stir in enough of the water to make a liquid the consistency of a thick soup. Continue to simmer over low heat, about 30 minutes. Correct seasonings and serve over rice.

Each serving provides:

41.67 calories; 170.23 g protein; 2.5 g fat; 10 mg cholesterol; 3.57 g carbohydrate; * dietary fiber; * calcium; * iron; 267.33 g sodium

* = data unavailable

PINTO BEANS (OR RED BEANS)

Serves 4–6

1½ cups dried pinto beans (or red beans)
¼   cup chopped yellow or white onion
1   teaspoon salt
6–7 cups water
¼   teaspoon black pepper
¼   teaspoon white pepper
¼   pound smoked turkey meat, diced
¼   cup chopped green onions
3   tablespoons minced fresh parsley
2   jalapeño peppers, seeded and minced
1   bay leaf

Pick over the beans by running a few of them through your hands at a time and removing anything that is not a bean. Wash beans well in a colander. In a deep pot, combine beans, onion, salt, and 6–7 cups water to cover. Bring to a boil. Reduce heat. Add black and white pepper and smoked turkey meat. Simmer uncovered at least 1 hour, stirring occasionally. Add more water if liquid evaporates too quickly. Add green onions, parsley, jalapeño, and bay leaf. Simmer uncovered, stirring frequently, scooping from the bottom of the pot to make sure beans do not stick and burn. Add more water if beans dry out too quickly. Simmer until a bean flattens when you barely touch it (about 1 hour longer). If the liquid has failed to thicken, increase the heat and boil rapidly until the consistency of a thin gravy. If consistency is too thick, add ½ cup water and simmer 15 minutes longer. Remove bay leaf before serving.

Each serving provides:

254 calories; 18.82 g protein; 1.3 g fat; 7 mg cholesterol;
43 g carbohydrate; 12.37 g dietary fiber; 102 mg calcium;
4.7 mg iron; 509 mg sodium

PRAWNS ÉTOUFFÉE

Serves 4

⅓ cup fish stock (or clam juice or water)

¾ cup finely chopped celery

½ cup finely chopped green bell pepper

1½ cups finely chopped yellow onions

¼ cup minced fresh parsley

¼ cup chopped green onions

3 cloves garlic, minced

3 medium fresh tomatoes, coarsely chopped

8-ounce can tomato sauce

1 cup water

4 teaspoons flour dissolved in about ⅓ cup cold water

1 teaspoon salt

1 teaspoon cayenne (or to taste)

¼ teaspoon black pepper (or to taste)

3 bay leaves

4 cups peeled and deveined prawns

Place a large skillet over high heat. Add ¼ cup fish stock (or clam juice or water) to the skillet with celery, green bell pepper, yellow onion, parsley, green onion, and garlic. Sauté over medium-high heat 10 minutes or so. If mixture becomes dry or starts to stick, add fish stock (or clam juice or add water) by the teaspoonful, being careful not to drown with too much liquid. Keep a tiny layer of moisture between the food and the skillet, not a puddle. Add the tomatoes, tomato sauce, water, flour paste, salt, cayenne, black pepper, and bay leaves. Bring the mixture to a boil, stirring constantly to dissolve flour thoroughly. Reduce heat and simmer uncovered until the vegetables are cooked through but not mushy (about 20 minutes), stirring occasionally. Taste carefully and correct seasonings; sauce should be quite spicy. Increase the heat to medium-high and add the prawns. Simmer just until they are cooked, about 5 minutes. Remove bay leaves and serve immediately over rice.

Each serving provides:

214 calories; 32.89 g protein; 3 g fat; 231 mg cholesterol; 11.6 g carbohydrate; 2.96 g dietary fiber; 37 mg calcium; 1.27 mg iron; 623 mg sodium

PRAWNS AND PASTA

Serves 4 as a main course, 8 as an appetizer

2 cups evaporated skim milk

2 tablespoons chopped onion

1/2 teaspoon cayenne

1/2 teaspoon white pepper

1/4 teaspoon salt (or to taste)

1 tablespoon arrowroot (or cornstarch)

2 teaspoons natural butter substitute, such as Molly McButter

3 tablespoons Parmesan cheese

9 ounces (approximately 1 cup) peeled, deveined, and coarsely chopped prawns

1 tablespoon parsley

2 cups dry pasta twirls

Reserve 2 tablespoons evaporated skim milk. Place the rest of the milk in a saucepan over medium heat. Add onion, cayenne, white pepper, and salt. Combine the reserved milk with the arrowroot (or cornstarch). Add arrowroot (or cornstarch) to the saucepan and mix well. Continue cooking, stirring until the sauce has thickened. Stir in prawns and simmer 3 minutes longer. Stir in butter substitute and parmesan cheese. Add parsley and correct seasonings.

Meanwhile, cook pasta according to package directions. Drain pasta and mix with the sauce. Serve hot or cold.

Each serving provides:

388 calories; 31.04 g protein; 4.2 g fat; 105 mg cholesterol; 57 g carbohydrate; 1.76 g dietary fiber; 443 mg calcium; 2.61 mg iron; 565 mg sodium

ROUX FLOUR

Yield: 4 cups

4   cups all purpose flour

Place the flour in a large skillet over medium-high heat. Using a wire whisk, stir the flour consistently for about 20 minutes. The flour will toast and begin to turn a light tan color. If the flour begins to darken very quickly, remove the skillet from the direct heat and continue to stir, allowing it to cool slightly. Return to the heat and continue to stir until flour resembles the color of light brown sugar. Remove from heat and continue stirring until flour is cooled down.

Place in a container with a tight fitting lid, and store in a cool, dry place. Roux flour will last a good 2 months when stored appropriately. Use in place of traditional roux for a fat-free alternative.

Per one cup:

455 calories; 13 g protein; 1 g fat; 0 mg cholesterol; 95 g carbohydrate; 3.45 g dietary fiber; 20 mg calcium; 5.5 mg iron; 3 mg sodium

RUSSELL'S BARBECUE BASTING SAUCE

Makes about 1½ cups

3/4	cup white or cider vinegar	1/2	teaspoon salt
1/2	cup water	1/2	teaspoon cayenne
1	teaspoon chopped garlic (or 1/2 teaspoon garlic powder)	1/2	teaspoon black pepper
		1/2	teaspoon onion powder
		1/8	teaspoon dried thyme leaves, crumbled
2	teaspoons Worcestershire sauce		

Combine all ingredients in a saucepan. Heat gently 10 minutes to blend. Brush on meats before and during grilling.

Each serving provides:

3 calories; 0.29 g protein; 0 g fat; 0 mg cholesterol; 0.6 g carbohydrate; 0.03 g dietary fiber; 3 mg calcium; 0.15 mg iron; 262 mg sodium

~~~~~~~~~~~~~~~~

SMOTHERED CHICKEN BREASTS

Serves 4

4 (4-ounce) chicken breast halves, boneless and skinless	2 tablespoons chopped onion
1¼ teaspoons salt	2 tablespoons chopped celery
1 teaspoon garlic powder	¾ cup water
¾ teaspoon cayenne	2 tablespoons chopped fresh parsley
¼ teaspoon black pepper Nonstick vegetable oil cooking spray	

Season chicken breasts with salt, garlic powder, cayenne, and pepper. Heat a large skillet and spray with nonstick vegetable oil cooking spray; add the chicken and brown on both sides. Add onion and celery and sauté until wilted. Add the water and bring to a boil over high heat. Reduce heat and simmer, covered, 15 minutes. Sprinkle the parsley over the chicken and simmer 5 minutes longer. Serve hot, with rice.

Each serving provides:

267 calories; 54.63 g protein; 3.1 g fat; 136 mg cholesterol; 1.5 g carbohydrate; 0.42 g dietary fiber; 37 mg calcium; 1.98 mg iron; 824 mg sodium

SPICY MEAT LOAF À LA REINE

Serves 6–8

3 slices bread
3 pounds ground turkey
   breast meat
¼ cup chopped celery
¼ cup chopped bell pepper
¼ cup chopped onion
3 cloves garlic, finely
   chopped

2 teaspoons cayenne (or
   to taste)
1½ teaspoons salt
½ teaspoon black pepper
3 egg whites, well beaten
   16-ounce can stewed
   or whole tomatoes,
   drained and chopped
½ cup water

Preheat oven to 350 degrees. Soak the bread in a little water a few seconds, then drain and squeeze out. Knead together turkey meat, celery, bell pepper, onion, garlic, and seasonings. Knead in the bread and add egg whites. Mix well. Place mixture in a 9″ × 11½″ baking dish and mold into a loaf about 2½ inches thick. Pour tomatoes over the loaf and add the water. Bake 30 minutes. Reduce heat to 325 degrees and cover with foil. Continue baking another 15 to 20 minutes, basting occasionally.

Each serving provides:

449 calories; 84.72 g protein; 5.1 g fat; 204 mg cholesterol;
10.4 g carbohydrate; 1.22 g dietary fiber; 78 mg calcium;
3.49 mg iron; 825 mg sodium

CORNICHONS DES TOMATES VERTES
(*Thelma's Chowchow*)

Makes 3 cups, 12 portions

1   cup fresh hot peppers
     (serranos, cayennes,
     summer-grown
     jalapeños), trimmed,
     seeded, and chopped
½   cup chopped onion
½   cup chopped bell pepper
½   cup peeled, chopped
     cucumber (preferably
     pickling cucumber)

1   medium green tomato
     (or slightly red, but still
     crunchy), chopped
1   teaspoon prepared
     mustard
     Pinch of salt

Combine all ingredients in a heavy saucepan and sprinkle a little salt on them to help draw out their water. Simmer uncovered over low heat until tender (about 30 minutes). Spoon the mixture into a jar, let cool, seal, and refrigerate several hours or days.

Each serving provides:

19 calories; 0.90 g protein; 0.1 g fat; 0 mg cholesterol; 3.9 g carbohydrate: 0.7 g dietary fiber; 9 mg calcium; 0.46 mg iron; 11 mg sodium

TURNIPS ÉTOUFFÉE

Serves 4

6	turnips, pared and thinly sliced	½	teaspoon salt
3	slices bacon, cut into cubes	½	teaspoon black pepper
	Water to fill bottom of steamer	½	teaspoon cayenne (or to taste)
		1	teaspoon sugar (or to taste)
		1½	cups water

Fill the bottom of a steamer with water, add the bacon, and bring to a boil, making sure there is not enough water to boil up through the holes in the bottom of the steamer basket. Place turnips in steamer basket, cover and steam for 10–12 minutes, or until they just become tender. Check to be sure there is enough water in the steamer basket to last through the steaming of the turnips.

Remove turnips from steamer and place in a saucepan. Discard the bacon and water left in the bottom of the steamer pot. Combine turnips with salt, black pepper, cayenne, sugar, and water. Bring to a boil, reduce heat, and cover. Simmer very slowly until they are cooked down almost to creamed turnips. Additional water may be added if turnips become dry.

Each serving provides:

51 calories; 1.26 g protein; 0.1 g fat; 0 mg cholesterol; 13.3 g carbohydrate; 4.28 g dietary fiber; 45 mg calcium; 0.46 mg iron; 365 mg sodium

APPENDIX

Ingredients, Techniques, and Sources

BACON As in most other Southern cooking, bacon or bacon fat makes strong, frequent contributions to the flavor of Creole dishes. (After bacon has been fried, pour its fat into a heatproof container. Keep it in the freezer and dig out small amounts as needed. It will keep about one year at 0 degrees.) The type of bacon traditionally used is deeply smoked bacon, which comes in slabs (rather than sliced supermarket bacon, which, too often, is merely injected with liquid smoke flavoring).

If smoked slab bacon is unavailable from a nearby delicatessen, mail-order sources include:

Bacon Champs
Burger's Country Hams
Highway 87 and South Route 3
California, MO 65019
(314) 796-3134

Early's Honey Stand
Rural Route 2
Spring Hill, TN 37174
(615) 486-2230

Jugtown Mountain Smokehouse
77 Park Avenue
Flemington, NJ 08822
(201) 782-2421

McArthur's Smokehouse
Litchfield on the Green
Box 190
Litchfield, CT 06759
(203) 567-4593

Meadow Farms Smokehouse
Box 1387
Bishop, CA 93514
(619) 873-5311

BUTTERMILK Buttermilk is used frequently in Southern cooking, even by people (like me) who wouldn't think of drinking it straight. It seems to interact with baking powder to make baked or fried foods lighter and to give them a little tang. If necessary, regular milk can substitute for buttermilk; however, since it is already sour, buttermilk apparently keeps much longer than regular milk (several weeks at least) when placed in the coldest part of the refrigerator, so that leftover buttermilk can be used up over a longer period of time. Do not, of course, use it if it has developed an off-color or spoiled odor.

CAYENNE Except when specified, "cayenne" here refers to dried, ground cayenne pepper. It is almost interchangeable with the "red pepper" of major spice companies. Once the box or bottle is opened, all dried, ground hot pepper gradually loses its spiciness; take this into account when measuring. Fresh cayenne peppers are long, narrow, and extremely hot; like other peppers, they are green when young, red when mature. Two serrano chiles can substitute for one fresh cayenne pepper.

CHOPPING VEGETABLES When chopped onion, celery, bell pepper, tomato, or potato is specified in a recipe, it is generally chopped in ½-inch dice; garlic is chopped much smaller. "Finely chopped" indicates ¼-inch dice, and "minced" indicates tiny pieces of about ⅛ inch (or, with garlic, about 1⁄16 inch). Typically, a medium-size onion, bell pepper, or potato (6–7 ounces) will yield 1 cup chopped. A peeled medium tomato of the same weight will yield a generous ½ cup chopped. One average rib of celery without leaves will yield ¼ cup chopped. Three medium cloves of garlic will yield about 1 tablespoon chopped.

COOKWARE FOR CAJUN/CREOLE COOKING If you do not have a **covered roasting pan,** substitute a large, round ovenproof casserole or Dutch oven, and set in the bottom of it a 7½-inch round cake-cooling rack to use in place of a standard roasting rack. (Alternatively, seal the roast and the roasting pan in foil.)

A **double boiler** can be improvised, if necessary. If you do not have a heatproof bowl that will fit neatly into the top of one of your saucepans without falling through, set several heatproof cups (such as Pyrex custard cups) upside down in the saucepan. Pour about ½ inch water around the custard cups. On top of the custard cups, place a heatproof bowl (steel, Pyrex, stoneware) that fits snugly inside the saucepan, and proceed with the recipe. If even this is impossible, just use a heavy pot on the lowest possible heat (preferably with a "flame-tamer" pad set over the burner) and stir constantly.

A **Dutch oven** is a deep, ovenproof, flameproof casserole pot with a tight-fitting cover. It should be of heavy material (such as cast iron or stainless steel), of at least 2½-quart capacity; some recipes will require a larger size (4–6 quarts). Those coated with enamel or porcelain are easiest to use and to clean, and will not react with acidic ingredients such as tomatoes.

The most typical **skillets** for Creole cuisine (and which are both heat-retentive and able to withstand high temperatures) are of uncoated cast iron,

11 or 12 inches in diameter and about 2 inches deep. To season new cast-iron cookware, follow directions included with the pan, if available. Otherwise, clean off any sticky labels, rinse the skillet, wipe dry, and fill it with 8 ounces of lard. Place pan over medium heat until lard melts, tip pan and swirl the lard to lightly coat the sides, then heat pan in a low oven (200–250 degrees) at least 8 hours. Discard lard and wipe out skillet with paper towels. Use the newly seasoned skillet for frying as often as possible, as this will set the seasoning. Avoid cooking acidic foods in it for the first year or so. To clean a seasoned skillet, use hot water and an unsoaped scouring cloth or scrub sponge; do *not* use soap or steel wool, or the seasoning will wash away. For the first several years of use, avoid soaking the skillet, and dry it after each washing. Should any rust appear, reseason as above. A well-cared-for cast-iron skillet will eventually acquire a hard, shiny, lavalike black coating that is not only rust-resistant and nonreactive, but virtually nonstick.

CRAWFISH AND OTHER LOUISIANA SEAFOOD It takes about 7 pounds of live crawfish (or about 120 crawfish) to yield 1 pound of meat. The easiest way to use crawfish in complex dishes such as Crawfish Étouffée is to buy peeled crawfish tails if they are available.

Oysters can be purchased in their shells (requiring shucking) or shucked and bottled in their own juices; do not buy oysters that have already been shucked but left dry. The Apalachicola oyster is the type found in Louisiana, but other oysters can substitute easily.

Mail-order sources for Louisiana seafood:

Bon Creole Seafood
Route 3, Box 518-D
New Iberia, LA 70560
(318) 229-8397

Catfish Wholesale
P.O. Box 759
Abbeville, LA 70510
(318) 643 6700

C.J.'s Seafood
Route 1, Box 1416
Breaux Bridge, LA 70517
(318) 845-4413

K-Paul's Louisiana Mail Order
501 Elysian Fields
P.O. Box 770034
New Orleans, LA 70177-0034
(800) 457-2857

CREOLE SPICES AND INGREDIENTS
Mail-order sources:

Central Grocery
923 Decatur Street
New Orleans, LA 70116
(504) 523-1620

Louisiana Catalog
Route 3, Box 614
Cut Off, LA 70345
(504) 632-4100

EGG WHITES, LEFTOVER Some recipes in this book result in leftover egg whites. These may be refrigerated in a jar up to 48 hours, or slipped into small plastic bags, sealed, and frozen almost indefinitely. (After freezing, defrosted egg whites lose some of their loft when beaten into meringue, so use about $\frac{1}{3}$ extra.) Leftover egg whites can go into Gin Fizz (page 42), scrambled eggs or omelets (such as Ray G's Special, page 212), dessert mousses, meringue cookies, and meringue tart shells (see any standard general cookbook or French cookbook for recipes).

FILÉ POWDER (or Filé Gumbo, or Gumbo Filé) A spice made of powdered dried sassafras, often blended with a smaller amount of powdered thyme. There is no substitute for it. See *Creole Spices and Ingredients* for mail-order sources if it is unavailable in your area.

FROGS' LEGS Although rarely found in supermarkets outside Louisiana, frogs' legs may be available from specialty butchers and poulterers, and are routinely available from butcher shops in neighborhoods with significant Southeast Asian populations. (They are a favorite meat of Thailand.)

GAME ANIMALS
Mail-order sources:

Czimer Foods Inc.
13136 West 159th St.
Lockport, IL 60441

D'Artagnan Inc.
399-419 St. Paul Ave.
Jersey City, NJ 07306
(800) 327-2462

Polarica Meats
P.O. Box 880204
San Francisco, CA 94188-0204
(800) 426-3872

HAM HOCKS Ham hocks, the front shins of a hog, are used for flavoring many dishes, especially vegetable dishes. Some of their flavorful cooking liquid is usually included in the dish, along with their meat. "Tight" ham hocks are the rather thin, bony ones with meat clinging tightly to the bones, and skin clinging tightly to the meat. These are liable to be very tough, and require 1–2 hours of simmering to tenderize. Looser ham hocks are meatier, with meat clinging loosely to the bones. These will cook in much less time.

HOG'S HEADS See *Organ Meats*

LEMONS Several recipes in this book call for fresh lemon juice. Store hard, pale lemons on a sunny windowsill for a few days to ripen and soften them. To maximize the amount of juice the lemon yields, microwave it on the highest setting 1 minute or drop it into boiling water for 1 minute.

ONIONS, GREEN (Scallions) In Louisiana cookery, both the white bulb (trimmed of roots) and the crisp parts of the green tops are used in cooking, unless otherwise noted. The more costly shallots are used interchangeably with the whites of scallions in Louisiana cooking.

ONIONS, PEARL To peel pearl onions, drop them into boiling water to cover, and lightly boil 5–7 minutes (depending on size). Drain and immediately cool under cold water. With a small sharp knife, thinly cut off the root of each onion; then pinch onion from the root end to slip it out of its skin through the pointed end.

ORGAN MEATS AND SPECIALTY MEATS (Ponce, Hog's Head, etc.) Although supermarkets rarely carry the heads, stomachs, or even livers of pigs, these items are often available from specialty butchers, and from butcher shops in African American, Chinese, Filipino, French, Hispanic, and/or Southeast Asian neighborhoods. Those supermarkets with butchers on the premises will sometimes special-order large items, such as a hog's head, at the customer's request.

SALT PORK Salt pork is a fatty portion of a pork belly (unsmoked bacon) that has been preserved by brining. It is often blanched, thinly sliced, and then added to vegetables to give them flavor. To blanch salt pork, cover it with water, bring it to a boil, and boil about 5 minutes to rid the meat of excess salt. Discard the cooking water.

SAUSAGES, SMOKED Smoked sausages can be mild or spicy. They are fully cooked during the curing and smoking process; they only need to be heated through, but may be cooked longer to contribute their flavor to a dish. Louisiana-style smoked sausages *(andouille* or *chaurice)* and/or "hot links" may be available from well-stocked delicatessens; if using supermarket deli-case sausages, try several brands and choose the smokiest one you can find. Mail-order sources for Louisiana-style smoked sausages:

Bruce Aidells Sausage Co.
1575 Minnesota St.
San Francisco, CA 94107
(415) 285-6660
(Cajun *andouille,* tasso ham,
   chaurice)

Old Grove Smoke House
Route 6, Box 133
Baton Rouge, LA 70815
(504) 673-6857
(Cajun *andouille,* tasso ham)

E.M. Todd Co.
P.O. Box 5167
Richmond, VA 23220
(800) 368-5026
(country-style smoked sausages)

Zingerman's
422 Detroit St.
Ann Arbor, MI 48104
(313) 663-3354
(Cajun *andouille,* tasso ham)

SAUSAGE CASINGS AND EQUIPMENT Homemade smokers can be constructed from discarded refrigerators, 55-gallon drums, or metal garbage pails, or can be built more elaborately out of brick. Plans for building these smokers can be found in do-it-yourself books and magazines; Jacques Pépin's *Art of Cooking, Volume II* (Knopf, 1988) includes a plan for a refrigerator smokehouse. Kettle barbecues can also be used for smoking. An excellent source of detailed information about sausage making is *Hot Links and Country Flavors* by Bruce Aidells and Dennis Kelly (Knopf, 1990).

Casings and sausage-making equipment can be mail-ordered from:

Aidells Sausage Co. (see
   Sausages, above)

Carlson Butcher Supply
50 Mendell St., #12
San Francisco, CA 94124
(415) 648-2601

Cook'n'Cajun Water Smokers
P.O. Box 3716
Shreveport, LA 71133
(318) 925-6933

The Sausage Maker
177 Military Road
Buffalo, NY 14207
(716) 876-5521

SHRIMP, DRIED Dried shrimp contribute a strong seafood flavor to cooking liquids. They must always be rehydrated by soaking or cooking in hot liquid. They come in cellophane packages of various sizes, and are available at many large supermarkets and at many groceries in African-American, Chinese, Hispanic, and Southeast Asian neighborhoods. See *Creole Spices and Ingredients* for mail-order sources.

TASSO Today's tasso is a spicy cured ham coated heavily with pepper (black and red), most often made from the pork loin (like Canadian bacon). It is typically used as a flavoring, rather than served on its own; usually it is chopped in fine dice and introduced into gumbos, jambalayas, étouffées, omelets, or vegetable dishes at the stage when the flavoring vegetables are sautéed. It is rarely found outside Louisiana and East Texas; see *Sausages* for mail-order sources.

TOMATOES, PEELED (see also *Chopped Vegetables*) Tomatoes are usually peeled before cooking because when cooked, the peels come off in tough, thin strings. To peel, drop tomatoes into boiling water and boil no more than 1 minute, or until the skin breaks at the touch of a knifepoint. Drain under cold running water, slip off peel, and cut out core. When fresh tomatoes are out of season, canned tomatoes can be substituted. Canned tomatoes are already peeled.

ABOUT ZYDECO

Quintessentially multicultural, zydeco music is a mixture of Cajun French and African-American traditions with plenty of help from Hispanic, German, Appalachian, and Caribbean influences. Zydeco music evolved in the Creole communities of southwest Louisiana. Although zydeco is emerging from obscurity and influencing popular culture, there are still only a handful of Creole artists touring nationally today. Of these, Queen Ida is unquestionably the best known and most widely traveled.

As it developed, zydeco repeatedly drew from and contributed to the neighboring Cajun tradition, which can be traced back over 200 years to France. Cajun waltzes and two-steps still make up the lion's share of a Queen Ida concert. The polkas and mazurkas that enliven Queen Ida's repertoire are a legacy of the German settlers and Jewish peddlers who brought the accordion to the area in the 1880s. Oldies such as Hank Williams's "Jambalaya" and some of Ida's recently composed songs have the flavor of the country western music that permeated the air waves of Louisiana during Ida's childhood.

The African-American blues roots of zydeco are clearly heard in the bass, drums, lead guitar, and saxophone of the Queen Ida band. The rub-board (washboard) is another hallmark of zydeco music not found in the Cajun tradition. The scratch-scratch rhythm of the rub-board echoes the sound of the African shakeree, a large gourd wrapped with strings of beads that is shaken as an accompaniment to singing.

The origin of the word *zydeco* is somewhat of a mystery. It is often used as a verb, as in "Let's go out and zydeco tonight!" There is some speculation that zydeco came from the French word "haricot," which means snapbean, thus connoting snappy music. In fact, one of the early zydeco hits was called "Le Haricot Ne Sont Pas Salées." On the other hand, Louisiana folklorist Barry Ancelet has observed that musics with names similar to zydeco occur in other areas where French and African culture coexist, including Haiti and the Seychelles islands.

Regardless of its origins, zydeco is now being heard throughout the American cultural continuum—in movies, TV commercials, popular music, major festivals, and concert halls. Zydeco, with its distinctive French accordion and exhilarating zig-zag rhythms, is winning the hearts and feet of audiences around the world.

RESOURCES FOR STUDY

Queen Ida Discography:

Cajun/Creole/Bayou Music (GNP/Crescendo, GNPS 2101)

Zydeco à la Mode (GNP/Crescendo, GNPS 2112)

Queen Ida and the Bon Temps Zydeco Band in New Orleans (GNP/Crescendo, GNPS 2131)

Queen Ida—On Tour (GNP/Crescendo GNPS 2147)

Queen Ida in San Francisco (GNP/Crescendo GNPS 2158)

Caught in the Act (GNP/Crescendo GNPS 2181)

Cookin' with Queen Ida (GNP/Crescendo GNPS 2197)

(These recordings are currently available in the U.S. European releases are on the Sonet and Vogue labels.)

GNP and Arhoolie Records are available by mail and telephone order from Down Home Music Inc., 6921 Stockton Ave., El Cerrito, CA 94530 (415/525-1494). Retail store: Down Home Music, 10341 San Pablo, El Cerrito, CA 94530 (415/525-2129). Extensive selection of Cajun and zydeco records.

Book:

Savoy, Ann Allen. *Cajun Music: A Reflection of a People, Volume I,* 1984. Bluebird Press Inc., P.O. Box 941, Eunice, LA 70535 (318/457-9563); available by mail from Bluebird, or through Flower Films (see Films, below).

Magazines:

Performance Magazine and *Pollstar* (available in many public libraries) frequently include Queen Ida's current touring itineraries.

Films on Cajun and Creole music and culture:

Aginsky, Yasha. *Blues de Balfa* (30 minutes, on the Balfa brothers); *Cajun Visits* (30 minutes, on Cajun fiddle music, with Dewey Balfa, Canray Fontenot, Dennis McGee, et al., in Cajun French with English subtitles). Videotapes available through Flower Films, 10341 San Pablo, El Cerrito, CA 94530 (415/525-0942).

Blank, Les et al. *Dry Wood* (37 minutes, on Bois Sec Ardoin and Canray Fontenot); *Hot Pepper* (54 minutes, on Clifton Chenier); *Spend It All* (41 minutes, on Cajun culture and music, including Marc Savoy, Balfa Brothers, Nathan Abshire); *J'ai été au bal* (84 minutes, traditional Cajun music, including Queen Ida and many others); *Yum, Yum, Yum* (30 minutes, on Cajun cooking, with Marc Savoy, Paul Prudhomme, et al.); work-in-progress on Marc and Ann Savoy (tentative title *Marc and Ann).* Available on 16-millimeter film or videotape through Flower Films (see above).

Spitzer, Nick. *Zydeco* (1 hour, with Bois Sec Ardoin, Dolon Carriere, Armand Ardoin); videotape available through Flower Films (see above).

INDEX